empirical studies

in the

Psychology of Learning

empirical studies
in the

Psychology of Learning

abstracted by
B. R. Bugelski

Hackett Publishing Company, Inc.
P. O. Box 55573
Indianapolis, Indiana 46205

ISBN: 0-915144-02-6
Library of Congress Catalog Card Number: 74-22867
Copyright © 1975 by Hackett Publishing Company, Inc.
Cover Design: Melissa Martin Goldsmith
First Printing

Printed in the United States of America

For Jamie

PREFACE

In the process of teaching a course in the Psychology of Learning, I found that I had occasion to refer to the work of more than a hundred different psychologists but that I rarely had the time to provide an adequate account of the work being cited. A hasty run through an experiment would result in an inadequate set of notes on the part of the students, with a consequent lack of appreciation of the points I hoped to make. The remedy of sending a class of 50 students to the library to read a journal article was impractical, since by the time they got around to reading the paper the course would be far along. The hoped-for book of readings containing all the papers I would like never appeared. The readings books that were available usually contained complete original papers which frequently were too long and complicated for undergraduate interests. The solution I finally arrived at is this volume of abstracts wherein I try to present the basic research operations and factual findings of some 123 experimental studies.

My goal was to provide students with materials they could handle within the time constraints under which they work. This meant, in the context of a three-meetings-per-week course, that I wanted them to read more than two papers per week in addition to text and other assignments. The imposed decision was to attempt to provide a summary of each assigned paper in the briefest possible form; i.e., in one or two pages of print. Accordingly, I abstracted and reproduced the materials included in this volume and distributed them to my class. The students' reports indicate that the abstracts are not easy to comprehend—that they must be studied, and call for at least two careful readings. But at least students now have the facts as "straight" as I can provide them. As a corrective to any sense that research reports always appear in one- or two-page summaries, I have each student execute and submit three abstracts (from three different journals) done in a similar style by himself. In this way I hope to get him acquainted with the original sources.

In this collection I have tried to include all of the creative, provocative, innovative, and seminal studies I could find. Many colleagues were helpful with their nominations of papers I had not really appreciated before, if I even knew about them. Many important papers were omitted because they could not be abstracted without undue violence to the subject matter, or because the theoretical issues could not be reduced intelligibly. Where important researches are overlooked, I can only regret my lack of insight and hope that copies of reprints will be directed to me for a revised and enlarged edition. One governor of the selection process was to look for papers that opened new areas of research, even if more important papers came later. Another governor was to find papers on two or more sides of an issue. The papers are not meant to solve the teacher's task of teaching; they are meant to serve as source material. The chronology covers the decades up to the 70's. Beyond that, I felt it would be presumptive to assume the impactfulness of various seemingly important papers.

Although this work was inspired by my students' needs, as it developed I became aware that together the abstracts provide an adequate, if not definitive, history of research in the subject matter. Thus, in this brief work, any curious reader will be able to perceive the bare bones of the psychology of learning as defined by the researchers in the field.

In offering this collection as a teaching aid to other teachers of courses in learning, I am keenly aware of my debt to those psychologists who produced the original papers. There is nothing here that is original on my part (with the exception of one paper) and I greatly appreciate the willingness of those living psychologists who kindly gave me leave to abstract their work. Some of the authors suggested clarifying changes, and to these colleagues I am especially grateful. I take full responsibility for whatever errors and distortions I was unable to perceive. I am also grateful to the American Psychological Association and to the publishers of the several journals containing the original papers who gave their approval to this effort. The publishers include, besides the American Psychological Association, the following: *The American Journal of Psychology, The Journal Press, Psychological Reports,* and *The Academic Press.*

In developing this volume, I happily had the highly competent assistance of Ms. Tracey Ricci, who not only prepared the manuscript and the materials for use in classes, but who also kept track of the multiple details involved in dealing with so many separate abstracts. Her participation was invaluable.

B. R. B

Buffalo, New York
December, 1974

CONTENTS

Contents

Contents

xi

Contents

INTRODUCTION

The papers summarized in this volume are presented in chronological order of their publication. An exception was made in the case of Pavlov, because his best-known work, *Conditioned Reflexes*, did not appear until 1927 in its English translation, while his actual research began in the period when his American contemporary, Thorndike, was investigating *Animal Intelligence*.

The choice of a chronological arrangement is deliberate. It is based not only on a personal fondness for history, but on a desire to demonstrate the developmental nature of research and the relative persistence of problems. Many current issues in psychology have their roots in the nineteenth century. Contemporary Behavior Therapy began in 1923, if not earlier. What emerges from the historial account is a sense of the growing sophistication in how to attack problems rather than a stockpiling of solutions.

The historical arrangement reveals another aspect of psychological research: that the same questions are raised again and again, the same problems raised over and over—the same questions about acquisition, retention, and transfer; questions about discrimination and generalization, and similarity; questions about the course of learning, the principles of association, and the role of reinforcement; problems of forgetting and retrieval, and problems of set and meaning.

The table of contents, that precedes, preserves the historical order of publication. In this table, authors are listed with a brief indication of the topics that engaged their interests. Such a listing, however, will be of little help to the instructor concerned with a special topic, and so a second "table of contents" is provided in the form of a "topical outline." (See pages 253-254) The topical outline lists by Abstract Number all of the abstracts that deal with a given subject matter. Because many abstracts deal with several topics, there are multiple listings. An index of topics is also provided at the end of the text for more detailed and specific topics. The index of authors at the end of the volume does not include bibliographical citations, since these are given in full with each abstract.

In all cases, where determinable, the original locale of the research done is listed with the authors in the abstracts. The current addresses of living authors can be obtained in most cases from the current Psychological Register. The use of the original addresses of the authors provides a sense of what was going on where and when, and this was presumed to be of some historical value.

Free Association

Sir Francis Galton, F.R.S.

"Psychometric Experiments," *Brain*, July 1879.

Ideas arise from association with objects perceived by the senses or with other ideas. Such ideas can be examined, timed, and recorded. When walking along Pall Mall for about 450 yards, I scrutinized a variety of objects and waited for thoughts relating to each object to occur. Thoughts from my entire life history were provoked by associations to such casual objects. Upon repetition of the walk, there was a great deal of repetition of the thoughts.

Method

For a more precise study, 75 words were written down in such a way that a book covering the sheet would expose one word at a time when moved slightly. As soon as a word was exposed, a stop-watch was started and allowed to run until two thoughts occurred. The thoughts had to be separate associations to the word. The thoughts were recorded on each of 4 trials at near monthly intervals.

Results

Five hundred fifty thoughts were recorded and the total association time was 660 seconds. (The rate was about 3000 thoughts per hour). There was a great deal of repetition in the 4 sessions. Only 289 different thoughts were recorded. Of these, 167 occurred once, 57 twice, 36 three times, and 29 four times. Where identification was possible, the thoughts came mostly (46%) from the period of manhood, 39% from boyhood and youth, and 15% came from recent experiences.

The character of the associations could be described in 3 general patterns:

1. A verbal or parrot-like memory, quite meaningless.
2. Sense imagery, especially visual.
3. Histrionic—imagery of acting out.

The thoughts could also be classified into 3 categories or series: 1) the "abbey" series, made up largely of mental imagery words (samples:

1

abyss, aborigine); 2) the "abasement" series, mostly "acting out" histrionic words (samples: abhorrence, ablution); and 3) the "afternoon" series, mostly abstract words (samples: ability, abnormal).

These categories could be broken down by character of reaction as in the table. Such associations to words are highly individual or idiosyncratic and the same word can give rise to "quick impressions" that will differ widely among people. Also: Such records "lay bare the foundations of a man's thoughts with curious distinctness, and exhibit his mental anatomy with more vividness and truth than he would probably care to publish to the world."

Functions or Operations (in percent)

			Purely Verbal	
	Sense Imagery	*Histrionic*	*Names of People*	*Phrases or Quotes*
"Abbey" series	43	11	30	16
"Abasement" series	32	33	13	22
"Afternoon" series	22	25	16	37

The Forgetting Curve

Hermann Ebbinghaus

"Retention and Oblivescence as a Function of the Time," Chapter 6, *Memory,* New York, Teachers College, Columbia University, 1913 (first published 1885; experiments started 1879).

Some theorists think nothing is forgotten, only overlaid or buried by later learnings. Others believe old memories are slowly destroyed, fragmented, components incorporated into other combinations. Still others hold that complex memories lose parts entirely and do not just fade or weaken as wholes. Probably there is merit to each of these views, but no proof for any. Proof can be found only through analysis of what remains. What remains can be determined by how much effort is required to relearn.

Method

Lists of 13 nonsense syllables (6 or 8 lists at each retention interval) were learned to a criterion of 2 perfect recitations. The lists were relearned to the same criterion after intervals listed in the table. Lists were relearned at 2 different times for the 30-minute and 9-hour intervals. This may involve problems of fatigue, etc.

Results

It required about 1100 seconds, or nearly 20 minutes, to learn the original lists. Relearning always took less time, depending upon the delay.

The results are reported as "savings scores" and % forgotten. (See next page.)

EBBINGHAUS'S FORGETTING CURVE

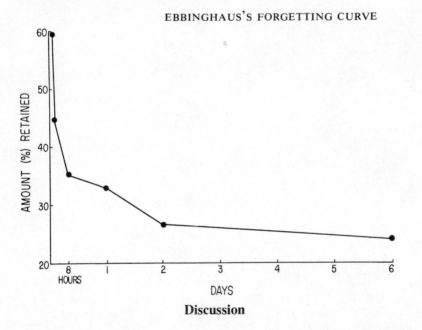

Discussion

Forgetting is extremely rapid in the 1st hour, but after 24 hours the rate of forgetting declines and the retention of about 1/5 of the material after 1 month suggests the material will remain at that level almost indefinitely. The small loss between 9 and 24 hours is a problem. The amounts retained after various intervals relative to the original work required "were about inversely proportional to a small power of the logarithm of those intervals of time."

Time of Relearning (after x hours)	Savings Score (%)*	Amount Forgotten (%)
0.33	58.2	41.8
1.00	44.2	55.8
8.8	35.8	64.2
24.	33.7	66.3
48.	27.8	72.2
6 x 24	25.4	74.6
31 x 24	21.1	78.9

*Savings scores are computed as original learning time − relearning time × 100.

The Learning Curve, Plateaus

W. L. Bryan and N. Harter
Indiana University

"Studies on the Telegraphic Language. The Acquisition of a Hierarchy of Habits," *Psychological Review*, 1899, **6**, 345-375.

Studies of receiving and sending telegraphic code may be informative about the formation of habits and habit hierarchies in other areas, as previous studies have shown similarities in learning curves between telegraphic code acquisition and other practice curves. A feature of telegraphic receiving practice curves is the appearance of plateaus at certain stages. This study is an intensive observation of one telegrapher trainee.

Method

Subject: John Shaw, with 6 weeks of practice prior to the 1st test.

Procedure: S was tested every Saturday from the 6th to the 35th week. Tests covered 3 kinds of materials: random letters, strings of unrelated words, and sentences. The testing rate was adapted to performance, and slowed or speeded depending on progress. Tests covered 2 minutes of American Morse Code. (Only receiving data will be considered in this abstract.)

Results

The improvement in receiving the 3 kinds of material is plotted in the figure. The curves for letters and unrelated words rise regularly. The curve for sentences, however, shows a period of no improvement in the December to March tests, followed by a second rise which continued till May.

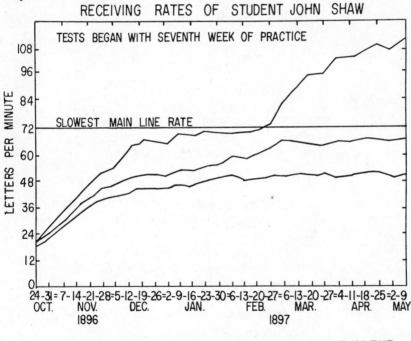

CONNECTED DISCOURSE CURVE AT THE TOP; CURVE IN THE
MIDDLE; LETTER CURVE AT THE BOTTOM

Conclusion: Receiving telegraphy consists of mastering a series or hierarchy of habits, namely the reception of letters, then words, and finally sentences. A rapid gain in the higher order habit cannot be attained until a lower level habit is well established. Only after lower level habits are automatized can an advance be made. The period of no improvement, a plateau, is a stage when "lower order habits are approaching their maximum but are not yet sufficiently automatic to leave attention free to attack higher order habits."

Interviews with other telegraphers confirm these findings. They report separate stages of acquisition, with a process described as "copying behind," i.e., having several letters, or words, kept in mind (up to 12 words) as the signals come in before they transcribe the message.

Transfer of Training

E. L. Thorndike and R. S. Woodworth
Teachers College, Columbia University
New York University Medical School

"The influence of Improvement in One Mental Function upon the Efficiency of Other Functions," *Psychological Review*, 1901, **8**, 247-261.

Note: This is one of the earliest, if not the earliest, study of the problem of transfer of training. In the same volume of the Review, *two more papers by the same authors extend the same findings to other skills (crossing out letters, locating verbs, detecting misspellings, etc.).*

In this study, a mental "function" will be trained and a determination will be made as to whether the learner benefits from such practice in even closely similar functions. A function here means "the mental basis of such things as spelling, multiplication, delicacy of discrimination of size . . . " etc. The present experiment is concerned with the influence of training on size judgments.

Method

Subjects: Six college students.

Material: A collection of pieces of paper of various sizes and shapes divided into a training series and two test series. Three squares—1, 25, and 100 square centimeters—drawn on a piece of cardboard served as a general guide for the *S*s. The shapes and sizes of the materials will be listed below.

Procedure: A *S* first looked at 127 pieces of paper (rectangles, triangles, circles, and irregular figures) one at a time, and estimated their areas in square centimeters, writing down his guesses without any information being provided. This constituted a pretest. He then underwent the training process by looking at 90 parallelograms ranging from 10-100 square centimeters, increasing in steps of 1 square centimeter. The pieces of paper were shuffled to provide a random order, and *S*s went through the collection time after time (1000-2000 estimates) until they showed improvement. As a *S* went through this collection, he wrote his estimate and saw the correct size measurement immediately thereafter. "The function trained was that of estimating areas from 10 to 100 sq. cm. . . . ." After training, the *S* went through a test series which included 2 kinds of items: Test series 1: 13 rectangles taken from the actual practice list. Test series 2: 27 triangles, circles, irregular figures within the same size limits taken from the pretest.

The basic question: Does training on one set of figures benefit the judgment of other identical, similar, or different figures?

Subject	Average Errors				End of Training	
	Pretest Series 1	Posttest Series 1 Identical Items	Pretest Series 2	Posttest Series 2	Total	Series 1 Items
T	9.0	6.0	15.8	11.1	2.3	2.1
Be	21.9	6.4	28.0	5.2	3.1	1.8
BR	24.2	14.7	22.5	18.7	3.3	3.7
J.W.	7.7	8.6	12.7	21.0	1.5	1.5
W	11.6	3.3	17.0	20.0	4.0	4.0
E.B.	9.8	4.1	10.5	7.5	0.4	0.4

Results

The basic findings appear in the table. The scoring was done in terms of average error—i.e., how far off from the actual measurement of each test item the Ss' estimates were (in cm^2). Note that by the end of the training series (column 5) the Ss were making relatively small errors. In the post-training tests the Ss did better on Test series 1, which contained items identical to those in the training, although they were not so good with these items as they had been with training items at the end of training (last column). The skill acquired with rectangles did not transfer effectively to the second test series (circles, triangles, irregular figures), compared to the skill with training items shown at the end of training (next to last column). There were no gradients of skill demonstrated. The Ss did as poorly or as well on items close to those used in the training series as on more distant items.

It is concluded that "the 'function' of estimating areas is really a 'function group,' varying according to the data (shape, size, etc.). Even judging sizes with correction supplied is a different task or function from judging without correction. When someone learns something it is always specific to a 'particular environment' for a person in a particular mental attitude or frame of mind. . . . " There is no mysterious transfer of practice to an unanalyzable property of mental functions. Different mental functions are separate and require their own special training for improvement.

Experimental Neuroses

I. P. Pavlov

Conditioned Reflexes (selected experiments), London, Oxford University Press, 1927.

Experimenter: Dr. Erofeeva. *Concern:* Noxious stimulation as a CS.

A strong electric shock is applied to the skin of a dog. After each stimulation the dog is allowed to eat for a few seconds.

After a few trials the dog salivates when the shock is applied, showing no motor defence reflex. A sample record:

Time	Number of Drops	
4:23 pm	6	usual place of stimulation
4:45 pm	5	
5:07 pm	7	
5:17 pm	9	new place (stronger shock)
5:45 pm	6	

Experimenter: Pavlov. *Concern:* Extinction.

After conditioning with a 30-second metronome beat, the US (food) is omitted, but stimulation with the metronome continues in 2-minute intervals for 30-second periods. The dog continues to salivate for some time but the amount of secretion is reduced and the time before the response increases.

Latency	Number of Drops
3 sec.	10
7	7
5	8
4	5
5	7
9	4
13	3

Experimenter: Dr. Shenger-Krestovnikova. *Concern:* Experimental Neurosis.

Procedure: Dog was trained with a circle as positive CS and ellipses of various ratios as negative. Experimentation began with a 2:1 ratio of the semi-axes, then 3:2, then 4:3 and so on. Dog could not respond appropriately at the 9:8 ratio. Three weeks of work resulted not only in the dog losing whatever discrimination had been attained but becoming violent, barking, fighting the apparatus, and losing all other discriminations. The table below shows records from some of the various stages of the research.

9

Date	Time	CS for 30 sec.	Drops of Salivary Secretion
August 4, 1914	4:10 pm	circle	4
	4:22	circle	6
	4:37	4:3 ellipse	0 (perfect discrimination)
	4:44	circle	4
Sept. 2, 1914	1:10 pm	circle	2
	1:27	circle	8
	2:6	circle	10
	2:16	9:8 ellipse	1 (discrimination almost established)
	2:30	circle	6
	2:48	circle	8
Sept. 17, 1974	3:20 pm	circle	4
	3:31	circle	7
	3:54	9:8 ellipse	8 (failure of discrimination
	4:9	circle	9
Sept. 25, 1914	2:17 pm	circle	9
	2:47	2:1 ellipse	3 (failure of discrimination)
	3:8	circle	8
	3:22	circle	8
	3:46	2:1 ellipse	3 (failure of discrimination)
Nov. 13, 1914	10:55 am	circle	10
	11:5	circle	7
	11:30	2:1 ellipse	0 (discrimination reestablished)
	11:44	circle	5

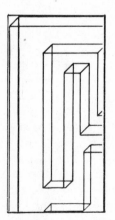

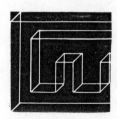

Concept Formation

Clark L. Hull
University of Wisconsin

"Quantitative Aspects of the Evolution of Concepts,"
Psychological Review Monographs, 1920, **28**, 85.

This extensive monograph describes a number of experiments dealing
with the formation of concepts and concentrates largely on the process
of *generalizing abstraction*. In this abstract only one of the studies, that
dealing with the differences in learning when proceeding from simple to
complex vs. complex to simple, will be considered.

Do we learn some difficult concept by beginning with simple examples, or can we benefit more by starting to practice with more complex sample situations or stimuli? The approach adopted in this monograph was to pick out 12 symbols to be learned (by naming each) and em-
bedding each of these symbols in a gradually increasing degree of com-
plicating embellishments. There were then 12 concepts in 12 degrees of
complexity. It could then be possible to have *S*s learn by starting with
relatively simple examples and proceeding to more difficult ones, or by
beginning with more complicated items and reverse the order, winding
up with the more simple forms. Tests could then be conducted with even
more complex examples to determine the merits of the two procedures.

Method

Subjects: Ten college students.

Apparatus, Materials, and General Procedure: Memory drum with a
5-second exposure rate. One hundred and forty-four Chinese characters
in 12 packs of 12. Each pack consisted of 12 separate but distinguishable
basic characters which were assigned nonsense syllable names like *yer,
deg, nez,* etc.(See illustration.) *S*s would learn a pack to a criterion of 1
perfect trial, then attempt 2 more trials with a different order. They
would then proceed to the next pack and so on through the rest of the
packs.

Specific Procedure: Each S learned 6 concepts in the simple-to-
complex (S-C) order and six in the complex-to-simple order (C-S). Six
new sets of packs were made up from the first 6 packs so that half of the

Word	Con-cept				Pack								
		I	II	III	IV	V	VI	VII	VIII	IX	X	XI	XII
A oo	氵	汫	沛	汖	沲	洪	漆	沼	沭	港	沛	淠	满
B yer	歹	殂	殁	珍	殆	殊	殫	殖	殁	殓	殘	殃	死
C li	力	劝	勁	功	勔	劼	势	劵	雁	脉	勦	助
D ta	弓	弦	弧	弔	弛	弴	弜	弓	張	弭	弱	弗	發
E deg	石	古	砂	矵	碧	碧	盾	磊	碧	砭	砧	砗	碾
F ling	穴	空	宊	宠	窂	窕	窨	窞	窺	窣	窼	窀	窨
G hui	⺄	延	延	延	与	㞷	閟	辷	念	归	邑	迠	仓
H chun	禾	秂	秎	稦	秠	秂	秂	秂	脈	脎	粼	舸
I vo	广	痲	莊	痈	疾	痆	痃	瘣	瘵	瘫	瘓	瘅	瘋
J na	尸	屍	屍	屙	尾	層	屁	屈	屍	房	屁	屢
K nez	立	竐	竗	章	竕	竖	竝	竕	育	竏	竞	竕	竐
L fid	米	粼	糶	粢	粺	粩	翠	穀	糉	精	粃	粲	糞

MATERIAL FOR STUDYING THE FORMATION OF CONCEPTS

first pack contained 6 items from Pack I and 6 items from Pack VI; the second pack contained 6 items each from Packs II and V; then packs were made up from Packs III and IV; and so on. Thus, each S had 6 concepts that he learned in the order I-VI and 6 learned in the VI-I arrangement. After all 6 packs were learned, the Ss were tested by being shown Packs VII to XII 3 times each, with no further prompting. All errors were noted.

Results

The table shows the number of promptings required by the 10 Ss to reach criterion with each kind of item in the 6 learning assignments. Note the relatively large drop on the second pack for the S-C items. Note also that the S-C items took somewhat more prompting on the first pack, which is interpreted to mean that more time was spent on the simpler exemplars, those which enjoyed maximal favorableness for learning. In the test trials there were 108 possible errors for the S-C or C-S items. The actual number of errors for the 10 Ss were 30.2 for the S-C items and 44.1 for the C-S items, a highly significant difference.

Conclusions: In the evolution of concepts, simple experiences are more efficient than complex ones, although the time factor must be ex-

12

Packs	I	II	III	IV	V	VI
Simple to complex	36.3	9.8	8.3	6.9	4.8	3.5
Complex to simple	34.8	17.0	11.1	7.8	3.9	3.9

cluded—i.e., with more time per item a C-S pattern might be just as effective. The conclusions thus far apply only to nonsense material and would have to be tested in other contexts before further generalization.

Conditioning of Fear

John B. Watson and Rosalie Rayner
Johns Hopkins University

"Conditioned Emotional Reactions," *Journal of Experimental Psychology,* 1920, **3**, 1-14.

There are few emotional reactions in infancy, probably just fear, anger, and love. To account for the complexity of adult emotional life there must be some simple method whereby the range of stimuli that call out these emotions and their compounds can be increased. The basis of such extension is likely to be conditioning.

Method

Subject: Albert B. an 11-month-old infant, in good health, stolid, showing no fear to a rat, rabbit, dog, monkey, masks, cotton wool, burning newspapers. Albert was in residence at a home for invalid children where his mother was a wet nurse.

Procedure: Albert placed on mattress on a table. White rat presented to Albert, 4-foot steel bar struck with hammer just behind Albert's head just as Albert reached for rat. Procedure repeated once more. One week later 5 more paired stimulations were given.

Results

On first 2 trials, child whimpered, jumped violently. On test, child avoided contact. After next 3 trials, child whimpered and withdrew on test with rat. After 2 more joint stimulations (a total of 7), child cried and crawled away from rat, "a case of a completely conditioned fear response."

On test 5 days later, Albert crawled away from rat. Transfer tests with a rabbit, dog, seal fur coat, cotton wool and Santa Claus mask were all positive—i.e., Albert withdrew, with strongest reaction to the rabbit. Five days later, Albert showed a less violent reaction to the rat but was "reconditioned" in 1 trial of paired stimulation. Conditioned fear responses were then established to the rabbit and dog in 1 trial by presenting the loud sound and animal together.

In later test trials the fear reaction was modified to turning away from the animals, raising hands, thumb in mouth, even after a 1-month period. Because of Albert's departure from the hospital no effort was made to remove the conditioned fears or "recondition" him, but the procedure of counterconditioning is suggested as probably an effective therapy. For example, candy could be presented along with the feared object or animal.

Abstract **8**

Forgetting during Sleep

John C. Jenkins and Karl M. Dallenbach
Cornell University

"Oblivescence during Sleep and Waking," *American Journal of Psychology*, 1924, **35**, 605-612.

Ebbinghaus was puzzled by his failure to forget proportionately more in the 15-24 hour interval after learning (8 hour score and 24 hour score) than he forgot in the 24 hour interval between 1 and 2 days after learning. The authors hypothesized that the early period included some sleep which might conserve the learning.

Method

Subjects: Two college students.

Materials and Method: The subjects lived in the laboratory from April to June and learned lists of 10 nonsense syllables early in the day or just before retiring. They were tested for recall (Ebbinghaus used re-learning) after 1, 2, 4 or 8 hours. The Ss learned to 1 perfect repetition. A memory drum presented the syllables at 0.7-second intervals.

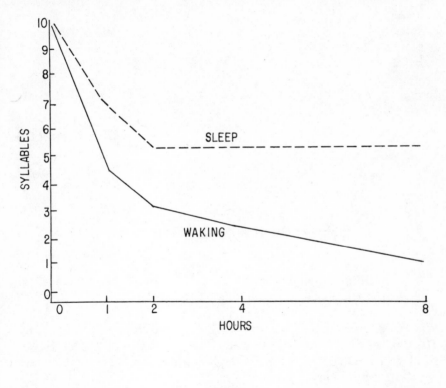

Results

The Ss did not differ significantly. Averaged recall data appear in the figure. Recall after sleep was superior at every test interval. After 2 hours of sleep there was no further decrease.

15

Conclusions: The decrease in waking recall is attributed to interference. Similar results are reported for a hypnotized S. Ebbinghaus's puzzle is stated to be solved, since most of the interval between the 9th hour after learning and 24 hours was spent in sleep. Ebbinghaus forgot nonsense syllables at the following rate (measured by relearning):

Time	20 min.	1 hr.	8.8 hrs.	1 day	2 days	6 days	31 days
% forgetting	41.8	55.8	64.2	66.3	72.2	74.6	78.9

Phobia Theory

Mary Cover Jones
Teachers College, Columbia University

"The Elimination of Children's Fears," *Journal of Experimental Psychology*, 1924, **7**, 382-390.

Watson has shown how fears might be acquired through conditioning. The next step is to discover how such fears can be eliminated. Seven methods have been described in the literature, and these methods are the subject of inquiry.

Method

Subjects: Seventy children, 3 months to 7 years of age in a temporary care institution. Children were normal in IQ, social status, etc. (Temporary residence due to illness at home, mother working, etc.)

Materials: White rats and rabbits, frogs, false faces, etc.

Procedure: All children were screened for possible fears (of the dark, being alone, animals, loud sounds). Those with readily elicitable fears were subjected to 1 of 7 different treatments (sometimes combinations, because the intent was to eliminate fears, not only to study techniques.) The techniques used will be described, along with results.

Results

One, 2, or 3 cases are described briefly in connection with each technique. The techniques used varied in numbers of attempts or hours, depending on progress.

1. *Method of Disuse:* Shield child from fear stimuli or situation for a time on the grounds that "he'll grow out of it." In 3 cases, waiting for weeks or months did not result in disappearance of fear. *Conclusion:* An unsafe method.

2. *Method of Verbal Appeal:* Talk the child out of it, pleasant stories in connection with feared object. Can be used only with older children. *Result:* Hours of talking proved ineffective.

3. *Method of Negative Adaptation:* Repeat stimulus monotonously; *S* should get used to it. *Result:* May be indifferent to formerly feared stimulus, but not a positive, pleasant reaction which was the objective.

4. *Method of Repression:* Ridicule, social teasing, scolding. *Result:* The emotion seems to be re-suggested and entrenched.

5. *Method of Distraction:* Offer a substitute activity; e.g., candy to a crying child. *Result:* Requires someone around to provide substitutes or distractions, which lead only to temporary forgetting.

6. *Method of Direct Conditioning:* Associate fear stimulus with a positive stimulus; e.g., food in presence of feared object. This method requires care and sensitivity in controlling the situation—e.g., keep a feared animal at a distance which will be tolerated. *Result:* There is a danger of reversed results but this is the only method, except for the next, which worked effectively.

7. *Method of Social Imitation:* Have a non-fearing *S* who shows positive behavior present along with the fearful one. *Result:* This method (with no. 6 above) was found to be productive in developing positive behavior.

Conclusion: Only the methods of direct conditioning and social imitation were found to be unqualified successes. The other techniques had some virtues, but they either did not lead to positive adjustments or had undesirable aspects.

Similarity in Retroactive Inhibition

Edward S. Robinson
Yale University

"The 'Similarity' Factor in Retroaction," *American Journal of Psychology*, 1927, **39**, 297-312.

The findings from retroactive inhibition (RI) studies indicate that as interpolated learning (IL) decreases in similarity from original learning (OL) there is less and less interference with recall of OL. More generally, if IL is the *same* as OL, there will be a strengthening in recall because this would amount to further practice. As IL changes from *identity* to something quite different, there will be at first a little interference, then more and more, up to some point of minimum interference; then a reversal of this gradient should occur as the IL becomes more and more dissimilar. This hypothesis is represented in the figure below where **A** represents identity of IL, B an intermediate degree of similarity, and C a minimum degree. Note that C will remain lower than A.

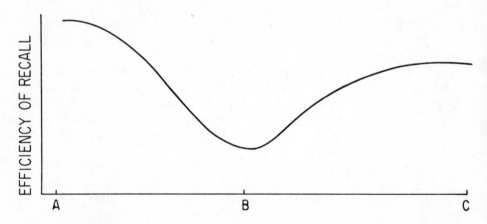

A test of this hypothesis requires that material of known (measured) degrees of similarity be available. Such material could be arranged from sets of letters, where the first half of the set could be thought of as OL and the second half as IL. The learner would not necessarily think of the set as being thus arranged and his task would be to recall the whole set. The first half of the set might run HLQR and the second HMZR, with the *S* hearing or seeing HLQRHMZR as a series. Recall would be tested on the first four letters where two are common and two are not. The number of common letters in the two halves would be a measure of similarity, which could thus range from 4 through 0 in an 8-letter set.

Method

Subjects: Twenty college students, each serving as *S* and *E* in 3 runs through 16 arrangements of letter sets in the first two experiments (visual and aural presentation of 8-letter sets) and 16 in the 3rd experiment with 12-letter sets.

Materials: Three experiments were conducted, 1 with 8-consonant sets (aural and visual presentations) and 1 with 12. The results were the same, and only the data on the 12-consonant sets will be reported here. Letters were presented as a letter-span test (both aurally and visually— no differences in this aspect). Each consonant was exposed for 0.5 seconds (or spoken at a 2/second rate).

Procedure: A prearranged set of consonants, where the first 6 conso-

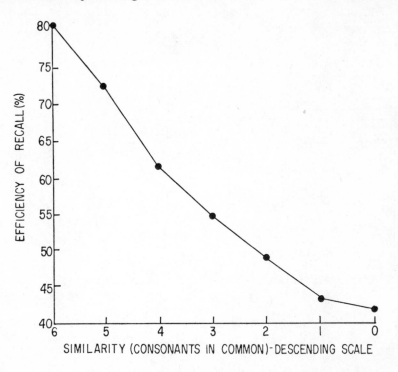

nants were always the same while the second 6 were the same or different, in varying numbers from 0-6, were read to the *S*s. As soon as the set was finished, *S* wrote out his recall.

Results

The results from all of the experiments did show the preliminary decline in the recall gradient, but there was no real evidence of any inversion or reversal of the recalls as similarity reached a minimum. The hypothesis may still be correct, but the supporting evidence is not available from these studies.

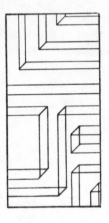

Representational Functions

Otto Leif Tinklepaugh

"An Experimental Study of Representative Factors in Monkeys," *Journal of Comparative Psychology*, 1928, **8**, 197-236.

In this report the behavior of monkeys in several delayed-reaction situations is described. In this kind of experiment the monkey sits in a chair while the experimenter places food in one of two cups at some distance from the monkey, who watches the experimenter bait the cups. The food can be in the cup on the left or the right, or the cups might be in a line with the monkey so that one cup is ahead of the other. The monkey can be made to wait for varying intervals. In general, the monkeys do well in these tests compared to rats, cats, and dogs. The experiment of special interest here is the study entitled "substitution tests with monkeys," the last study in the series described in this paper.

Method

Subjects: Five monkeys (Macacus), 1 male, 4 females. Two 5-yr-old twin boys.

Apparatus: Tin cup, wooden board, slices of banana, carrot, pieces of lettuce. Three boxes.

Procedure: For 2 of the monkeys, *E* displays a piece of banana to a seated monkey and pretends to put it in a cup behind a board. He actually places some lettuce in the cup. The monkey is then permitted to approach and pick up the cup. Tests are conducted with 2 monkeys with several-day intervals between tests. For the other 3 monkeys, a piece of carrot is placed in one of 3 boxes when a piece of banana is displayed.

Results

When the monkeys picked up the cup and saw the lettuce instead of the banana, they typically reacted in the following way: "She extends her hand to seize the food. But her hand drops to the floor without touching it. She looks at the lettuce, but (unless very hungry) does not touch it. She looks around the cup and behind the board. She stands up and looks under and around her. She picks up the cup and examines it thoroughly inside and out." Occasionally the animals would show apparent anger, walk off and leave the lettuce on the floor. Two of the monkeys behaved in this fashion (one in 13 tests out of 15, the other in 8 out of 11 tests).

When a piece of carrot was substituted for a piece of banana in the view of three monkeys, the monkeys rushed to the box and one grasped the carrot and ran off with it. When she saw what she had, she dropped it. The other two monkeys, who had pursued her, rejected the carrot. All three returned to the box and fully examined it. When *E* gave the piece of banana to one, they all gave up the search, and the unrewarded monkeys pursued the one with the banana piece.

When the twin boys were given the same treatment, with a chocolate drop substituted for a pink jelly bean they had seen being placed under a cup, they reacted with the same signs of bewilderment or surprise.

Conclusion: Monkeys gave evidence of "representative factors" standing for qualitative aspects of the food.

Latent Learning

Hugh Carlton Blodgett
University of California

"The Effect of the Introduction of Reward upon the Maze Performance of Rats," *University of California Publications in Psychology,* 1929, **5**, 113-134.

Is reward necessary for learning? If an *experimental* group of rats is run through a maze without reward as often as a *control* group which is rewarded, what will be the effect of introducing food rewards for the experimental group at a later stage (after the control group has demonstrated learning)?

Method

Apparatus: Three different kinds of mazes: A with 6 choice points, B with 4, and C with a long or short path to the goal box. All mazes had trap doors which closed after a correct turn (see first figure).

Subjects: Six groups of black and white rats. For Maze A, Group I (control), N = 36; Group II (experimental), N = 36; Group III (experimental), N = 25; Group IV, N = 10. For Maze B, 23 rats from Group I and 22 rats from Group II. For Maze C, Group V (control), N = 23 and Group VI (experimental), N = 21.

Procedure: Part I. Group I ran for seven days in Maze A, with one rewarded run per day. Group II ran for six days without reward, and were rewarded on the 7th day. Group III ran for two days wtihout reward, and were rewarded on 3rd day. *Results:* On the day after being rewarded, Groups II and III showed no significant difference in errors from Group I's performance (see the second figure).

Part II. In Maze B, rats from Group I and II showed no differences in learning ability.

Part III. With Maze A, Group IV rats showed no benefit compared to Group I after running through the Maze for 7 days in a backward direction before learning trials in the forward direction, thus demonstrating that the original results of Group II were not due to general familiarity with the maze.

Part IV. Control rats (rewarded) in Maze C, with a long and short path to the goal, gradually, over 16 days, learned to choose the short path. Unrewarded rats (experimental) showed no preference for 16 days. When rewarded on the 16th day they immediately showed the same preference as the controls.

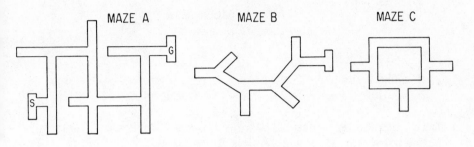

MAZE A   MAZE B   MAZE C

THE THREE MAZES

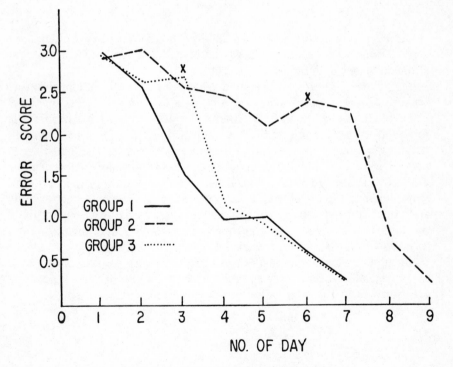

THE PERFORMANCE CURVES

Retroactive Inhibition

John A. McGeoch
University of Arkansas

"The Influence of Degree of Learning upon Retroactive Inhibition," *American Journal of Psychology,* 1929, **41**, 252-262.

Data obtained by other investigators suggests that when material is better learned it is less susceptible to retroactive inhibition (RI). The purpose of this study is to determine whether any such continuous relationship exists.

Method

Subjects: Eight students and 2 faculty members in psychology.

Materials: Lists of 9 nonsense syllables. Chicago memory drum set at a 2-second per syllable exposure rate.

Procedure: The design involved 2 kinds of sessions, a learning-rest session and a learning-work session. In a learning-rest session the S learned a list of 9 syllables for either 6, 11, 16, 21, or 26 trials. This was followed by a 5-minute "rest" period during which S rated jokes in a humor magazine. At the end of 5 minutes S relearned the list to 1 perfect recitation. Under a learning-work condition S again learned for either 6, 11, 16, 21, or 26 trials. He then learned another list of 9 nonsense syllables to an 11-trial level. Following this interpolated learning (IL), he relearned the first list to 1 perfect recitation. Any time not filled by learning was occupied with joke rating. Each S had 2 sessions per day (1 work-rest, 1 work-work). Each S went through each of the 5 different levels of original learning (OL) twice. All degrees of OL were systematically varied, as were the work-rest and work-work periods. Learning was by the anticipation method. Ss spelled out the syllables.

Results

The basic findings are the scores of correct responses under the rest and IL conditions in the 1st relearning trial. These are shown later.

Total Recall Scores on the First Relearning Trial
(total possible = 20 × 9 = 180)

| | *Number of OL Trials* | | | | |
	6	11	16	21	26
Rest	73	102	108	143	134
Work	13	22	38	55	72
Relative RI	82%	78.4%	64.8%	61.5%	46.2%

Although the 2nd cycle of sessions showed some practice effects, the trends were the same, and the results were combined for the 2 cycles. There are, thus, 20 readings for each entry in the tables.

The relative RI is found by dividing the difference between the rest and work scores by the rest score. Note the better learning and smaller RI as OL learning increases. The relearning of the 1st list to a criterion of 1 perfect recall showed the same trends. When relative RI was computed by the relearning measure—i.e., by Savings Scores—the rest sessions were followed by relatively faster relearning than the work sessions. In addition, the relative RI scores for the 5 training levels were 108.5, 23.5, 13.0, 10.5, and 5.3%, showing that RI decreased sharply between 6 and 11 repetitions and then more slowly as repetitions of OL increased.

"The conclusion is clear that measured in terms of saving score, retroactive inhibition varies inversely as the number of presentations given the material to be learned."

Early Experience

Harold E. Burt
Ohio State University

"An Experimental Study of Early Childhood Memory," *Journal of Genetic Psychology*, 1932, **40**, 287-294.

Are impressions formed in infancy retained in any form?

Method

Subject: The author's 15-month old son.

Materials: Eighteen original Greek selections from Sophocles' *Oedipus Tyrannus.*

Procedure: Three 20-line (iambic hexameter) passages wre read to the boy every day for 90 days; then 3 more were substituted for 90 days; and so on till the child was 3 years old. At the age of 8 years and 6 months, the child was asked to memorize 7 of the 15 "old" passages and 3 (presumably equivalent) new ones. The child was tested again at age 18.

Results

At age 8½ the boy required 435 repetitions to learn the "new" passages; those presented in infancy took 317. Some of the passages heard earliest in infancy took more trials than those nearer the 3-year level, but even the earliest showed a "savings" of about 30%. When tested at 18 years, there was no "savings."

Intent to Remember

Olive P. Lester
University of Chicago

"Mental Set in Relation to Retroactive Inhibition," *Journal of Experimental Psychology,* 1932, **15**, 681-699.

What is the effect of epectation of recall on the efficiency of learning? If we intend to remember something, will it be remembered better?

If we are aware of the possible factors that influence retention, can we learn in such a way as to overcome these factors? In this study the effect of a mental set, "that mental attitude which is the result of specific work instructions," is explored.

Method

Subjects: College students, naive with respect to nonsense syllables.

Apparatus: Hull memory drum, lists of 12 nonsense syllables, 3-second exposure per syllable.

Procedure: Ss appeared for 4 successive days, the first 2 for familiarization with nonsense syllable learning and for purposes of equating groups. On the 3rd day Ss learned a list of 12 syllables (List A) under varying instructions to a criterion of 1 correct trial. On the 4th day Ss in all but he control group learned another list (List B) of 12 syllables, after which they were tested by recall and relearning for the 1st list.

Results

The table shows the instructions, the original learning, recall, and re-learning scores for the 7 groups. The first group is a control for assessing the amount of RI. Group II and Group IV are the same except for the expectation of recall. Groups V, VI, and VII all expect an interpolated learning task prior to recall of list A. Each group has progressively more information, with Group VII aware of the interference effects of inter-polation and with an instruction to try to learn List A in a way that will avoid confusion with the second list.

The amount of simple RI can be estimated from Group III. The RI was quite pronounced. Simply expecting a future recall (Group II), helped recall significantly. Interpolated learning of List B reduced recall in all of the groups (III-VII). But as Ss had more and more awareness of recall, the fact of interpolated mterial and its possible effects, the re-calls improved, with Group VII being significantly superior in recall to Groups VI, V, and IV, and significantly superior to Groups IV and V in the relearning operation. Note the slight improvement in original learn-ing scores with increasingly detailed instructions.

Group	N	Conditions	Instruction	Trials to Learn A	Trials to Relearn A	Svings Score	Recall of A
I	21	Learn A	No recall expected.	24.33	8.15	66.6	4.24
II	21	Learn A	Recall expected.	24.14	6.05	79.4	4.57
III		Learn A					
		then B	No interpolated task expected.	25.30	11.35	55.2	.40
IV	33	Learn A	Recall expected.				
		then B	No interpolated task expected.	24.42	8.21	66.4	1.18
V	34	Learn A	Expect Recall.				
		then B	Expect interpolated task.	24.32	8.79	63.9	1.23
VI	35	Learn A	Expect recall and interpolation.				
		then B	Told of possible effects.	22.91	7.48	67.4	1.54
VII	35	Learn A	Expect recall and interpolation.				
		then B	Try to prevent effects.	23.48	6.83	70.9	3.08

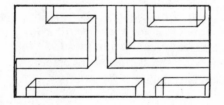

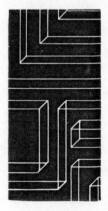

Reward and Punishment

Edward Lee Thorndike
Teachers College, Columbia University

"The Influence of Rewards and Punishment," Chapter 11,
The Fundamentals of Learning, New York, Teachers College, Columbia University, 1932.

The Fundamentals of Learning describes more than 100 experiments on
such aspects of learning as repetition, sets, knowledge of results, and
especially the influence of rewards. This abstract of parts of Chapter 11
deals with experiments 71-73 which are concerned with the effect of rewards and punishments on vocabulary learning.

Method

Subjects: College students. Experiment 71, N = 9, Experiment 72,
N = 9; Experiment 73, N = 8.
Materials: Experiment 71—200 Spanish words, each with 5 accompanying English words, 1 of which would be the correct translation. Experiments 72, 73—200 relatively rare and difficult English words with 5
other more common English words, 1 of which would be the appropriate
"translation" or synonym.

Examples

Spanish: abedul (ameer, birch, couch, carry, punch)
English: eidolon (laziness, benefice, gift, duck, phantom)
Procedure: At each of 12 runs through a list of 200 ords, *S* would
pick and underline a word from the set of 5 accompanying the key words.
If he chose correctly, *E* would say "right." If he chose incorrectly, *E*
would say "wrong." These announcements were regarded as rewards
or punishments.
*Data analysis: S*s had a 20% chance of selecting any word.
On the 1st trial, some word might have some special appeal to the *S*.
If such a word happened to be the correct answer, that word would
be ignored in the analysis. On the 2nd trial, all the selected words
were checked for correctness or error if they had not been correct on

the 1st trial. The next step was to examine Trial 3 and note the effect of the announcement in the 2nd trial. If reward had no effect, one would expect a repetition on Trial 3 of a word that was correct on Trial 2 only 20% of the time. Similarly, if a word selection had been punished, one would expect only a chance repetition unless punishment had a negative efect.

Results

The percent of choices of the same word if it were correct or incorrect on Trial 2 and on Trial 3 are given in the table. The same analysis is made for changes from Trial 3 to Trial 4. The data are recomputed from Thorndike's original figures for present uniformity.

	Subjects									
	1	2	3	4	5	6	7	8	9	Mean
Correct on 2, correct on 3	43	24	30	38	54	56	56	32	30	40
Wrong on 2, same wrong choice on 3	26	20	22	30	35	32	18	16	26	25
Correct on 3, correct on 4 but not before	27	23	50	56	87	25	58	29	27	40
Wrong on 3, same wrong on 4	29	22	25	19	34	26	24	17	22	24

Individual data are not provided for Experiments 72 and 73, but the same trends are observed. Note that 1 reward of "correct" raises the proportion of repetitions approximately 20% above chance. On the other hand, 1 punishment by "wrong" also raises the proportion of repetitions of the punished choice by about 5%.

Conclusion: Punishment does not weaken connections and may have little or no real direct effect. Indirectly, punishment may lead to other responses which are themselves strengthened by reward.

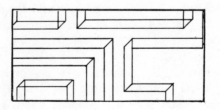

Disproof of the Law of Effect

E. C. Tolman, C. S. Hall, and E. P. Bretnall
University of California

"A Disproof of the Law of Effect and a Substitution of the Laws of Emphasis, Motivation, and Disruption," *Journal of Experimental Psychology*, 1932, **15**, 601-614.

The purpose of this study was to determine what would happen in a trial-and-error learning situation if an "annoyer" (electric shock) were applied after a correct response rather than after a wrong one. According to Thorndike, such an annoyer should weaken tendencies to respond in the way that was followed by shock.

Method

Subjects: One hundred eighty-six beginning psychology students (106 men, 80 women) in 5 groups.

Apparatus: Punch-board maze—a 3-foot square board with 30 pairs of holes in a path curving back and forth across the board. The pairs were numbered from 1 to 30. The holes were backed by brass contact plates so that when S inserted a stylus in one hole of each pair he could be shocked, hear a bell (buzzer), or both. The shock was administered through a contact held by S in his non-preferred hand and was as strong as he felt he could stand.

Design and Procedure: The Ss learned the maze according to 1 of 5 conditions to a criterion of 1 errorless trial (or 20 trials). The conditions were:

1. Bell-wrong group (N = 46): Ss were to avoid holes which resulted in buzzer sound.
2. Bell-right group (N = 47): Ss to select buzzer holes.
3. Bell-wrong (a) group (N = 25): Same as (1) except opposite holes were wired for sound.
4. Bell-shock-wrong (N = 34): Same as (1) except for shock added to buzzer.
5. Bell-shock-right (N = 34): Same as (2) except for shock added to buzzer.

Groups 1, 2, and 3 were control groups for assessment of shock effect.

Group 3 was a control over pattern difficulty.

Results

By the 20th trial, all groups had learned to a mean value of 2 or fewer errors. The basic findings are shown in the cumulative error curve. The

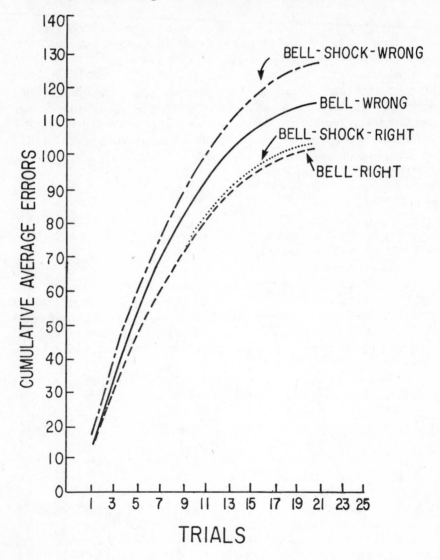

bell-right and bell-shock-right are better than the bell-wrong and bell-shock-wrong groups. The difference between the bell-shock-right and bell-shock-wrong groups also is greater than that between the bell-right and bell-wrong groups. These findings are contrary to "any ordinary formulation of the Law of Effect." Group 3's results are not shown here. They were only slightly better than Group 1, but not as much better as were the bell-right and bell-shock-right.

Interpretations

Bell alone. This "signal" assists learning when it follows correct responses more than when it follows incorrect responses. A bell is neither a reward nor punishment—it is an "emphasizer" and a signal. It "accents" the to-be-selected hole. When it accents the wrong hole, it seems to act "as a baleful fascination which attracts the performer. . . ."

Shock. When the shock is added, it also serves to emphasize and motivate (the faster the learning, the fewer total shocks). But since it did not help learning any more than the bell for correct responses, it must be regarded as a distractor for the shock-wrong group (would disturb the recall of wrong responses). For the shock-right group it would also disturb recall and counteract the "emphasis" effect of the bell alone.

Conclusion: The Laws of Motivation, Emphasis, and Disruption, as tentative hypotheses, provide a better account of the findings than does the Law of Effect.

Mediation

Walter C. Shipley
Yale University

"An Apparent Transfer of Conditioning," *Journal of General Psychology,* 1933, **8**, 382-391.

Pavlov's description of how second order (higher order) CRs are set up suggested the present attempt to elicit a CR or, at least, an *apparent*

CR, by a stimulus which, by itself, had never been paired with the response involved. The experiment, in short, is one where a transfer of a CR from one stimulus to another will be attempted.

Method

Subjects: Thirty-six male college students in 3 groups—1 experimental, 2 controls.

Apparatus: S sat in a Morris chair with a large black hood over his head and upper body to prevent seeing the experimenter and what he was doing. Inside the hood (2 feet from S) a small blackened light bulb could be illuminated to provide a faint light. A small padded hammer inside the hood could be released from a holding device to strike the S on the right cheek, producing an eyelid blink. Eyelid blinks could be recorded on a kymograph by means of a fine thread attached to the eyelid and to a marker. Electrodes on wrist and finger pad allowed for shocks to the finger pad sufficiently intense to insure finger withdrawal. Any lifting of the finger from a pressure button was recorded on the kymograph paper. Signal markers recorded the presentation of stimuli.

Procedure: There were 3 groups of Ss—an experimental group and 2 control groups. The basic design for the experimental Ss was to condition a blink reflex to the light by pairing a light and tap to the cheek, then using the tap as a CS, pairing it with shock to elicit finger withdrawal. The inter-stimulus interval was .4 sec. After the finger withdrawal was conditioned, the Ss could be tested with the flash alone to see if finger withdrawal had transferred to the flash. Control Groups B and C were given the same treatment, except that Group B had no preliminary conditioning to the light and Group C had no conditioning to the tap stimulus. The procedure took 3 days, with the following steps:

	Experimental group A (N = 15)	*Control B* (N = 10)	*Control C* (N = 11)
First Day	5 flashes alone 15 flash and tap pairs 5 taps alone 10 flash and tap pairs	5 flashes alone 15 taps alone 5 taps alone 10 taps alone	5 flashes alone 15 flash and tap pairs 5 taps alone 10 flash and tap pairs
Second Day	15 flash and tap 10 taps alone 5 flash and tap pairs	15 taps alone 10 taps alone 5 taps alone	15 flash and tap pairs 10 taps alone 5 flash and tap pairs
Third Day	5 flash and tap pairs 25 tap and shock pairs 2 flashes alone	5 taps alone 25 tap & shock pairs 2 flashes alone	5 flash and tap pairs 25 shocks alone 2 flashes alone

Note: The underlined conditions in B and C show the different treatments in B and C which were otherwise the same as in A.

Results

Nine of the 15 Ss (60% in the experimental group gave 1 or more finger withdrawal responses to the flash alone, indicating a transfer of the CR to a stimulus never paired with the US for that response. Group B, who never had the flash paired with the tap, gave no responses of finger withdrawal to the flash-alone tests. In Group C, there was no conditioning of tap and shock. In this group, only 1 S responded to the flash with finger withdrawal.

Because a majority of the experimental Ss responded by finger-withdrawal to the flash, it appears that conditioning was established in the absence of temporal contiguity of the two stimuli (flash and shock).

The results are open to three interpretations:
1. The flash could have become a functional equivalent of the shock, in what amounts to a "pre-established" second-order CR.
2. The reaction could be the result of chaining. The elicitation of a blink by the flash would also produce a kinaesthetic stimulus from blinking. This stimulus could then serve as a CS along with the shock as US for producing finger withdrawal.
3. There might be some inherent generalization in the conditioning process itself, so that once a stimulus has been conditioned to one response it becomes capable of generating other conditioned responses, perhaps limited to a given setting.

Spread of Effect

Edward Lee Thorndike
Teachers College, Columbia University

"A Proof of the Law of Effect," *Science,* 1933, **77**, 173-175.

Opponents of the Law of Effect have proposed alternate principles of learning (frequency, recency, intensity) but when such variables are held constant, satisfying after-effects are still the basic condition for the strengthening of connections. This report presents an entirely independent experimental proof.

Method

Subjects: Ten college students.

Material: Lists of words, 10 words to a list.

Procedure: The experimenter would read a word and *S* would announce a number from 1 to 10. *E* would then say "right" or "wrong." *E* would then continue with the next word and so on "again and again" until the list was learned, when a new list would be presented. Words were presented about 2½ seconds apart, including the time for response and "reward" or "punishment."

Results

The chance of being correct on any words was 1 in 10. When a reward followed a stated number, the percentage of repetitions of that number on the next trial was 50 (in 905 cases of correct reponses).

When a number was labeled "wrong" its probability of repetition could be estimated at 10%, but in this study the percentage of repetitions of wrong items varied as a function of how *close* the word was to one called "right." The closer in time a response was to one called "right" the more likely it was to be repeated. Thus the strengthening of a response by calling it "right" spreads to adjacent responses even if they are wrong. This "Spread of Effect" is evidence for the validity of the original law. A single instance of hearing "right" strengthens the tendency to repeat an adjacent wrong response about 4%.

Repetition of Wrong Responses in Terms
of Steps away from a Rewarded Response

Steps Removed	# of Cases	% of Repetitions
1	4136	26.4
2	2250	23.6
3 or 4	1933	21.0
5 or more	1228	20.8
3 or more	3161	20.7

The strongest evidence comes from those instances when a "wrong" response falls between two correct ones. The spread of effect in both directions raises the repetition rate by 7½%.

Conclusion: A satisfactory after-effect strengthens directly the connection producing it, and also those in close proximity.

The Goal Gradient

Clark L. Hull
University of Wisconsin

"The Rat's Speed-of-Locomotion Gradient in the Approach to Food," *Journal of Comparative Psychology*, 1934, **17**, 393-422.

In formulating the goal gradient hypothesis, it is assumed that reactions occurring near the goal are more strongly conditioned to the surrounding stimuli than preceding reactions, and that the stronger the excitatory tendency, the more rapid the reactions stemming from it.

Method

Subjects: Twenty-eight male Albino rats—on a 24-hour hunger drive with scanty rations.

Apparatus: A 42-foot-long alley of seven 6-foot sections with hanging hinged doors every 5 feet, providing 8 sections of 5 feet for timing the speed of running. The alley was 4 x 4 inches in its other dimensions and had starting and goal sections making up the rest of the length. It was possible to use the alley as a 20-foot run by blocking off the middle section.

Procedure: Rats were first guided through the alley twice, then given 5 trials each night for 7 nights. The time of passing each 5-foot marker was automatically recorded. Some rats first ran to a goal box 20 feet away and were then run to the 40-foot goal. Others were trained at the 40-foot goal throughout. After 7 days of training, some rats were given extinction trials. Others were run when satiated for food and water.

Results

The typical findings are shown in the figure on the next page.

Note that in the early trials the rats ran faster with each succeeding section until the last. As the training continues, the gradient flattens out. With extinction trials (after frustration and/or satiation), the gradient reappears at a higher level. The slowing down at the end could be due to

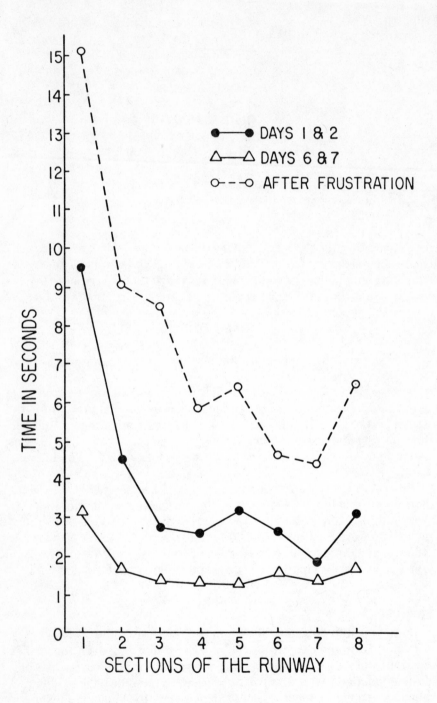

antedating of eating responses, as it appears not to be merely precaution-
ary (slowing up in slow runs as well as fast ones).

When rats were trained at the 20-foot goal and switched to the 40-foot
alley a double gradient appeared which would also flatten out with training.

The extinction (frustration) and spontaneous recovery effects parallel
Pavlov's findings on inhibition in conditioned reflex studies. Analysis of
the speed-of-running gradient suggests a positively accelerated "gradient of excitation."

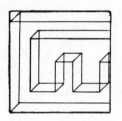

Abstract **21**

Sensory-sensory Conditioning

E. Lowell Kelly
Stanford University

"An Experimental Attempt to Produce Artificial Chromaesthesia by the Technique of the Conditioned Response," *Journal of Experimental Psychology,* 1934, **17**, 315-341.

Ever since Goethe (1810), there have been reports of people who
state that they see certain colors when they hear certain tones. This is
known as chromaesthesia, a form of synaesthesis, or combined sensory
reactions to a single stimulus which normally evokes one kind of sensory
report. Some people report tastes accompanied by color. Are such syn-
aesthetic experiences physiologically (hereditarily) determined in some
rare individuals, or is the joint sensory experience a result of some en-
counter(s) where two stimuli have become conditioned by being paired
together so that one can evoke the sensory reaction of the other?

Method

Subjects: Eighteen undergraduate and graduate college students, 13 as members of a group study, 5 participating in individual sessions.

Apparatus: A square screen (about 100 × 100 centimeters) surrounded by a black border and 7 projectors which permitted filling the screen with white or 1 of the 6 spectral colors; R, O, Y, G, B, V. Behind this screen was placed an automated keyboard accordion designed to produce the 8 musical tones from middle C to upper C. The same mechanism which depressed the keys also controlled the projectors. White was paired with both C and C', and each other note of the musical scale was paired with the color occupying the corresponding position in the spectral series.

Procedure: Group study. Ss met 4 times a week at 5:00 PM for 7 weeks. They were asked to look at the screen and listen to the tones. The tones were presented simultaneously, or just slightly before the colors, and the pair of stimuli lasted 2 seconds. The tonal stimuli were presented in ascending and descending scales with ½ second between tones and 2 seconds between scales. Ss were presented with 2 series of 40 tone-color pairs (5 scales) per session, a total of 80 paired stimulations.

Individual study: Five Ss were shown only 1 color accompanied by 1 tone, 5 pairings per minute, for 10 minutes. Two or more series of 50 pairings were presented per session up to 1000 trials. On the 4th day of each week, Ss in the group study took a test of 40 tones-only stimulations, with the request to report any color experience and to report what color "went with" each tone (a test of learning to name the tones by color).

Results

Not all Ss could meet for all sessions. The number of Ss and their scores for identifying the tones by color name are shown in the table.

Since a chance score on this test was only 5.7, it is obvious that considerable learning of paired associates did occur; the mean was 22.5 after only 360 paired presentations and increased to 31.7 after 2000 presentations. (The range of scores was 12 to 38 on test 1 and 22 to 40 on test 6.) However, none of the Ss in either the group or individual experiment ever reported a sensory experience of color on hearing a tone. "The results of the experiment with regard to chromaesthesia were certainly negative." Later, 5 of the subjects ingested mescal, a hallucinogenic drug. Although 4 of the 5 subjects experienced synaesthesias, their spontaneous colored imagery was in no way influenced on hearing the musical tones used. Thus not even "latent chromaesthesia had been established by the experimental procedures used."

Color Matching Performance of *S*s to 40 Randomly
Presented Musical Tones

Test Numbers (Week)

	1	2	3	4	5	6
No. of subjects	8	9	7	4	4	4
No. of previously presented tone-color pairs	360	680	1000	1320	1640	2000
Mean No. of correct matchings	22.5	23.1	28.0	26.0	31.0	31.7

Positive Effects of Punishment

Karl F. Muenzinger
University of Colorado

"Electric Shock for Correct Response in the Visual Discrimination Habit," *Journal of Comparative Psychology,* 1934, **17**, 267-277.

The usual pattern of research in discrimination studies is to reward responses to one stimulus (the correct) and punish responses to the wrong stimulus. No one has controlled the research properly because punishment of the correct response has not been included in the design. In this study, animals are punished for correct as well as wrong responses and compared with animals that are not punished for incorrect or correct responses. All correct responses are rewarded.

Method

Subjects: Three groups of 45-day-old Wistar rats. N = 25/group. The 3 groups were:
a. no-shock control
b. shock for correct turn
c. shock for wrong turn

Apparatus: T-maze with doors leading to food compartments on the ends of the T. Light bulbs at each end. The bulb for the correct path on any trial would be lighted. Grid floors *after* the choice point could be electrified to provide a mild shock. Cheese rewards.

Procedure: After preliminary habituation, feeding, and trial runs, animals mals were given 10 trials per day until reaching a criterion of two days of domly in any 10 trials.

	Mean Errors	S.D.	Mean Trials	S.D.
No shock group	30.0	5.6	114.4	43.7
Shock correct	13.8	6.7	48	16.25
Shock wrong	10.8	7.9	38.8	19.2

Results

The 3 groups varied in the number of trials to reach the criterion and the average number of errors per animal. The table provides these data.

The differences between each shock group and the non-shock group are significant, but the 2 shock groups do not differ significantly.

Conclusion: Moderate shock has a weakening effect (compared with non-shock) on a wrong response and a facilitatory effect on a correct response. Compared with reward alone, the effect of shock is to make the animal respond more readily to significant cues. It is not a cue itself because it was not presented before the choice was made. Annoying after-effects are not dynamically opposite to satisfiers.

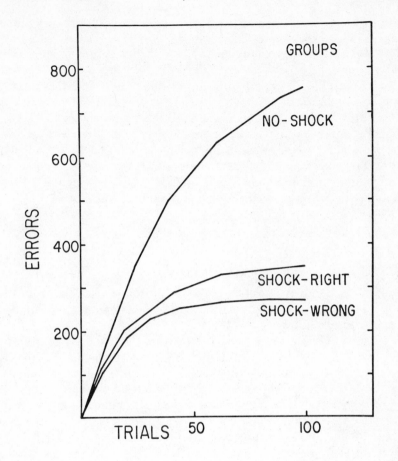

Abstract **23**

Response Substitution in Conditioning

Ernest R. Hilgard and Donald G. Marquis
Yale University

"Acquisition, Extinction, and Retention of Conditioned Lid Responses to Light in Dogs," *The Journal of Comparative Psychology,* 1935, **19**, (No. *1*), 29-58.

The closure of the eyelid in mammals is an almost ideal response for conditioning and other reflex studies. The closure can be recorded photographically, along with indicators of stimuli, and the latency, amplitude, and form of the response can be observed. Dogs were chosen in this study to provide comparison with Pavlovian subjects.

The lid response as observed in the dogs studied varies with stimulation. To a flash of light, the lids open slightly in about 65 milliseconds followed by a secondary partial closure. To a puff of air, the reaction is predominantly unilateral and occurs quickly, 15-30 milliseconds. These characteristic features were the main concern of this study.

Method

Subjects: Four normal dogs.

Apparatus: Dodge pendulum photochronoscope—an apparatus that permits single photographic recording of some simple brief movement on one strip of photosensitive paper.

Procedure: The dog, encased in a box with only the head protruding, was fitted with artificial eyelids (strips of paper which cast shadows on the photo paper). A puff of air serving as an unconditional stimulus, could be directed at one eye and a 300 candle power, 1 square centimeter light could be exposed as a CS. The light was presented 375 milliseconds before the puff in conditioning trials. After preliminary habituation to both light and puff (separately presented) conditioning trials were started, 50 trials per day for 5 days. On the 5th day after the last training trial, 60 trials of light alone were included as a test of extinction. From 3 days to 3 months later, tests were made to determine the degree of forgetting.

Results

Conditioning proceeded slowly but regularly on the five training days. The amplitude of the conditioned response rose, while the latency decreased; there are, of course, limits on these measures. By the 5th day, frequencies of response to the CS were 94, 76, 92, and 94% for the four dogs. The mean latency score had gone down to 158 milliseconds from a 3rd day peak of 171 milliseconds. On the 5th day in an extinction series of 60 light presentations, the dogs took from 11 to 50 trials to reduce the frequency of CRs by 30%. The dogs who were the first to acquire the CR were the first to extinguish.

44

An unexpected result was the finding that as conditioning began to develop, the bilateral lid opening response began a corresponding decline. With extinction of the unilateral closure, the bilateral opening response returned.

The CR was not forgotten up to a 3-month test. Reconditioning took place with a 90% savings.

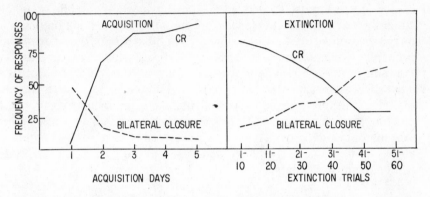

ACQUISITION AND EXTINCTION OF AN EYELID CLOSURE TO A LIGHT CS.
(Note the decrease in bilateral closure during acquisition and its return in extinction.)

Drive Discrimination

Robert Leeper
University of Chicago

"The Role of Motivation in Learning: A Study of the Phenomenon of Differential Motivational Control of the Utilization of Habits," *Journal of Genetic Psychology*, 1935, **46**, 3-40.

Is motivation important only in the *acquisition* of habits, as Thorndike's Law of Effect seems to imply, or is it vital also in *performance*—

in determining how habits are used? And, in addition to effects demonstrated by Tolman's group, can motivation have a directive influence? The pioneer experiment on this problem was provided by Hull, who hypothesized that rats, trained in a two-way maze, could probably learn to take one route when hungry and the other route, on alternate days, when thirsty. Hull's experiment yielded positive results, but Hull concluded that his rats learned so "exceedingly slowly" that, if other studies got comparable evidence, this would "place distinct limitations on the theoretical implications which might otherwise be drawn from the principle." Independently, the present author started an experiment on the same problem before Hull's article was published. By good fortune, *most* of his experimental setup was very similar to Hull's. However, planning his experiment in terms of Tolman's theory of learning, he used one function which most psychologists would have said would be unimportant, but which proved to make a powerful difference in the outcome, clearly demonstrating the phenomenon of differential motivational control of the use of habits.

Method

Several mazes of basically the same design were used for various controls, but only the basic maze, I-A, is shown here. As the diagram indicates, the maze had two goal boxes. Both were open on every trial. For a given rat, food was always available in one, water in the other. In Hull's maze, there had been only 1 goal box, accessible from the correct arm, but closed off from whichever was the wrong arm on the given day. Blocked from entering the end box from the wrong arm, the rat could retrace its path, as though out of an empty blind alley, and go around through the correct arm to get the appropriate reward-material. Both experimenters gave 5 trials daily, but put most emphasis on the daily first trials as showing most clearly whether motives can govern the use of long-term habits.

Results

The graph shows the detailed record for Leeper's 23 rats in his main experiment (with small circles indicating hungry days and triangles the thirsty days). Learning was clearly rapid. Hull's rats, over an even longer period, had less than half of their first runs correct—his rats were learning to some degree to use the route correct on each *previous* day, but not the route required when their motivation was changed. To reach a level of 80% correct, Hull's rats required twenty-five 8-day periods of training, whereas, in the present study, this level was reached after one

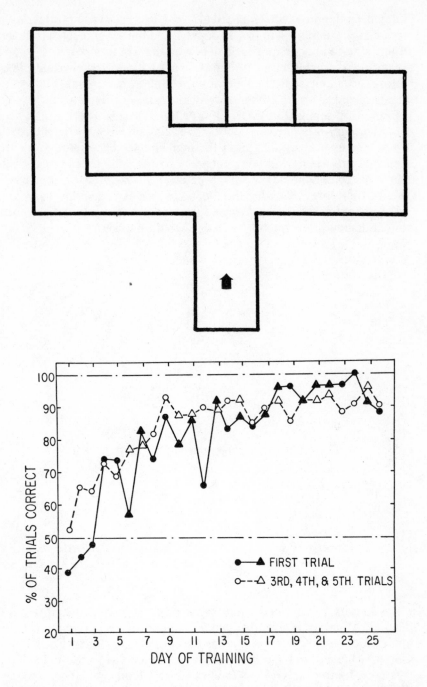

PERCENTAGE OF CORRECT CHOICES ON SUCCESSIVE DAYS OF TRAINING.

8-day period, and a 95% level after two 8-day periods. A partial replication of Hull's experiment (for 32 days) found the same results as those of Hull. Other control experiments showed that, in mazes with 2 or 3 end boxes, it did not matter whether rats were confined in the wrong end box before the next trial or whether, as with Hull, they were allowed to leave that area and go around to the correct end box. From the whole set of experiments, it seems that the learning required in this sort of situation can be either very rapid or very slow, depending on whether the alternative routes and end boxes are readily distinguishable and whether, on wrong runs, the rats are permitted to enter the wrong end box and see or smell (they never consumed) the goal-material not wanted on that day. It seems, therefore, that what the rats were learning was "knowledge" of what behavior led to what consequences, and that motivation at later points decided how such knowledge would be used.

Extinction as Response Competition

G. R. Wendt
Yale University

"An Interpretation of Inhibition of Conditioned Reflexes as Competition between Reaction Systems," *Psychological Review,* 1936, **43**, 258-281.

"An activity is inhibited when some other behavior system takes its place." All inhibitions of the spinal cord are reciprocal inhibitions. Antagonistic reflex systems compete. This principle of Reciprocal Innervation may have broad implications for more complex reflex and behavior systems. Inhibition is not, as Pavlov viewed it, an independent process. What needs to be demonstrated is that as one reaction system seems to drop out or cease, another system has been developing and replacing the first.

Experiment I. Habituation to rotation.

Method

Subjects: Monkeys and humans (total of 102).
Apparatus: Rotating chair, eye-movement photographic equipment.
Procedure: Ss are repeatedly rotated through short arcs (15 to 65 degrees).

Results

Original response to rotation is a nystagmoid eye-movement during rotation, with little after-movement. As habituation proceeds, a new eye movement system begins to intrude. "Instead of making a compensatory response at the onset of rotation, an opposite response may be made so that the eyes move toward the direction of rotation. . . . The normal uninhabituated response to a rapid short rotation to the right (65 degrees) is a compensatory drift to the left interrupted by several saccadic movements to the right. At a certain stage of habituation this reflex is replaced by an irregular or tremulous shift to the right at onset of rotation." Compensatory reaction has been replaced by an antagonistic eye-movement system.

Experiment II. Inhibition of Food-taking responses by monkeys.

Method

Subjects: Eleven monkeys.
Apparatus and Procedure: A monkey is trained to open a drawer to get a piece of food when a tone comes on. The monkey is in a cage, the drawer outside. The cage area through which the monkey reaches can be covered by a curtain. The training in sequence is: Ready signal. After 5 seconds the curtain is raised. After either 8 or 16 seconds the tone occurs and the monkey can open the drawer. If the monkey fails to wait for the tone he finds an empty drawer. The experimental question: How does a monkey wait?

Results

If Pavlov were correct, there should be signs of an irradiating inhibition. Actually the monkeys filled "the delay interval with other substitute responses natural to the situation." The kinds of response varied with monkey species, ranging from grooming to fear responses. Activity included scratching, cage manipulation, vocalizing, galloping, climbing, biting sides of the cage, circling about the opening. With continued practice, the activities became more localized (in the vicinity of the drawer); e.g., manipulating the curtain cords and sides of the food-box, placing a foot on the drawer handle, etc. As training was continued the responses became even more intimately related to the drawer handle, sliding the paw on it, giving it a slight pull. One baboon learned to pull the curtain back so as to hide the drawer or to cover the drawer handle. Instead of Pavlov's concept of "inhibition of delay," a better description might be "activity of delay."

Conclusion: The observations support the interpretation of inhibition as instances of competition between reaction systems, analogous to the reciprocal inhibitions of the spinal cord.

Generalization Curves

Carl I. Hovland
Yale University

"The Generalization of Conditioned Responses: I. The Sensory Generalization of Conditioned Responses with Varying Frequencies of Tones," *Journal of General Psychology*, 1937, **17**, 125-148.

Precise data on the form of the curve of generalizations is not available, yet it is of great importance for theories of transfer. The purpose of this study is to ascertain the way in which generalization spreads. Is it concave, convex, flat? Does it decrease sharply at some point? Does extinction follow the same laws of generalization as hold for the CR?

Method

Subjects: Sixty college students—20 in the generalization study and 40 in the extinction group.

Apparatus: Oscillator for sound stimuli, galvanometer for recording CSRs, inductorium for presenting shocks.

Procedure: A preliminary procedure was employed with 10 Ss to determine their sensitivity to sound frequencies in order to establish a scale of frequencies that could be described as equally distant. Just noticeable differences from a tone of 1000 cycles were found by the Method of Limits. Tones of 25 j.n.d.s were then selected as CSs. The tones were 153, 468, 1000, and 1967 cycles. They were checked for their tendency to elicit GSRs and found essentially equal. They were also checked for effectiveness as CSs and again found essentially equal. They appeared, therefore, to be basically different only in their pitch qualities. The tones were also equated for loudness.

For the generalization study, the highest tone (1967 cycles) was used as a CS for half the Ss, the lowest for the other half.

The US was an "unpleasant but not painful" shock. CS and US were paired 16 times. The CS lasted 400 milliseconds, and 495 milliseconds after CS onset the brief (75 millisecond) shock was given. After the 16 conditioning trials, 2 tests were made of the CSR at each of the other frequencies.

Extinction Study: All 4 sound frequencies were used as CS, with 6 paired stimulations (tone and US). Then the highest and lowest frequencies were subjected to extinction (each for half the Ss) for 16 extinction trials, following which the other stimuli were tested for spread of extinction.

Results

The curves for generalization and generalization-of-extinction are shown in the figures. In both cases they indicate clear-cut negative acceleration. In the extinction curve it should be noted that the CS furthest away from the extinguished one shows the least loss.

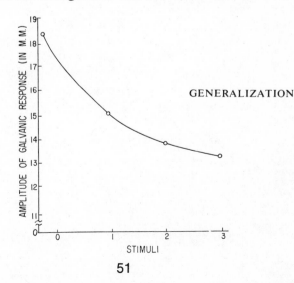

51

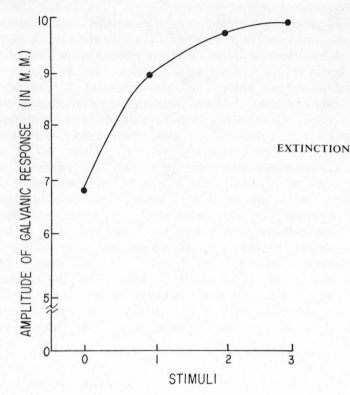

Transposition

Kenneth W. Spence
Yale Laboratories of Primate Biology

"In a Single Dimension," *Psychological Review*, 1937, **44**, 430-444.

Gestalt psychologists emphasize that organisms respond to not only the absolute, physical properties of stimuli, but to relationships between stimuli, such as *larger than, brighter than,* etc. Support for such an assumption would come from transposition tests after training. If an *S* is trained to select the larger of two stimuli with a given pair of training items, he should continue to select the larger of any other two items differing in the same dimension. Evidence from such test trials may indeed show an apparent response to relationships, but if the tests are carried out at greater and greater distances, the proportion of positive selections appear to drop off. What may be happening can be accounted for in terms of the figure, where a stimulus dimension of size (square centimeters) is arranged on the abcissa. A stimulus value of 256 is made positive, 160 is negative; i.e., an organism will be reinforced for responding to 256 and not reinforced if it responds to 160. Curves of generalization of excitatory and inhibitory tendency extend from each stimulus, and their stimulus value at any point on the abcissa can be read as the algebraic summation of the two. Note that although 256 is always reinforced, it has a value of only 4.84 because it is subject to the negative generalized tendency from 160, which, although consistently non-reinforced, has a value of 3.16. All these values are arbitrarily based on assumptions about generalization curves and sensory stimulus values. The values indicated are only suggestive and subject to correction from appropriate data-gathering studies. The diagram is designed only to explain how responses to relationships might appear to be made, when, in fact, the responses are being governed by net excitatory value of stimuli. Thus, in the diagram, the stimulus value at 655 exceeds that at 409, and the organism should select the larger stimulus. But at 1049 the stimulus value is less than at 655, and the smaller value would be chosen.

Experimental Findings

In a study with 5 chimpanzees the animals were trained to find food left behind one of two white metal squares differing only in size. Three were trained to select the larger stimulus (a white metal square shielding a food compartment) and 2 were trained to select the smaller. The animals were then tested with squares of other values. The results are shown in the table. Note that the animals Pati, Mona, and Pan were trained to react to the larger stimulus, while Soda and Benita had to choose the smaller. The results of this preliminary study (there should be more Ss and only 1 test per S over a larger range) show a decreasing average tendency to select the stimulus with the original positive value sign. On the basis of such data the proper generalization curves could be drawn to determine more accurate prediction.

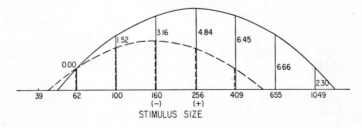

STIMULUS SIZE

Showing the Percentage of Responses Consistent with the Original Training,
i.e., to the Larger (or Smaller) Stimulus of the Combination

Training Stimuli		*Test Stimuli*	
160 (+) vs. 100 (−)	256 vs. 160	320 vs. 200	409 vs. 256
Pati	100%	80%	80%
	100%	100%	60%
Mona	50%	40%	80%
	100%	70%	60%
Pan	80%	90%	90%
	100%	100%	100%
	Mean = 88.3%	Mean = 80%	Mean = 78.3%
256 (+) vs. 409 −)	160 vs. 256	100 vs. 160	
Soda	50%	40%	
	70%	50%	
Benita	40%	30%	
	60%	40%	
	Mean = 55%	Mean = 40%	

Secondary Reinforcement

B. R. Bugelski
Yale University

"Extinction with and without Sub-goal Reinforcement,"
Journal of Comparative Psychology, 1938, **26**, 121-133.

In sequential or serial responses, the occurrence "along the way" of
stimuli related to goal behavior may function as subgoals. Failure of

such stimuli to occur could be frustrating and hasten extinction. Bar pressing in the Skinner Box is a sequential series of stimuli and responses (when the bar is pressed, the food-dispensing equipment generates a variety of sounds or clicks before the food appears in the receptacle). Following the press, the rat turns to the food-cup where the food (preceded by the mechanical clicks) will appear. The "click" can become conditioned to the food-approach response. Failure of the click to occur should create some frustration. If the press is not reinforced, as in an extinction trial, the additional frustration of silence added to the basic frustration of nonreinforcement should hasten extinction.

Method

Subjects: Sixty-four albino rats.
Apparatus: Four Skinner-type boxes, recording tape.
Procedure: All rats were given the same 3-day preliminary training schedule.

Day 1. Three ½-hour periods in the box with 10 pellets of food. Then 30 pellets of food supplied by E operating the dispenser from outside the box. With each pellet the dispenser "clicked."

Day 2. Two bar-press periods separated by 10 minutes. In each period the rat had to press the bar 15 times. Total reinforced presses = 30. Time for earning 30 pellets served as the basis for equating groups.

Day 3. *Extinction*. Rats placed in boxes and kept till 5 minutes passed without a response. After a 10 minute out-of-box rest, the animals underwent a second extinction. For the extinction runs the animals were divided into 4 groups. For the 1st extinction, 32 rats worked under normal conditions (except for no food); the other 32 rats got no food but also heard no clicks from the dispenser because it was disconnected from the bar. For the 2nd extinction, half of each group (N = 16 per group) had the same condition as for the first extinction; the other half had the reverse.

Results

The number of bar presses produced by each group appears in the table. Groups I and III comprised 1 group for the first extinction, as did Groups II and IV.

In the first extinction, the click groups averaged about 77 responses to about 54 (a 30% difference) for the non-click groups, a significant difference. Note that Group II is the strongest in the second extinction, as if revived by the click. But, note also that this group had not expended

N	Group	Extinction Condition		Means	
		First	*Second*	*First Extinction*	*Second Extinction*
16	I	click	no click	63.12	11.88
16	II	no click	click	43.12	27.14
16	III	click	click	91.90	14.38
16	IV	no click	no click	65.00	7.17

much activity in the first extinction. Group IV included some older, larger rats who were originally quite resistant to extinction in the first session, but a·second period of silence following bar presses quickly stopped the bar pressing.

Conclusion: The non-nutritive noise served as a subgoal in the bar-pressing situation and helped maintain the response. Its absence added frustration and hastened extinction.

Pseudo-conditioning

W. F. Grether
University of Wisconsin

"Pseudo-conditioning without Paired Stimulation Encountered in Attempted Backward Conditioning," *Journal of Comparative Psychology,* 1938, **25**, 141-158.

As the title implies, the original study was an attempt to attain backward conditioning. Animal *S*s were chosen because humans can verbalize and perhaps effect a backward conditioning study in which the CS *follows* the US. The actual observations led to an examination of "pseudo-conditioning."

Method

Subjects: Four Rhesus monkeys.

Apparatus: One-way vision screen, restraining chair for monkeys. Two USs (flashlight powder, and a toy snake blowout—a toy that uncurls, producing a rattling noise) and a bell as a CS.

Procedure: The bell was pretested and found to produce only an orienting response or none at all.

Two *experimental* animals were then given 10 paired stimulations (2 to 5 minutes apart) of 1 of the USs and the bell CS. The CS followed the US in 3 seconds.

The 2 *control* animals were given only the 10 USs. No CS was introduced.

Tests for conditioning were run on the 11th trial.

Results

1. *Experimental group.* Both animals reacted to the bell alone. Responses (sudden backward movement of head and torso, struggling, vocalization) were almost identical to responses to US.

2. *Control group.* Both monkeys reacted just like the experimental monkeys. Because they had no paired stimulations, their reactions could not be considered backward conditioning and, by the same token, the experimental animals' behavior is suspect as far as conditioning is concerned.

3. *Generalization.* Almost any moderately loud sound could produce the reaction for several days if the monkeys were in the experimental chair, but not outside the experimental chamber.

4. Because the explosion of the flash powder was accompanied by a sound, as was the unfolding of the snake, these sounds were tested without their visual aspects with the control animals behind a screen. The animal stimulated by flash powder gave no response; the other reacted violently to the sound of the blowout as it did to other sounds of equal intensity.

Conclusion: The results suggest caution in interpreting results of conditioning experiments. The animals may have been conditioned to adopt an expectancy attitude in the experimental quarters and might give a fear response to any sudden noise. The pseudo-conditioning might then be considered a kind of facilitation except for its long-term duration. Certainly there was a modification in behavior, but not of a backward conditioning variety. And other experiments purporting to support backward conditioning might be susceptible to the explanation offered here.

Field Orientation

Donald O. Hebb
Harvard University

"Studies of the Organization of Behavior: I. The behavior of the rat in a field orientation," *Journal of Comparative Psychology*, 1938, **25**, 333-351.

The experiment was designed to follow up on preliminary work which suggested "a peculiar dependence of the rat upon remote environmental cues in seeking food, with an apparent complete disregard of the more immediate ones." While human observers may consider certain stimuli they have arranged to be the stimuli affecting their subjects, the actual stimuli may be something quite different. Any accurate analysis of neural activity depends on a precise appreciation of the stimuli that are actually functioning. The study reported here is one in a series planned to relate behavior to brain functions. (In this particular report, brain-damaged rats were used in part of the work, but, because the rats with brain lesions showed no significant differences from normal rats, only the normal rats will be considered in this abstract).

Method

Subjects: Nine hooded male rats, 3 to 5 months old.

Apparatus: A circular black table 4 feet in diameter, with a 26×26 inch black plywood square in the center of the table. At each corner of the square there was a compartment or shield consisting of two walls (see figure) 4 inches high. The shields were painted black. One of the shields had a 5½-inch-high structure, painted white, fitting around the black sides so that to a human observer it was an outstanding feature of the apparatus. The table was in a constant position in the windowless room, with a ceiling light directly above it. An open door allowed light from a large window to provide some remote illumination, and an air-shaft at one side of the room provided a constant hum.

Procedure: The apparatus is shown in reversed colors. Note the numbers and letters. These will be referred to later.

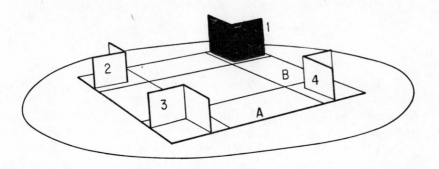

The rats, after preliminary training on a long, narrow table were trained to find food in the distinctive white compartment. In the training trials they were placed at point A, facing away from the shield, and released. Approach and/or entry into any of the other 3 compartments were scored as errors. There were 10 trials per day until a criterion of 19 out of 20 successive correct runs was reached.

Testing. On reaching criterion, the animals were given 30 test trials. On the following day, they were retrained and given 30 more test trials. Thus, each animal had 20 test trials of 3 different kinds, as follows:

Test A. (20 trials) The white cover was removed from the goal compartment.

Test B. (20 trials) White cover was retained but the rats were started from point B, a 90° rotation of the starting point.

Test C. (20 trials) The plywood square was rotated 90° and rats were started at Point A, as in training, so that Shield 4 now occupied the former goal position.

(There were some other tests for some of the rats, but these will not be covered here).

Results

The results, in terms of which shield the animals approached in the 20 trials of each test, are shown in the table on the next page.

In Tests A and B the rats preferred Shield No. 1, the original test

Test A Shield No.				Test B Shield No.				Test C Shield No.			
1	2	3	4	1	2	3	4	1	2	3	4
16.1	1.1	2.0	0.8	15.3	1.6	0.8	2.3	1.0	0.4	2.8	15.7

shield, despite the missing white structure in Test A. In Test C, the rats preferred the original geographical, or absolute, location of the former goal.

Conclusions

1. Test B and C indicate that the rats were not depending upon olfactory or kinaesthetic cues; in Test C, kinaesthetic cues would have led the rats to the original goal in its new position; in Test B, they should have gone to Shield 2 on the basis of kinaesthetic cues.
2. "The preference was for a shield lying in a certain direction from the center of the apparatus rather than for the shield distinguished by size and color, by position in the room, or by any relation to the position of the rat at the starting point."
3. Remote auditory and visual cues could not be directly responsible for the preferences (established by other tests), so that the animals must have been dependent upon the immediate visual cues in relation to or as "polarized by" the cues from the remote environment." In brief, auditory and visual room cues determine an orientation which, in turn, gives differential value to the visually perceived parts of the immediate situation."

Amounts of Reinforcement

Stanley B. Williams
Yale University

"Resistance to Extinction as a Function of the Number of Reinforcements," *Journal of Experimental Psychology,* 1938, **23**, 506-522.

Pavlov, Hull, and Skinner all agree that resistance to extinction is an appropriate measure of learning strength. Few studies have explored the relationship between number of reinforcements and extinction measures. In this study 3 measures of extinction (number of responses, time to extinction, and rate of response) will be observed in relation to 4 values of reinforcement.

Method

Subjects: One hundred forty male albino rats, 60-100 days old.
Apparatus: Skinner-type lever-press box.
Procedure: Preliminary training: one week of scheduled eating at the same hour. Last 3 days in the box without the lever.

Experimental pre-training: Three days of feeding on pellets in the box, with 60 pellets in groups of 10. The feedings were spaced 5 minutes apart. The pellets were dropped 1 at a time and the animals learned to come to the food dish at the sound of the delivery mechanism.

Experimental training: The next day, the lever was introduced into the box and different groups of 35 rats received either 5, 10, 30, or 90 pellets, 1 for each bar press. The time for the first 5 presses in all groups was about 3 minutes. The mean total time for each group was 3.1, 6.2, 11.5, and 29.6 minutes respectively for the 5, 10, 30, and 90 pellet groups.

Extinction: Twenty-two hours after training, each rat was placed in the box and left there until 5 minutes went by without a bar press. One hour later the animals underwent a second extinction.

Results

In the table are the means of the 3 measures for each group of *S*s.

	Groups (No. of Reinforcements)			
Measure of resistance to extinction	5	10	30	90
No. of responses to 5 min. criterion	19.00	35.00	48.30	62.70
Time to reach criterion (minutes)	7.90	15.00	17.10	20.60
Rate of response (in minutes)	.64	.64	.47	.40
Second extinction				
No. of responses	6.70	10.40	12.30	19.80
Time (minutes)	3.90	5.30	5.70	8.40
Rate (in minutes)	.75	.58	.52	.41

The data for numbers of responses are plotted in the figure. In general, these data are most closely correlated with number of reinforcements. The ratio of extinction responses to reinforcements becomes progressively smaller with increasing amounts of reinforcement. Rate of response is the poorest of the 3 measures. In the second extinction, the amount of recovery is roughly proportional to the original reinforcement.

In the original learning of the 90 reinforcement group, the only one with enough trials to be useful in this connection, the animals appear to have reached asymptotic performance by the first 30 reinforcements.

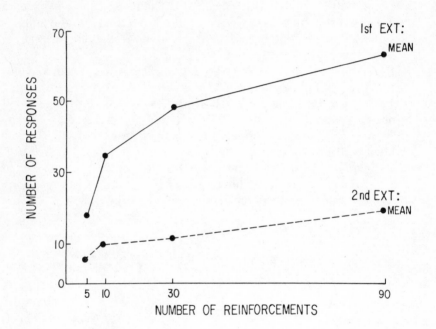

Sensory Pre-conditioning

W. J. Brogden
University of Wisconsin

"Sensory Pre-conditioning," *Journal of Experimental Psychology,* 1939, **25**, 323-332.

Prior Russian and American experiments in sensory conditioning failed to control for motor responses to one of the stimuli. Can two stimuli which do not evoke some phasic reaction be associated together so that when one is conditioned to evoke flexion to shock, the other will elicit the same response when tested later?

Method

Subjects: Sixteen mongrel dogs—8 experimental, 8 control.

Procedure: Experimental animals were given combined stimulation for 2 seconds by a bell and a light 20 times a day for 10 days. Then 4 dogs were given conditioning trials (shock to forelimb as US) with the 2-second light as CS, and 4 with the 2-second tone as CS. Conditioning proceeded with 20 trials per day until there were 20 CRs in one session. Control animals were similarly conditioned to light or bell, but with no prior association of light and bell. After conditioning, all animals were tested to an extinction criterion of 0 responses to the stimulus which had not been paired with shock. Twenty extinction trials were given per day.

Results

The 8 experimental animals required 10-18 sessions to give 20 CRs in a session. The bell was a somewhat better CS than the light. Of the 4 dogs with the bell as CS only 2 responded in test trials with the light. They responded 27 times in 11 test periods. Control animals gave no responses to the novel stimulus. Dogs with the light as CS gave 56 flexion responses in 16 test periods. One control dog responded to the bell (not a CS) 4 times in 5 test periods. The 6 experimental animals required 27 test periods (20 stimulations per period) to extinguish, giving a total of 78 flexion responses.

Discussion and Conclusions

Some connection must have been formed between the bell and the light as a result of contiguous stimulation. The relationship of the bell and light is difficult to appreciate in view of Kelly's (1934) failure to demonstrate chromaesthesia by pairing colors with sounds. Sensory pre-conditioning presumably occurs in natural environments whenever stimuli are experienced together, and one later becomes a CS for some response.

Abstract **33**

Partial Reinforcement

Lloyd G. Humphreys
Stanford University

"The Effect of Random Alternation of Reinforcement on the Acquisition and Extinction of Conditioned Eyelid Reactions," *Journal of Experimental Psychology,* 1939, **25,** 141-158.

It is commonly assumed that the strength of conditioned responses is a function of the frequency of reinforcement. Skinner, among others, has challenged this view with his findings from "schedules" of reinforcement. Pavlov, himself, reported faster conditioning by a partial reinforcement procedure. In this study the influence of reinforcement frequency on the acquisition and retention of conditioned eyelid blinks will be examined.

Method

Subjects: Three groups of 22 college students (9 men, 13 women per group); total N = 66.
Apparatus: Photographic recording of eyelid closures by reflections of light from a mirror attached to a lever which would move slightly via a

string attached to the eyelid. The CS was an increase in illumination (approximately 15 foot-candles) behind a flash glass panel. The US was a puff of air. Interstimulus interval: 400 milliseconds.

Procedure: The *S*s were divided into 3 treatment groups:

1. Continuous or 100% reinforcement for 96 trials.
2. Partial reinforcement—48 reinforced trials interspersed with 48 non-reinforced (CS alone) trials.
3. A spaced reinforcement group—100% reinforcement of 48 trials with rest pauses corresponding to Group 2 non-reinforced stimulations.

For all 3 groups, 24 extinction trials followed acquisition. Half the acquisition trials were given on one day, half the next.

Percent of Conditioned Responses

	Acquisition	Extinction
Group 1 (100% massed reinforcement)	.65	.31
Group 2 (50% reinforcement)	.59	.60
Group 3* (100% spaced reinforcement)	.64	.34

* *This group had only 48 paired stimulations.*

Results

Acquisition and extinction data appear in the table (only frequency data are reported, although amplitude measures were also made).

There were no significant differences in the acquisition scores, and Group 1 and 3 are virtually alike. Forty-eight spaced trials provide the same percent of CRs as 96 massed trials. The learning curves, especially on the 2nd day, are very similar.

In the extinction scores, Group 2 was "strikingly more resistant to extinction" than the other groups which hardly differ. The differences between Group 2 and the others is highly significant.

Conclusion: "It is obvious that comparable performance during acquisition does not lead in all cases to comparable performance during extinction." The classical theory of the correlation between number of reinforcements and conditioning strength appears to be refuted. As an account of the findings an "expectancy" hypothesis is favored. The *S* in Group 2 *expects* the puff although he knows it may not come. During extinction he may continue to expect the US. The non-reinforced trials may be more impressive, for the 100% reinforced groups, in leading to a changed expectancy.

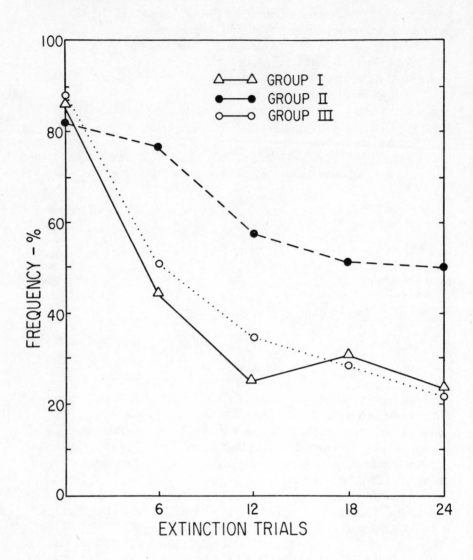

Insight

Louis A. Peckstein and Forrest D. Brown
University of Cincinnati

"An Experimental Analysis of the Alleged Criteria of Insight Learning," *Journal of Educational Psychology*, 1939, **30**, 38-52.

The insight theory of learning proposed by Gestalt psychologists has been contrasted with Thorndikean trial-and-error theory. The criteria of insight are generally accepted to be:

1. immediate solution (if within the capacity of the learner)
2. sudden solution (in situations too complex for immediate solutions)
3. response to situation as a whole
4. response to meaningful relationships in a situation
5. evidence of mental activity (inspection, pause, concentrated attention)
6. absence of random activity and chance as primary factors.

Such criteria were developed from work with the great apes. The present study examines some problem-solving situations with great apes and children as subjects.

Method

Subjects: A female gorilla, male chimpanzee, eight children (2 years, 6 months to 7 years, 3 months).
Apparatus: Puzzle box locked with iron bars under catches. The bars had to be withdrawn before the hinged top could be opened. Sticks, 1 hollow which could receive the other as an extension.

Procedure: The first experiment with the 2 apes was a replication of Kohler's study with chimpanzees. Both single- and double-stick problems were arranged for. The second problem was the puzzle box. Both apes and children were used in this situation. The procedures will be described with the results.

Results

Single-stick problem. A stick long enough (2 feet) to reach food was placed half-in and half-out of the cage. This turned out to be no problem for the chimpanzee, who used the stick effectively after first reaching for food by hand. The chimpanzee had had considerable experience using heavy rice straws as tools, and his success could be interpreted as transfer from such experience. The gorilla required 14 trials over 6 days to *learn* to use the stick. By waving the stick around, in play, the food would be struck accidentally at first. The learning was not sudden or immediate.

Double-stick problem. Only the chimpanzee was used in this situation. The problem was solved in 11 trials over 4 days. The first trial was terminated unsuccessfully after 30 minutes, with the chimp using the sticks separately in futile attempts. The chimpanzee, in play, put the sticks together and waved the larger stick about. In the second trial he happened to approach the food with the longer stick in hand and raked it in. The chimpanzee "gradually learned the relation between success in obtaining food and the two sticks joined." He displayed "insight" at the end of the learning process which "was essentially trial-error in nature."

Puzzle-box. The children and both apes were given the problem of opening the box to get food or a ball. Opening the box called for moving 1, 2, or 3 bars out from under catches. The problems were arranged in difficulty so that each S started with only 1 bar to move. The gorilla solved the easy problem by chance, without the S even knowing the problem was solved. The gorilla handled the 2-bar problem easily, but the 3-bar problem proved too difficult even after 8 chance solutions, until further practice with the 2-bar problem. The chimpanzee and the older children also solved the problems by trial-and-error. The 2½-year-old child's behavior resembled that of the gorilla.

Conclusion: None of the learning was immediate. Any sudden solutions were the results of transfer of past experience. Reactions to significant elements emerge from reactions to the whole situation. Chance plays a dominating role. Insight is the end-product of learning and not a principle of how learning takes place.

Semantic Conditioning

G. H. S. Razran
Columbia University

"A Quantitative Study of Meaning by a Conditioning Salivary Technique (Semantic Conditioning)," *Science*, 1939, **90**, 89-90.

Although conditioning to verbal stimuli has been reported before, it should be realized that words are visual or oral signs in their physical form, but they also have meanings. No one has determined if the conditioning has been to the physical features or the semantic, or meaning, features of the verbal stimuli. This study proposes to assess the relative strengths of the meaning versus the physical aspects of words used as conditioning stimuli. An approach to such a distinction is available by the use of generalization tests with synonyms and homonyms.

Method

Subjects: Three college students who were told the study dealt with digestion and vision.

Apparatus: Dental cotton rolls, scale for weighing cotton rolls. Set of words for CSs (*style, urn, freeze, surf*). Sets of generalization words (a synonym and homonym of each CS word). Candy, gum, and tea-sandwiches for UCs.

Procedure: Ss chewed gum, licked at lollipops, or ate sandwiches for five 3-minute sessions (to generate salivation). During the eating period CS words were flashed 15 times each. In the following 8 minutes the Ss were tested with CS words alone to determine amounts of conditioning. This was done by weighing the cotton rolls after they were held under the tongue for 1-minute periods after a word was shown. In a series of 5 test sessions, the Ss were tested for transfer to the synonyms or homonyms.

Results

The entries in the table are averages for 3 tests for each of the 3 Ss (9 tests). Note that the data for the responses to the CSs are given in milligrams (net amount of salivation after subtraction of control amounts) and the entries for homonyms and synonyms are entered as percentages of the response to the CS.

Conditioned Salivations in Milligrams of 3 Adult Human Subjects to Words That Have Been Flashed on a Screen while the Subjects Were Eating and to 4 Homophones and 4 Synonyms of These Words

Words	*Experimental Session*				*Mean*
	2	3	4	5	
style	234	276	293	218	255
stile	57%	51%	43%	49%	50%
fashion	64%	76%	66%	69%	69%
urn	186	199	234	223	211
earn	41%	34%	26%	34%	34%
vase	50	54	48	44	49
freeze	268	308	314	246	284
frieze	38%	32%	45%	46%	40%
chill	43%	56%	68%	72%	60%
surf	190	230	240	310	243
serf	24%	20%	18%	28%	23%
wave	46%	52%	68%	58%	56%
Mean for conditioned words	220	253	270	249	249
Mean for homophones	40%	34%	33%	39%	37%
Mean for synonyms	51%	60%	63%	61%	59%

The transfer or generalization was greater to synonyms (59%) than to homonyms (37%). The conclusion that verbal conditioning is primarily semantic seems justified, although there is an important degree of conditioning to the visual-auditory aspect. As tests continued, the transfer to meaning seemed to increase while the homonyms appeared to lose power to elicit the salivation.

Images as Conditioned Sensations

Clarence Leuba
Antioch College

"Images as Conditioned Sensations," *Journal of Experimental Psychology*, 1940, **26**, 345-351.

Can sensations be conditioned to objective stimuli in the same automatic, mechanical, and unconscious fashion as objective responses?

Method

Subjects: Eight college students over a 10-year span.

Procedure: Each *S* was deeply hypnotized and given suggestions for post-hypnotic amnesia. Additional suggestions were given to produce complete concentration on the stimuli provided by the experimenter. Two sensory stimulations would then be given to *S*, such as: bell and pin-prick on the back of the hand, some sound and some visual stimulus, a cutaneous and olfactory stimulus, etc. When *S* was awakened, 1 of the paired stimuli would be presented and *S*s reactions would be noted. There were several pairings of each set of stimuli, usually about 6.

Paired Stimuli	Post-hypnotic *Test Stimulus*	*Reaction*
Pin prick to hand and bell	bell	hand movement, report of feeling something there
Phonograph record; picture of pagoda	record	*S* asked to draw something, drew pagoda
Six taps on hand with ruler; sound of can being struck	can sound	*S* jerked back head first two times
Poke in side with ruler; shown a stop watch	poke	*S* reported silver ring with dot in center when shown a blank card
Cricket snap; hand prick	cricket	hand jerked away, felt hand prick
Ruler rub on hand; creosote odor	ruler rub	report of "tarred road"
S moves arm while looking at a drawing of a cube	arm movement	cube drawing reported to be on blank card
Cricket snap and creosote	cricket	odor of creosote reported

Results

A total of 17 different tests (15 successful) were carried out with the 8
*S*s. The results are shown in the table. The test stimulus was usually
given only after a series of irrelevant stimuli.

The sensory reactions (images) reported were frequently preceeded
by some movement, e.g., arm withdrawal, nose wrinkling, or sniffing.

In general, *S*s reported being puzzled by their unusual sensory experiences, which, though brief and fleeting, were frequently intense. It is
concluded that after several presentations of paired stimuli (under the
conditions of limited attention developed here) one of the paired stimuli
can "automatically, and without the intervention of any conscious processes, produce these sensations. An image can therefore be considered
as a conditioned sensation."

The Unlearning Hypothesis

Arthur W. Melton and Jean McQueen Irwin
University of Missouri   Scripps College

"The Influence of Degree of Interpolated Learning on Retroactive Inhibition and the Overt Transfer of Specific Responses," *The American Journal of Psychology*, 1940, **53**,
173-203.

Does retroactive inhibition (RI) develop in the early or intermediate
stages of interpolated learning (IL)? Some published data suggest that
RI decreases with overlearning of IL. Different methods of measuring
RI (writing out responses, vocalizing in limited time, trials to relearn)
show different results. This experiment is designed to explore the locus
of RI in serial learning.

Method

Design: Ss learned 2 lists of nonsense syllables under different conditions in 6 learning sessions. The 1st list, original learning or OL, was relearned after the 2nd list for a determination of RI.

Subjects: Twenty-four college males, paid for participation.

Materials: Twenty-four lists of 13 nonsense syllables were prepared from Glaze's lists of 24.5 to 29.3% association value. The lists were carefully balanced for letter content so as to assure stable differences between any 2 lists used in any 1 session. A 2-second-per-item memory drum was used with an anticipation method for serial learning. Ss spelled out each syllable or as much of it as they could anticipate.

Procedure: S was given 5 trials on a 1st list and then learned a 2nd list for 5, 10, 20, or 40 trials. In 1 (control) condition no 2nd list was learned. Ss "rested" in this condition by looking at humorous magazines for 30 minutes, as they did following their ILperiods, up to a time measured to 30 minutes, from the completion of OL. The average rest times for the different IL conditions were 25.5, 22.0, 15.0, and 1 minute for the 5, 10, 20, and 40 IL trial conditions respectively. Each S went through the 5 conditions twice. A 6th condition of learning 1 list to 2 errorless trials was included to balance the distribution of conditions.

Results

Original Learning: The original learning did not vary significantly among conditions although there was a gain between the 1st and 2nd cycles. In the 1st cycle, Ss learned between 5 and 6 of the syllables. In the 2nd cycle they learned 7 to 8 items of the OL lists. More than 50% of the syllables were not correctly anticipated at any time in OL.

Interpolated Learning: With different numbers of trials the attainment varied appropriately; the Ss in the 5, 10, 20, and 40 repetition conditions averaged 7.5, 14.7, 17.7, and 18.0 syllables respectively in the 2nd cycle, with somewhat lower averages in the 1st cycle. There was an indication of proactive interference in the IL, in that learning did not proceed as quickly in the first 5 trials of IL as in the 5 OL trials.

Retroactive Inhibition: The original lists were relearned to a criterion of 2 perfect recitations. RI, measured by the formula

$$\frac{\text{Rest} - \text{work}}{\text{work}} \times 100$$

for the 4 different IL conditions in relearning to a criterion of 1 perfect recall, was 1.5%, 7.7%, 1.0%, and 4.6% for the 5, 10, 20, and 40 IL trial conditions respectively in the 1st cycle. In the 2nd cycle the percents of RI for the 4 conditions were 8.8, 16.8, 19.2, and 1.6. In the 2nd cycle the differences were reliable. The most significant feature here was the highly significant difference between the 20 and 40 IL trial groups indicating the transitory nature of RI after a considerable amount of IL.

When RI was measured by recall on the 1st relearning trial the percentages of RI for the 2 cycles were: 1st cycle, 57.1, 79.7, 85.7, and 80.9, for the 4 conditions 5, 10, 20, and 40 IL trials; second cycle, 63.4, 76.2, 83.5, and 72.4 for the 5, 10, 20, and 40 IL conditions respectively; again showing the transitoriness of RI with greater IL learning.

Analysis of the first 4 relearning trials showed a strong tendency for Ss to recover from RI as the amount of IL learning increased. The strongest influence of RI, in general, was with the 20 IL trial condition.

Intrusions: An analysis of the number of kinds of intrusions is presented in the original paper. In this abstract we mention only the intrusions on the 1st recall trial. According to McGeoch, RI could be interpreted as interference with recall of OL because of intrusions from IL. When RI is plotted along with an adjusted score value for intrusions it is evident that there are not enough intrusions, nor do they follow the curve of RI sufficiently, to account for the total RI.

It is concluded that some other factor (Factor X), which can be called "unlearning," is responsible for the RI not attributable to intrusions.

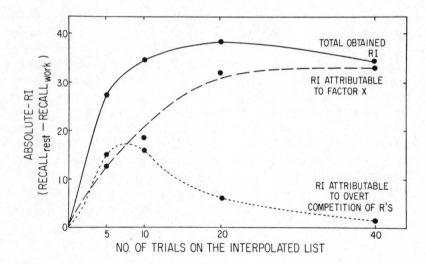

When Ss learn the IL list, and OL responses occur to them, they must be extinguished or *unlearned* if IL is to be learned. Beyond some point of IL learning (20 trials in this study), the unlearning tendency begins to decline as the IL is mastered. The data of this study, then, indicate in two ways the correctness of the hypothesis that RI increases up to some intermediate point and then declines as IL trials or experience increase.

Imitation

C. J. Warden, H. A. Fjeld, and A. M. Koch
Columbia University

"Imitative Behavior in Cebus and Rhesus Monkeys," *The Journal of Genetic Psychology,* 1940, **56**, 311-322.

Students might be familiar with the expression, "Monkey see, monkey do." But psychologists have been reluctant to accept the proposition that monkeys (or any other organisms) actually imitate their fellows. Thorndike and Watson both renounced or denounced imitation as a behavior principle with considerable influence on their followers. This study reopens the question. The criteria for imitation must be appreciated before the study can be considered pertinent. Imitation can be presumed if 1) the task is novel and sufficiently complex to involve a genuine learning process; 2) responses appear promptly after observation; 3) prior practice is excluded; 4) the responses are substantially the same; and 5) there are enough observations to exclude chance.

Method

Subjects: Six monkeys—3 Rhesus, 2 Cebus, 1 Capuchin as imitators; a 7th monkey (Rhesus) was trained as the imitatee.
Apparatus: Warden Duplicate Cage—a cage partitioned in the middle by a screen, with a puzzle box in one wall on each side. A spotlight can be used to illuminate one box or the other. The puzzle box involves a

panel which has to be opened for access to a raisin reward. Four different ways of opening the door are available, providing 4 problems. Each problem is originally solved only after considerable time (not stated) and trial and error. The problems are described in the Results section.

Procedure: An imitator monkey was first habituated to the cage for 4 days. When the imitatee was introduced on his side, he promptly solved the problem of the day, having learned the solution previously. When the imitatee finished and obtained his raisin, the light over his panel was extinguished and the imitator's light was turned on. The imitator had been restrained by a cord during the observation period, but had a profile view of the imitatee. There were 6 tests on each of 4 problems, providing 144 tests for the 6 monkeys. Data obtained included time of solution, number of solutions, and partial successes. Trials were limited to 60 seconds.

Results

The observations were classified as: 1) immediate solution; 2) P+, partial imitation—proper act, but not enough force; 3) P, partial imitation—contact with proper part, but incomplete; 4) P−, partial imitation—approach, inspection, but no contact; 5) failure.

There were no failures in the 144 trials. The problems and results are shown in the table.

	Problem	*Type of Solution*			
		Imitation	P+%	P%	P−%
I	Pull chain to raise door	69.4	19.4	11.2	0.0
II	Open door by turning knob	91.7	2.8	5.5	0.0
III	Operate latch	72.2	5.5	22.3	0.0
IV	Operate 2 latches, upper and lower	72.2	0.0	16.6	11.2
	Mean	76.4	6.9	13.9	2.8

There were 110 cases of immediate solution in the 144 tests. The median time was 7.3 seconds. In 57 cases (51.8%), the solution occurred in under 10 seconds; in 38 cases, in under 5 seconds. There was no practice effect from Test 1 to Test 2, although there was such an effect from Test 3 to Test 6.

Conclusion: There is a high level of imitative capacity in the cebus and rhesus monkey.

Neonate Conditioning

Delos D. Wickens and Carol Wickens
Ohio State University

"A Study of Conditioning in the Neonate," *Journal of Experimental Psychology,* 1940, **26**, 94-102.

The problem of conditioning the newborn is complicated by the question of what would have occurred naturally. Careful, objective controls are essential. Previous studies with small numbers of infants have left the question open. In this study, the leg withdrawal reflex of neonates will be observed under suitable controls for the possible independent effects of CS and US.

Method

Subjects: Thirty-six infants less than ten days old—18 girls, 18 boys. One third with at least partial Black parentage. The study began when infants were 3 to 4 days old.

Apparatus: A soundproof isolation cabinet where infant could be observed; inductorium with electrode for shocking the sole of one foot; a muffled buzzer (CS) 2 feet from *S*s head.

Design: Infants were divided into 3 matched groups (sex, race). The experimental group (N = 12) received 12 paired buzzer-shock stimulations each day for 3 days. The first control group (N = 12) received only the shocks (no buzzer) on the same schedule. The 2nd control group (N = 12) was tested with the buzzer alone on day 1 and day 8.

Procedure: All infants were first tested with the buzzer to be certain that no leg withdrawal would occur directly to this stimulus. The conditioning group received its 36 paired stimulations with the CS preceeding the US by ¼ second and continuing during the ¼-second shock. Trials were 1, 2, 3, or 4 minutes apart. Two experimenters observed each infant and recorded any leg withdrawal movements (each E watched one leg). Both legs consistently responded when the infants were shocked and, therefore, a dual leg response was necessary to qualify as the CR. At the end of the 3rd day of conditioning trials the buzzer was presented

Experimental Subjects

Subjects	1	2	3	4	5	6	7	8	9	10	11	12	Total
Day 3	2	2	4	0	3	1	5	2	0	1	0	3	23
Day 4	8	9	0	0	4	10	7	1	8	1	0	0	48

Control Subjects

Subjects	1	2	3	4	5	6	7	8	9	10	11	12	Total
Day 3	2	1	0	2	3	2	5	2	3	2	2	1	25
Day 4	2	10	0	9	3	2	3	0	5	0	2	1	37

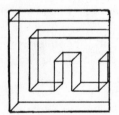

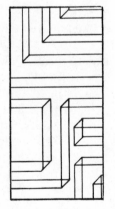

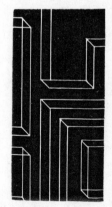

alone until the CR, if present, extinguished (3 buzzers without a response). On the 4th day the buzzer alone was again tested for spontaneous recovery and a second extinction.

Results

The number of leg withdrawal responses by the infants in the experimental and first control group on the 3rd and 4th day are shown in the table.

Because the experimental *S*s did respond to the buzzer after the paired trials, and showed both extinction and spontaneous recovery, one would conclude that conditioning had occurred. The control *S*s, however, responded, if anything, even more frequently to the buzzer alone on both test days. It can be inferred that the control group was sensitized by the shock trials to respond to any unexpected stimulus and that this might also be true of the experimental group, although they might also have been, in fact, conditioned. The second control group did not respond to the buzzer alone on the 3rd day (except for one *S*) and thus any "growth" factor could be ruled out.

Conclusion: Caution is required in interpreting results from CR studies. It could be that the CS itself was not correctly identified, that any sudden, novel change in stimulation could have been the CS; and this description would apply to the shock as well as the buzzer. In that case the shock would have been, in effect, both CS and US. The results of this study leave the question of conditioning withdrawal in the neonate unresolved.

Generalization in Verbal Learning

Eleanor J. Gibson
Smith College

"Intra-list Generalization as a Factor in Verbal Learning,"
Journal of Experimental Psychology, 1942, **30**, 185-200.

When a list of verbal items is to be learned, it is necessary to differentiate the items, one from another, before associations can be formed effectively. The items are difficult to identify because they appear one at a time and do not permit direct perceptual comparisons. If the items are at all similar, stimulus generalization may occur so that responses may become associated to incorrect stimuli. Put otherwise, wrong responses may block out correct responses. Differentiation through extinction of generalized response tendencies may lapse with time, leading to spontaneous recovery of incorrect associations. Such a recall could result in impaired retention over time. This study is designed to check the assumption that generalization will first increase and then decrease during learning, and that more differential reinforcement is required for associations with greater competition from generalizing tendencies.

Method

Subjects: Fifty-six Smith College psychology majors in 4 groups of 14.

Materials: Four lists of paired-associates wherein the stimulus style consisted of a figure and the response side was a nonsense syllable. List I contained 12 dissimilar nonsense figures, easily discriminable. Lists II, III, and IV each contained 4 of the figures of List I and 2 variations of each of these. The figures in Lists II, III, and IV, were, of course, different from each other. The variations were previously tested with other *S*s and found to be responsed to as if they were the original figures 41.1% and 9.7% of the time. These percentages are considered measures of the similarity of these variations to the original figures. Thus, the materials provide 2 levels of homogeneity or similarity along with the originals.

Procedure: The 4 lists, 1 of low generalization among the stimulus items (all response items were alike in the 4 lists) and 3 of high internal stimulus generalization were presented to *S*s by memory drum at a 2-second per pair rate. Each learning trial was followed by a test trial with only the stimulus side exposed. The pairs were presented in 6 random orders. Criterion was 1 perfect recall. The *S*s recalled and/or relearned the list on the following day.

	Low Generalization List	High Generalization Lists		
		List II	List III	List IV
mean trials to learn	8.86	22.29	14.36	22.79
mean trials to relearn	2.00	2.64	2.79	2.79
mean number recalled	9.31	8.86	8.50	8.71

Results

The mean learning and recall scores appear in the table. The original learning trials are significantly fewer for the low generalization list than for the other 3. The relearning and recall scores show the same trend but are not statistically reliable. Analysis of the items showed that the same items (from List I) were much more difficult to learn when they were members of the other lists. Overt intrusion errors followed the expected pattern; i.e., where generalization was likely (lists II, III, and IV) it occred in the form of "right answers to wrong stimuli." They formed the bulk of the confusion errors (88% in II, 80% in III, and 80% in IV). When the 2 degrees of similarity of stimuli were analyzed, it was found that the highly similar stimuli accounted for 42% of the errors in learning while the lower degrees of similarity evoked 21% of the errors. The remaining errors were between the 2 levels of similarity (19%), or of other types. It was also noted that, as predicted, the generalization errors tended to occur early in learning and then dropped off as learning ensued, with the less similar stimuli being more rapidly differentiated.

Conclusion: Differentiation of items is an essential component of verbal learning, and differential reinforcement of right and wrong (generalized) responses is the process whereby a differentiated series is achieved.

Retroactive Inhibition

Leland E. Thune and Benton J. Underwood
University of Wisconsin

"Retroactive Inhibition as a Function of Degree of Interpolated Learning," *Journal of Experimental Psychology,* 1943, **32**, 185-199.

Various studies with serial lists have shown that retroactive inhibition (RI) increases with the degree of interpolated learning but begins to decline with additional trials on the interpolated list. In this study the generality of this conclusion is tested by using lists of paired associates as the learning material. The procedure followed also lends itself to a check on the Melton-Irwin two-factor theory of RI.

Method

Subjects: Twenty-four male undergraduates.

Materials: Lists of 10 paired-associates made up of adjectives. The adjectives were unrelated. Each *S* learned an A-B list, then an A-C list where the "stimulus" adjectives were the same. Each *S* learned 6 sets of such A-B, A-C lists under different conditions (see Procedure). The lists were presented on a memory drum which presented the stimulus item for 2 seconds, then the response item for 2 seconds more. The anticipation method was followd.

Procedure: S learned an original list (A-B) for 5 trials and relearned it after 20 minutes. During the 20-minute period he either rested or had 2, 5, 10, or 20 repetitions of the interpolated (A-C) list. In a sixth condition (to balance the procedure, data not used) he learned the original list to 2 perfect recitations. Thus, each *S* participated in 6 learning sessions. In the 20-minute period the *S*s rested after the lists were presented for either 17½ minutes or 15, 11, or 3 minutes, depending on the number of interpolated list trials. Relearning of the original list (OL) was then carried out to 1 perfect recitation, but only the data from the first 4 trials were analyzed.

Results

All of the A-B lists (OL) were learned to a relatively uniform degree—i.e., there were no significant differences. In the 5 trials each *S* would learn some but not all of the 10 pairs, averaging between 4.4 and 5.8.

Retroactive Inhibition. As in other experiments the most reliable data came from the 1st recall trial and not the number of relearning trials. The percent of RI ($100 \times \frac{rest - work}{work}$) for the first 4 relearning trials is shown in the table.

RI was obviously and significantly present on trial 1 but began to de-

Percent RI

| Interpolation Condition | *Relearning Trials* | | | | *Intrusion* |
	1	2	3	4	Errors
2 IL trials	20.1	−1.4	−2.7	−2.3	1
5 IL trials	43.8	31.9	14.8	10.3	20
10 IL trials	55.3	20.1	9.3	7.2	45
20 IL trials	57.1	27.5	8.7	8.5	10

Note: The control group (No IL) recalled 4.38 of the A-B list which has been learned to the level of 4.96.

82

cline as relearning progressed. There were no differences as a function of IL by the 3rd relearning trial.

The *S*s in relearning the OL made overt intrusion errors; i.e., they responded with items from the IL list. The number of such intrusion errors is reported in the table where it can be seen that with 10 trials of IL the *S*s responded with the greatest number of such errors. The *S*s also reported that they frequently had a conflict between two responses, saying neither, and that (with greater learning of IL) they knew the response that occurred to them was wrong and consequently they would not pronounce it. In addition there were a number of partial overt errors. The combination of overt, covert, and partial intrusions was analyzed in terms of the number of times the *S*s had responded correctly in the OL to a given stimulus item. It was found that when the IL had relatively more correct responses (from 1 to 8) than the corresponding OL pair, the IL responses intruded at a greater frequency and accounted for the great bulk of the intrusions on the first relearning trial.

Conclusions: The present data reflect the same kinds of finding that have been reported with serial lists. As IL increases so does the RI, up to a point at which, with further learning of IL, RI does not increase. When the number of intrusions noted here was treated as in the Melton-Irwin study, the RI attributable to intrusions closely followed the total RI curve, supporting the interference hypothesis and contradicting the Melton-Irwin Factor X (or "unlearning") hypothesis.

Autonomic Conditioning of a Response

R. L. Roessler and W. J. Brogden
University of Wisconsin

"Conditioned Differentiation of Vasoconstriction to Subvocal Stimuli," *American Journal of Psychology,* 1943, **41**, 78-86.

Autonomic responses have been conditioned to verbal (vocal) stimuli, but the reports have been equivocal. In this study an attempt will be made to condition vasoconstriction to compound stimuli, then verbal stimuli, and finally to sub-vocal stimuli.

Method

Subjects: Four male college students out of an original group of 15. Eleven *S*s were dropped because they did not respond to the US, responded to the CS before conditioning, or for other reasons.

Apparatus: A plethysmograph for measuring blood volume changes encased *S*'s right hand. *S*'s right arm was strapped to the arm of a chair to reduce movement. The left arm of *S* hung loosely with the hand immersed in warm water (90°-110° F) to help vasodilation. The experimental room was kept at 80° F. A buzzer served as part of the CS in the first conditioning trials. A red light served as a signal in later stages. The US for *vasoconstriction* was an electric shock to the left wrist. Changes in blood volume were recorded on a kymograph, along with indications of stimulation. A minimum change of .05cc had to occur to be recorded.

Procedure: All CSs were 20 seconds long. A 5-second shock was used as US in the last 5 seconds of the CS duration. There were 5 stages of conditioning:

1. A buzzer CS sounded for 20 seconds. At the sound of the buzzer, *S* said "WEK" aloud repeatedly throughout the 20-second period, including the 5-second shock time; the CS was, therefore, a combination of buzzer and nonsense syllable recitation. Trials were run in blocks of 5 until *S* gave 4 CRs in 5 trials.

2. When *S* met the criterion in the first stage, a red light became the signal for saying "WEK" (the buzzer was now omitted) until the shock stopped. Again the shock took up the last 5 of the 20 seconds. The criterion was again 4 CRs out of 5 trials in a block.

3. Blocks of 5 trials of saying "ZUB," without shock, were alternated with blocks of trials of saying "WEK" with shock. Training continued until *S* gave no more than 1 CR out of 5 trials to "ZUB" and continued giving 4 CRs out of 5 trials to "WEK." This was "differentiation" training.

4. *S* repeated "WEK" *subvocally* for 20 seconds when signalled to do so by the red light. The criterion remained as above.

5. *S* repeated either "ZUB" or "WEK" subvocally in alternate blocks until the same criteria as in 3 were met.

Results

All Ss attained the conditioning criterion in stage 1 (buzzer and "WEK" spoken aloud). They required 20, 60, 25, and 25 trials for Ss 1, 2, 3, and 4 respectively.

Ss 2 and 3 did not meet the criterion in stage 2 ("WEK" aloud) in 110 and 70 trials. Ss 1 and 4 reached criterion in 30 and 10 trials.

In stage 3 (Differentiation), S 1 reached criterion immediately. S 4 required 30 trials of "WEK" and 35 trials of "ZUB" to reach the criterion.

In stage 4 (Subvocal conditioning) S 1 reached criterion in 10 trials and S 4 in 30 trials.

In stage 5 (Subvocal differentiation) both Ss reached criterion immediately.

In general the CRs resembled the URs in magnitude and latency, although the CR latency was shorter (by definition a CR was not counted as such unless it antedated the US).

Conclusion: Subvocal (voluntary?) control of an autonomic response can be attained by conditioning.

Punishment and Suppression

William K. Estes
University of Minnesota

"An Experimental Study of Punishment," *Psychological Monographs*, 1944, **57**, Whole No. 263.

Note: This is a long monograph with 12 experimental studies, only 5 of which are abstracted here.

Thorndike's revised theory of punishment asserts no weakening effect of punishment on a response (or stimulus-response connection), but

Thorndike used very mild punishments in situations with alternate responses available. While it is well known that a response can be weakened by punishment, little is known of the dynamic properties of punishment and its functional relations.

Method

Subjects: Albino rats.

Apparatus: Skinner box, food reinforcement, wire grid floor through which rat could be shocked for a fraction of a second.

Procedure: Preliminary. All rats used were first habituated to the compartment, trained with 100% reinforcement, then put on several hours of periodic reinforcement (4-minute intervals) to establish stable response rates. Experimental procedure for the punishment studies varied and will be specified for each.

A. Effects of mild punishment on extinction.

In the extinction period, 8 experimental rats were shocked in the period 5-20 minutes after extinction began. Shocks were received when the bar was pressed (circuit took 30 seconds to reset), but not all presses were followed by shock. The shock was just strong enough to depress the response rate but not eliminate it. After the 20th minute, normal extinction continued to complete an hour. Additional extinction sessions were run for 2 more days.

Results: Immediate effect of shock period was to depress the rate of pressing, but by the end of the hour the rate increased to equal that of 8 control rats. On the 2nd day of extinction, experimental rats equalled the controls, and on the 3rd day they exceeded the controls, with the total number of presses in the 3 extinction periods being the same.

Conclusion: The effect of a short period of punishment is a temporary suppression followed by a compensatory increase in response rate.

B. Severe punishment.

A 10-minute punishment session, with shock strong enough to prevent any response by the end of the 10-minute period, was followed by 50 minutes of extinction for 5 experimental rats. Control rats (4) were not shocked. By the end of the hour, the control rats had reduced their response rates to the low rate of the experimental rats. Four days of extinction followed.

Results: By the 4th day, the experimental rats did not differ from control rats in response rate.

Conclusion: Following punishment, there will be a negatively accelerated process of recovery. Because the recovery process proceeds more rapidly than the extinction, the total amount of time for complete extinction will not be affected by punishment.

C. Prolonged Punishment.

Severe punishment was continued for an experimental group (N = 4) for 1 hour, with rate of responding virtually at zero in this period. A control group (N = 5) received ordinary extinction. Additional sessions were held 1, 2, and 20 days later. In another pair of groups, the 2nd extinction was held 8 days later.

Results: In this latter pair, the experimental and control animals did not differ in the 4th extinction session; i.e., severe punishment for an hour did not extend the extinction. In the original E and C groups the E group did not recover to the C group level. This is attributed to spaced extinction. With retraining, the E group made more responses than the controls.

Conclusions: A periodically reinforced response cannot be eliminated by punishment. It can only be suppressed. Time for completed extinction could be reduced, although total number of responses will be fewer.

D. Effects of several short periods of severe punishment on extinction.

One group (N = 4) of rats is punished in 3 successive extinction sessions for 10 minutes. Control rats had simple extinction.

Results: On the 4th day in simple extinction the E group equalled the C group in responses and matched the C group on the 3rd extinction.

Conclusion: After punishment stops, there is a recovery in the strength of the response so that the response rate is about equal to what would have been shown without punishment.

E. Effects of periodic punishment.

Five rats were shocked during the 1st, 4th, and 7th 5-minute periods of a 40-minute extinction session. Five control rats were shocked continuously (if they pressed the bar). Five days of 1-hour extinction sessions followed.

Results: The periodically punished group was somewhat slower in recovery, but not significantly so. Recovery from periodic punishment is no more rapid than from continuous punishment.

The monograph includes 7 more studies on various aspects of punishment of responses of different strength, discriminated responses, the effect of adding positive reinforcement, non-contingent punishment, punishment without response elicitation, and punishment where more than one response is available. These additional studies generally confirm the conclusions already drawn but should be read for their own intrinsic values.

Conditioning of Autonomic Sensations

E. Airapetyantz and K. Bykov

"Physiological Experiments and the Psychology of the Sub-conscious," *Philosophy and Phenomenological Research,* 1945, **5**, 577-593.

Sensory reactions related to visceral activity or stimulation can be conditioned to external stimuli.

Method

Subject: Comrade F., a Russo-Finish war soldier with a fistula attached to the middle region of the small intestine.
Apparatus: A small rubber balloon which could be inserted into the intestine via the fistula and filled with cold or warm water. Flashing red and blue lights.
Procedure: The warm or cold water served as US. *S* reported sensory reactions corresponding to these stimuli. A red light was paired with cold water and a blue light with warm.

Results

When tested with either CS alone, *S* reported sensory reactions of the intestine corresponding to those initiated by the related US.

Cats in a Puzzle Box

Edwin R. Guthrie and George P. Horton
University of Washington

Cats in a Puzzle Box, New York, Rinehart and Co., 1946.

Associations are formed between stimuli and movements, not acts. Acts are definable in terms of end results, but there are many ways to achieve an end result, and each way consists of a separate pattern of movements. Only the "muscular contractions . . . are directly predicted by the principle of association." To provide an experimental illustration of this conclusion, an act—e.g., escape from some environment by some manipulation—must be examined in detail on numerous occasions with a variety of performers.

Method

Subjects: Thirteen cats, 1 dog.

Apparatus: A box 60 inches wide, 54 inches deep, and 36 inches high, made of metal with one glass wall. A glass door was fitted into the glass wall. The door would open only if a pole (about 16 inches high, mounted on a rounded base) was moved at least ½ inch. At the moment the pole was so moved, a camera mounted outside the box would automatically photograph the animal in stop-action. Motion pictures were also taken. A starting box at the rear of the box permitted access to the larger escape box.

Procedure: The 13 cats were given varied numbers of trials (20-71) over a period of months (1936-1939) so that more than 800 photographs were obtained. Twenty trials were also run on the dog.

Results

The basic data are the 800 photographs which are reproduced in an appendix. The 2 experimenters watched most of the trials together and recorded their observations. Ideal results would consist of exactly duplicate photographs for any one cat, showing complete stereotypy. The actual results amount to judgments about the degree of similarity of the pictures. The experimenters recognize the difficulties, asserting that observers will often see what they wish. Frequently, the photographs show a great many similar movements on the part of the cats (from one trial to the next). Some cats demonstrate several, but limited, patterns. It is concluded that stereotypy of movement is the rule, with exceptions traceable to malfunctions, distractions, or different entries, etc. "The behavior of the cat on one occasion tends to be repeated on the next. . . . The most stable response is the one which ends in a release from the box. . . . *The cat learns to escape in one trial* and could repeat the specific movements of its first escape except insofar as new trials by accidental variations of situation cause new associative connections to be established."

CAT A, TRIALS 21-24.

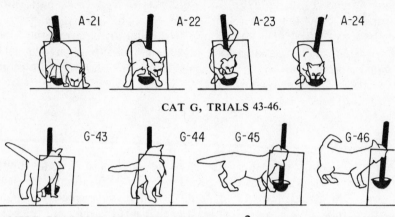

CAT G, TRIALS 43-46.

SAMPLE TRACINGS OF PHOTOGRAPHS OF 2 OF THE CATS INDICATING
THEIR UNIQUE BUT CONSISTENT MOVEMENT PATTERNS IN ESCAPING
FROM THE GUTHRIE PUZZLE BOX

Abstract **46**

Mental Set

A. S. Luchins
Yeshiva University

"Classroom Experiments on Mental Set," *The American Journal of Psychology,* 1946, **59**, 295-298.

When you solve a problem in some particular way, you are inclined to attack similar problems in the same way. Such an inclination is called a "set" or *Einstelling*. When an individual continues to handle problems in a characteristic routine, we may refer to him as being "in a rut" or demonstrating a "stereotype." When a routine approach fails, a person who has fallen victim to a stereotype may find himself unable to solve a given problem, even if it is quite easy and would present no difficulty if he could get rid of his "set."

Method

Subjects: Experimental group—1039 students from grammar school through graduate school; adults with no formal education. Control group—970 more of the same range of education. The Ss were run at various times, individually or in groups.

Apparatus: Pencil, paper, 11 water-jar problems. (In such a problem, you try to get a specific amount of water by using various size jars.) The problems are such that all (except 1 and 9) can be solved in the same fashion. Problem 1 is a demonstration problem; problem 9 is an "extinction" problem. All the remaining problems can be solved by figuratively filling the big middle jar (b) in a set of 3 and by subtracting the 1st jar (a) once and the 3rd jar (c) twice. The formula or "set" solution is b minus a minus c minus c or b minus a minus 2c.

Problem 9 cannot be solved in this fashion; it represents an "extinction" experience. Problems 7-11, in fact, can be solved in other ways (a minus c for problems 7, 9, and 11; a plus c for 8 and 10).

Procedure: Ss are allowed 3 minutes per problem, each being written on a blackboard. The procedure for problem 1 is explained; Ss write out their operations, and E writes out the solution to problem 1 as 29 minus 3 minus 3 minus 3. Control Ss are then given problems 7-11 only. The set of problems is listed in the table.

Water Jar Problems
THE TASKS

Problem	containers given			to get
	a	b	c	
(1)	29	3	—	20
(2)	21	127	3	100
(3)	14	163	25	99
(4)	18	43	10	5
(5)	9	42	6	21
(6)	20	59	4	31
(7)	23	49	3	20
(8)	15	39	3	18
(9)	28	76	3	25
(10)	18	48	4	22
(11)	14	36	8	6

Results

Eighty-three percent of the experimental Ss used the Einstelling procedure in problems 7 and 9, while only 0.6% of the controls did so. Sixty-four percent of the experimental Ss failed problem 9, but only 5% of the controls failed.

Set and Incidental Learning

Leo Postman and Virginia L. Senders
Harvard University

"Incidental Learning and Generality of Set," *Journal of Experimental Psychology,* 1946, **36**, 153-165.

When one learns something without intent or instruction to learn, he demonstrates "incidental" learning. Yet such learners must be stimulated in some way by the material to be learned. When Ss are instructed to learn, they are also *set* to learn. "Set" implies a readiness to respond selectively. Incidental learners may have other sets. Sets are habits and, as such, are learned. In incidental learning studies, the uninstructed Ss may be more or less set to learn other materials or features of a situation. Unless different sets are experimentally explored, the influence of type of set cannot be assessed. If all learning occurs under some set from explicit or self instructions, or from *covert* sets deriving from more general sets, it might be possible to dispose of the concept of *incidental* learning altogether. This study tries to determine what specific additional (covert) sets are generated from the explicit instructions given to learners.

Method

Subjects: Fifty Harvard and Radcliffe undergraduates.
Material: Three hundred fifty word selection from Chekhov's *The Bet*.
Procedure: Five sets of instructions were given to separate groups.
  A. E is interested in your reading speed. Read at your own speed. Raise your hand when finished.
  B. Read carefully; you will be tested for *general comprehension*.
  C. Read carefully; you will be tested for specific sequence of individual events.
  D. Read carefully; you will be tested for details of content.
  E. Read carefully; you will be tested for details of wording.
  F. Read carefully; you will be tested for details of physical appearance of print (errors, etc.).
     When finished with reading (about 90 seconds), Ss were distracted with another task (drawing 4-inch lines) for 3 minutes. They

then took a 50-item multiple choice test on the material, with 10 questions related to each instruction, except for A (the control group). Correct answers to questions other than those related to the explicit instructions would be evidence of a covert set.

Results

The percentage of correct responses for each type of question is shown in the table. The % differences indicate that *S*s learn different material under different instructions. Some instructions (e.g., E) are not effective. With no instruction to learn (A), the *S*s still learn something, presumably due to a covert set which aims at some general comprehension with little concern for detail. In B, the specific instruction was not greatly needed, but a covert set for C was prompted. Instruction E proved ineffective with the text, as the materials were very similar. Instruction F proved suitable, but the good score for general comprehension suggests a covert set; perhaps a lack of satisfaction with the instruction.

Conclusion: Learning and memory are not restricted to those materials *S* has been instructed to learn. The additional learning is not haphazard or "incidental." It is due to covert sets. Calling such learning incidental suggests that the term is a euphemism for ignorance of the sets that were operating. Such covert sets derive from our general sets to understand and structure environmental stimuli.

Question Category		*Instruction*					
		A	B	C	D	E	F
B	General comprehension	60	75	83	57	65	81
C	Sequence of events	50	65	46	79	44	55
D	Details of content	49	62	54	56	37	53
E	Details of wording	34	31	33	36	30	33
F	Physical appearance	31	26	26	31	38	39

Abstract **48**

Place vs. Response Learning

E. C. Tolman, B. F. Ritchie, and D. Kalish
University of California

"Studies in Spatial Learning. II. Place Learning versus Response Learning," *Journal of Experimental Psychology,* 1946, **36**, 224-229.

In learning a maze, does a rat learn a series of motor responses (turns), or does he learn to go to a certain place? On a T-maze, does the rat learn to turn to the right (a response), or to go toward the east (a place)? The question might be answered by training rats from two starting positions (say, North and South on different trials), with one rat being forced to turn right at a choice point while the other would be required to go to the same location (East), regardless of turn. The "response" rat would thus be going to two different places when making the same direction of turn, while the "place" rat would always be going to the same place but making different turns.

Method

Subjects: Two groups of pigmented rats (N = 8 for each group).
Apparatus: Elevated T-maze with food cups at each end but with one end blocked. The maze was in a large room with animal cages about 15 feet from F2.

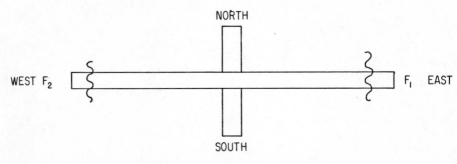

THE T-MAZE WITH MOVABLE STARTING LEG

Procedure: After preliminary training on the runway, the "place" rats were tested for position habits and forced to learn to run down the non-preferred alley. The response rats were forced to turn right. There were 6 daily trials, 3 from each starting point. Running more than 12 inches down the wrong alley was scored as an error. Rats were run to a criterion of 10 correct trials.

Results

Five of the 8 response rats failed to meet the criterion in 12 days (72 trials). The failing rats learned to go to the same place. The 3 successful rats averaged 17 trials. All place rats reached the criterion within 8 trials or less (mean = 3.5).

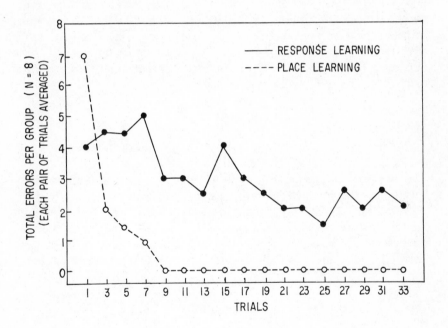

RESPONSE AND PLACE LEARNING COMPARED

Conclusion: Both place and response learning is possible, but place learning in this situation is simpler and more primitive. Such an advantage for place learning depends on marked external cues.

Interstimulus Intervals in Conditioning

Gregory A. Kimble
University of Iowa

"Conditioning as a Function of the Time between Conditioned and Unconditioned Stimuli," *Journal of Experimental Psychology*, 1947, **37**, 1-15.

Hull proposed that the rate of acquisition of a conditioned response was a function of the interstimulus interval—i.e., the time between CS and US—and that the curve of acquisition would be a negatively accelerated one up to some maximum. In this study both the level of conditioning and its rate were investigated to test Hull's proposal. Because it was already fairly well established that eyelid conditioning seemed to be most effective at about a 500-millisecond interval, this study explored intervals at and below 400 milliseconds.

Method

Subjects: Sixty-nine college students in 6 groups of 10 each, with 3 extra *S*s for the fastest time intervals.

Apparatus: Dodge pendulum-photochronograph. CS: a 53 millilambert light which reached full brilliance in 1/1000 second. US: puff of air.

Procedure: A test-trial procedure was used; on every 10th trial, only the CS was presented. Each *S* received 60 acquisition trials and 20 extinction trials. The 6 groups of *S*s had interstimulus intervals of 100, 200, 225, 250, 300, and 400 milliseconds. Intertrial intervals averaged 1 minute.

Results

While there was some variability because of the small N's, all the groups showed the negative acceleration expected and a higher level of conditioning with the increasingly longer intervals. The figures show the limits of conditioning and the rate of conditioning as a function of time interval between CS and US. The same finding was noted in the extinction runs. The 100-millisecond group responded 29% of the test trials, the 400 millisecond group 73%, with the other groups appropriately in

96

between. The data support Hull's view that the asymptote of habit strength, as well as the rate of learning in arriving at the asymptote, are negatively accelerated functions of the interstimulus interval.

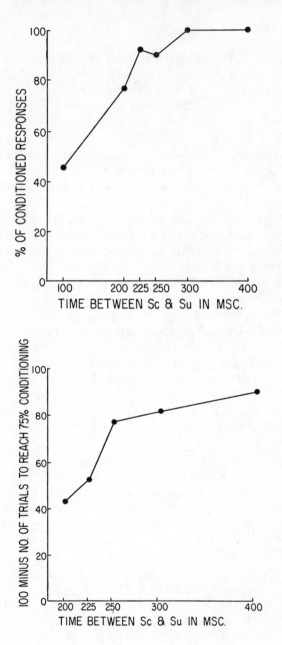

The Continuity Hypothesis

David Ehrenfreund
University of Iowa

"An Experimental Test of the Continuity Theory of Discrimination Learning with Pattern Vision," *Journal of Comparative and Physiological Psychology*, 1948, **41**, 408-422.

In 1936, Spence announced the "continuity" theory, which asserts that learning is a continuous process, each reinforcement adding to the learning strength, each nonreinforcement adding an increment of inhibition. The theory was challenged by Krechevsky, who argued that in discrimination learning an animal will test hypotheses in succession, and that it does not learn anything about the cues until it begins to respond systematically in terms of the cues. A test of the continuity theory could be mounted if a difficult discrimination was set up so that an animal would react at a chance level for some time while the cues are differentially reinforced. If the reward values were then reversed, the continuity hypotheses would predict retardation in the learning. Krechevsky had tried just such a set-up, using a pattern of horizontal or vertical black squares on a white background. Reversing values after 20 trials showed no retardation. Reversing after 40 trials did. The evidence is equivocal.

It is possible that in the Krechevsky experiment the animals were not actually responding to the pattern features of the stimuli because, with the apparatus used (The Lashley Jumping Stand), a rat tends to look where it will leap and usually leaps straight ahead. If the figures to be discriminated do not vary strikingly in the limited focus of vision, a rat might well ignore them. To test this notion, 2 repetitions of the Krechevsky type of experiment were run using white triangles on black backgrounds as the stimuli. One triangle pointed up, the other down. In 1 experiment the jumping stand was lined up with the base of the doors of the food platform. In the second experiment, the jump stand was raised 2 inches so that the rat looked straight at the base or apex of a triangle when looking directly forward.

Method

Subjects: Sixty hooded rats, 30 in each experiment, 15 experimental, 15 control.

Apparatus: Lashley jumping stand. Triangle targets. Variable-height jump platform.

Procedure: After preliminary training (walking through open doors, stepping across, then jumping gaps), all animals were induced to adopt a position habit by reinforcing 5 jumps to 1 side of a neutral cue. With the triangle stimuli in place, all animals were given 40 presolution trials. The experimental groups were consistently reinforced for jumping to 1 of the stimuli, but these amounted to only 50% of the 40 trials because of the position habit. The control animals were rewarded equally often (half the time) for jumping at either card so that they could not develop a cue preference. The position habit was then reversed and formal training started. The training up to this point can be called presolution.

In the regular training the control animals were now consistently reinforced for 1 of the triangles (up to now they had been reinforced half the time for each). The experimental group was trained under reversal of reinforcement—i.e., the cue that was positive in the presolution period was now negative and vice versa.

Results

The results for both experiments are shown in the table. Note that the experimental groups (with reversal of cues) have more difficulty in learning the discrimination than do the controls, especially in Experiment 2.

In Experiment 1, the differences are not significant; in Experiment 2, they are at the .001 level.

	Experiment 1 (Standard Lashley technique)		Experiment 2 (jumping stand raised)	
	Errors	*Trials*	*Errors*	*Trials*
Experimental 1	30.33	68.27	26.55	62.73
Control 1	23.73	59.33	16.86	37.13

Conclusion: When the stimuli to be discriminated can be effective from the beginning of training, there will be an effect from the early reinforcements, even though learning is not evident and shows up only on a reversal of the cues.

Conditioned Stimulus Intensity

David A. Grant and Dorothy E. Schneider
University of Wisconsin

"Intensity of the Conditioned Stimulus and Strength of Conditioning: I. The Conditioned Eyelid Response to Light," *Journal of Experimental Psychology,* 1948, **38**, 690-696.

The role of intensity of the CS has not been established because of difficulties in experimental design which heretofore could not separate measures of conditioning (association) from those of response strength. The correct design requires that measures of conditioning be independent of response strength. This can be achieved by a block design wherein CS intensity can vary during conditioning and vary in intensity during *extinction*. Extinction measures of frequency and magnitude would then reveal any differences due to strength of conditioning and response strength, and any interactions.

Method

The design involved 4 intensities of CS during conditioning (rows), and the same 4 intensities during extinction (columns), in a 16-cell square. The design is apparent in the table of results.

Subjects: Sixty-four men and women from elementary psychology classes. There were 4 *S*s in each treatment condition.

Apparatus: Photochronoscope by means which stimuli could be presented and responses recorded. An air puff was the UCS. The 4 light intensities were 7, 70, 320, and 1050 millilamberts in brightness. They were added to a standard 27 millalambert illumination brightness which was used for adaptation purposes before and between trials. The CS lasted for .75 seconds.

Procedure: *S*s appeared for 2 sessions on successive days. On day 1 they were given 25 reinforced trials with UCS and 1 of the CS intensities. On day 2 they received 25 more reinforced trials, 2 minutes rest, then 15 extinction trials with 1 of the extinction CS intensities, 2 more minutes rest and 5 re-extinction trials with the reinforced CS. Trials occurred at 30-50 second intervals.

Results

The CRs developed normally in all Ss in negatively accelerated curves. Extinction occurred rapidly in negatively decelerated curves. The results of interest are shown in the table. These are extinction data only.

Note that the *row* values represent the strengths of conditioning. The values do not show any regular trend and the results are essentially negative; i.e., the strength of conditioning is not related to CS intensity. Similarly, the column values, representing response strength, show no regularity and are again essentially negative. The data also show no significant generalization effects, although there are some trends. The re-extinction data were again not significant, though highly reliable for individual scores. There were no significant interaction effects.

Conclusion: Strength of conditioning is not affected by CS intensity. Because of the completely negative findings, it appears that the role of the CS is as Pavlov originally suggested—that of "a signal which sets off a conditioned triggering mechanism in the organism." Theories based on variations in stimulus trace strength (which would be a function of stimulus intensity) should be treated with caution.

Summary of Mean Frequency and Mean Total Magnitude (mm.) of CRs during Extinction

Stimuli		Conditioned Stimulus Intensity during Extinction (Millilamberts)				Row Marginals
		7	70	320	1050	
1050	Freq.	0	3.25	5.00	5.25	3.38
	Mag.	0	31.75	55.00	60.75	42.50
320	Freq.	1.25	3.75	3.50	4.25	3.19
	Mag.	29.50	111.00	42.75	61.75	61.25
70	Freq.	4.25	1.00	4.50	1.25	2.75
	Mag.	38.25	2.00	71.50	14.00	31.44
7	Freq.	5.25	2.00	2.25	1.75	2.81
	Mag.	77.50	36.00	55.50	26.50	48.88
Column marginals	Freq.	2.69	2.50	3.81	3.12	3.03
	Mag.	36.31	45.19	61.81	40.75	46.02

Conditioned stimulus intensity during reinforcement (Millilamberts)

Expectancies and Perceptual Learning

G. Robert Grice
Brown University

"An Experimental Test of the Expectation Theory of Learning," *Journal of Comparative and Physiological Psychology,* 1948, **41**, 137-143.

Does learning consist of the formation of stimulus-response associations, or the acquisition of knowledge or cognitions? The controversy divides Tolman and Hull and their followers. Woodworth's proposal of "perceptual learning" is an effort at the resolution of the conflict. Such perceptual learning might be arranged for by forcing animals to traverse both arms of a T-maze where one arm leads to water, the other to food. If the animals are *either* hungry *or* thirsty they should learn to go to the proper end. But, at the same time, having been exposed to the satisfier of the other drive at the other end, they should have learned it is there, and, when changed from one drive to the other, they should make the appropriate adjustment. Observations on rats in such experimental set-ups have not been definitive. This study is a further test of the possibilities of perceptual learning.

Method

Design: Two control features not previously explored are these: 1) Animals might learn that one end is the place where "needs are satisfied" and not specifically that hunger or thirst is satisfied. This requires that a thirsty rat, for example, find water at each end, but food only at one. Also, 2) If rats are run in free-choice situations, they will overlearn the need-satisfying route; both routes must be equally exercised.

Subjects: Twenty-three naive albino female rats, 80-100 days old.

Apparatus: Enclosed T-maze (19-inch starting alley, 15-inch runway alleys) with starting and goal boxes 15 inches long. The end panels were removable. One set of end panels contained water bottles with a glass tube projecting into the goal box. The T-maze was painted black throughout.

Procedure: The animals were put on a 20-hour deprivation-of-water schedule and given preliminary training in drinking in the detached goal boxes to which they learned to run in a gray alley. After preliminary training, the animals were given 4 trials per day in the T-maze under 20-hour water deprivation. Trials were 5 minutes apart. The 1st and 3rd trials were free choices; the 2nd and 4th were forced runs to the other side—i.e., the one not chosen in the "free" run. Both goal boxes had water bottles. The floor of the left goal box was covered with large food pellets so that the rats were forced to walk over the food to get to the water. They sniffed and pushed the food, but no animal ever was observed eating the food. They were permitted to drink for 5 seconds. Entrance to the goal box was prevented by a sliding door which was not opened until a choice of alley had been made. The animals were given 12 days of training (48 runs, 24 to each goal box). After the 12 days of thirst training, the animals were shifted to a 24-hour hunger drive (water available) and began a new training series of 4 trials per day (all free choices) to find food. The food location was reversed for 11 of the 23 rats and remained on the right for the non-reversal group. The criterion was 7 successful choices out of 8 trials.

Results

The 1st hunger-day trial was the major focus of interest. Would the animals "know" where the food was, having been at the place 24 times in the preceding series? In fact, 12 of the 23 rats took the left path which had led to food, and 11 took the right path, which had led only to water. This is not significantly different from a chance number.

In the new training series there were no significant differences between reversal and non-reversal groups before reaching criterion. Each group made 3.3 errors in the series of trials.

Conclusion: If the animals had learned anything about the location of the food, they did not demonstrate such "expectancies" on either the 1st test trial or the new learning series. On the contrary, the results support Hull's S-R reinforcement theory in that 2 competing responses were involved and each response had to be learned by its own reinforcement arrangements. In the water training series, each turn had been equally reinforced, and the habit strengths were, therefore, equal. One would have to predict a 50% probability of turning in either direction on the first test, and one also would predict equal learning of the new habit because of equal starting backgrounds for the new habit.

Acquired Drives

Mark A. May
Yale University

"Experimentally Acquired Drives," *Journal of Experimental Psychology,* 1948, **38**, 66-77.

Thorndike has equated wants, interests, and attitudes with habits. Such "motivational states" are responses, learned like any other responses. Miller and Dollard have described such states as drives, conditions of strong stimulation. Because responses can produce stimuli, a weak stimulus could result in a response that produced strong stimuli, and therefore qualify as a "secondary" drive. Any response (neural, emotional, motor) can be conditioned and, in appropriate cases, generate strong (drive) stimuli. In this experiment, a strong stimulus-producing response (the reaction to shock) will be conditioned to a weak (buzzer) stimulus to demonstrate the acquisition of drive characteristics by a previously inadequate stimulus.

Method

Subjects: Albino and hooded male rats, 3-6 months old.

Apparatus: Miller-Mowrer demonstration box—a glass-front box 30 inches long, 6 inches wide, and 18 inches high. The floor is a steel grid. The right and left halves of the floor can be electrified separately. In the middle of the box there is a 4-inch high barrier with a swinging door over it suspended from the top of the box. The door can be swung out of the way or pushed aside by the Ss when they go over the barrier. For part of the training, a small pen 6 inches square by 18 inches high was placed in the middle of the box. Rats would be shocked in this small enclosure without being able to avoid the shocks. A buzzer could be sounded over the pen for 10 seconds. During the last 5 seconds, a shock would overlap the buzzer for some Ss.

Procedure: Two experimental groups were used. Group A was trained to escape shock in the box with the door over the barrier closed. For Group B the door was swung out of the way. The experimental Ss were given buzzer and shock paired in the confinement pen. There were 4 control groups; 1 for Group A treatment and 3 for the Group B treatment. The control groups received either buzzer or shock (alone) or buzzer and shock, but not paired. All animals followed the same schedule of training, which involved 15 trials per day. The schedule consisted of—

1. five shock trials in the barrier box.
2. five stimulations in the confinement pen.
3. five more shock trials in the barrier box.

Training continued until the *S*s crossed the barrier in less than 3 seconds in the last 5 shock trials. When this criterion was met, each *S* received 25 test trials with buzzer alone. The conditions of training are shown in the table under Results.

Group	N	Confinement Pen Treatment	Mean Number of Test Crossings
Experimental A	12	buzzer plus shock	18.23
Control A	12	shock alone	2.25
Experimental B	7	buzzer plus shock	21.1
Control B_1	7	shock alone	8.6
Control B_2	7	buzzer *or* shock (5 each)	3.4
Control B_3	7	buzzer alone	2.7

Results

The results of interest are the number of responses to the buzzer alone following the different kinds of treatment in the confinement pen. Mean crossings are shown in the table.

Conclusion: In the confinement pen, no consistent response was paired with the buzzer. (It is assumed that some pattern of neural excitation was produced by the shock in whatever responses occurred, and that this pattern was conditioned to the buzzer. The buzzer thus acquired a drive power it did not previously possess.)

Fear as an Acquired Drive

Neal E. Miller
Yale University

"Studies of Fear as an Acquirable Drive: I. Fear as Motivation and Fear Reduction as Reinforcement in the Learning of New Responses," *Journal of Experimental Psychology*, 1948, **38**, 89-101.

If fear is learned as a new response to a novel situation, does it show drive properties as motivation of random behavior, and, when reduced, does it reinforce an immediately preceding response?

Method

Subjects: Twenty-five naive, 6 month old albino rats.

Apparatus: A 36-inch × 6-inch × 8½-inch box, divided into 2 compartments by a wall. One area had a grid floor and was painted white. The other area had a wood floor and black walls. A door in the wall separating the comparments could be left open or closed, and could be opened by rotating a small paddle-wheel above the door or by pressing a little bar in the back wall of the white "room."

Procedure: 1. Test the animals for preference of sides with door open; no preference shown.

2. Ten shock trials. On the 1st intermittent shock for 1 minute, door was opened by *E*. On the next 9 trials, the shock was turned on and door opened by *E* when animal was placed in white compartment. Animals escaped shock by going through the open door. Between trials, rats rested in wire cages for 60 seconds. This phase was followed by 5 non-shock trials with *E* opening door.

3. Non-shock training trials. Door closed between compartments. Animal had to rotate wheel to open door. Time to open door was recorded for 16 trials; no shock was administered in this or the next stage (see the figure).

4. Bar press required to open door. Wheel no longer operative. This procedure required extinction of first learning and acquisition of a new habit.

Results

Twelve animals learned to crouch or do things other than stand at the wheel and move it. The animals that moved the wheel enough to open the door got faster and faster at it, as shown in the figure. Extinction of wheel turning proceeded systematically and quickly. By the 6th trial, the rats were no longer turning the wheel.

SPEED OF WHEEL TURNING OVER THE 16 TRIALS AND LATER FOR
PRESSING FOR 10 TRIALS (----). AVERAGE FOR 13 RATS.

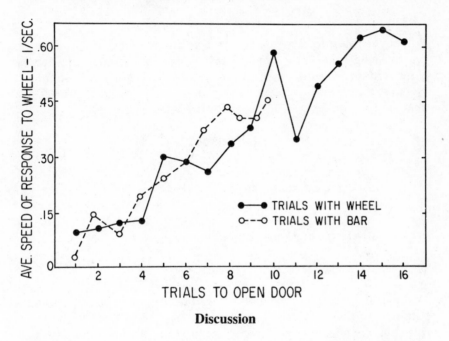

Discussion

The learning of two new responses in the absence of shock, but with a presumed learned or acquired fear, indicates that the fear had begun to function as a drive and its reduction as a reward. The fear is a stimulus-producing response. Acquired drives make behavior more adaptable and, at the same time, more puzzling when the prior history of acquisition of the drive is unknown but the reactions based on it are observed. This is likely to be especially so when the cues that initiate the drive are obscure and not obvious as in this study.

Superstition in the Pigeon

B. F. Skinner
Indiana University

"Superstition in the Pigeon," *Journal of Experimental Psychology*, 1948, **38**, 168-172.

Whenever a reinforcement follows a response, we must assume that conditioning takes place regardless of how the reinforcing agent is generated and regardless of the response that it followed. Reinforcements that occur by accident work like any others. The responses need bear no relationship to the occurrence of the reinforcers.

Method

Subjects: Eight pigeons.
Apparatus: Experimental cage with food hopper that is arranged to swing into the cage every 15 seconds for 5-second feeding periods.
Procedure: Pigeons were not required to do anything. Food was presented regardless of pigeons' activities.

Results

In 6 of the 8 cases, the pigeons began to behave in obviously unique patterns. Individually, the patterns were—turning counter-clockwise; thrusting the head into a cage corner; lifting of the head in a "tossing" fashion; pendulum-like swinging of the head (2 birds); brushing movements toward the floor. The conditioning develops as the bird happens to be engaged in some action just before the food hopper appears.

The effect of conditioning in this manner depends on short intervals between reinforcement appearances. After a response is set up, the interval can be increased. High rates of responding can be attained with extended intervals. The response can be extinguished and reconditioned readily. The illustration shows a reconditioned stepping response established in one bird (moving from one foot to the other). With 1 minute intervals between reinforcements, the behavior resembles ordinary training data. More than 10,000 responses were obtained before extinction appeared complete.

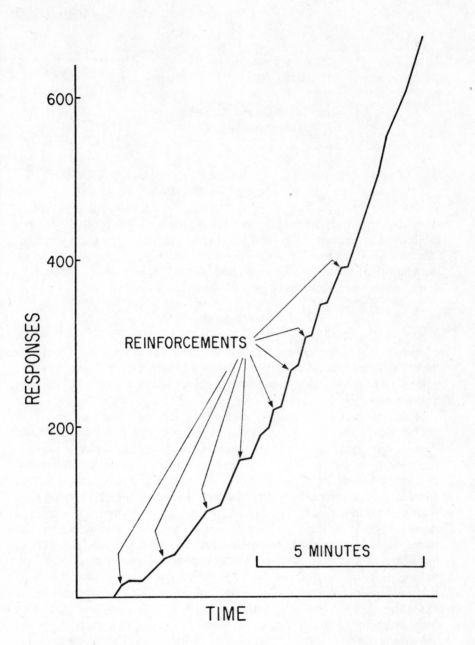

RECONDITIONING OF A ''SUPERSTITIOUS'' HOPPING RESPONSE.

Intrauterine Conditioning

David K. Spelt
Muhlenberg College

"The Conditioning of the Human Fetus *in utero*," *Journal of Experimental Psychology,* 1948, **38**, 338-346.

Can conditioning techniques be applied to the unborn fetus to learn about the impact of environmental factors without resort to surgery? The fetus is known to respond to a loud sound. Can the sound be used as an Unconditioned Stimulus (US) and, when paired with a suitable CS, can learning before birth be demonstrated?

Method

Subjects: Thirteen pregnant and 3 non-pregnant women. The pregnant women were at or beyond the 7th month of gestation. The responses recorded came from these Ss, but the real Ss were, of course, the fetuses.

Apparatus: A large, hollow pine box about 30 inches square × 10 inches deep served as a sound chamber when struck with an 8-pound force by an oak clapper. The sound (which did not evoke startle responses in the mothers) served as the US and was effective stimulus for a movement of the fetus. A gongless doorbell was strapped to the abdomen. The striker from the doorbell served as the CS, producing a vertical vibration on the surface of the mother's abdomen. Tambours were attached to the abdomen at points where X-rays indicated the head, arms, and leg positions of the fetus. The mothers could detect fetal movements almost perfectly. All fetal movements were recorded by tambours connected to pens writing on a kymograph drum.

Procedure: It was necessary to provide controls for movements of the abdomen that were not made by the fetuses. This was done by testing non-pregnant women (N = 3). Controls were also necessary for pseudo-conditioning and the possible effects of CS alone because of advanced pregnancy (N = 6). Two more Ss before the 8th month of gestation were tested to see if the fetus would react to the sound before the last 2 months. The controls were effective in that none of the Ss reacted inappropriately. The conditioning procedure consisted of presenting the CS (vibrator) for 5 seconds followed by the US (loud noise). Trials were spaced at least 4 minutes apart, and 2 experimental sessions were held daily for 30-75 minutes for varying numbers of days with different Ss (because of their entering labor or other reasons).

Results

For the 5 Ss who were used in the conditioning study (conditioning) proper, these were the findings:

S 10——Sixteen US, followed by 10 CS—no response to CS (control for pseudo-conditioning). After 8 sessions of paired stimulation, 3 successive CRs.

S 17——Three successive CRs after 8 sessions.

S 16——After 21 pairings, 1st CR. After 59 pairings, 7 successive CRs. The following day, 4 CRs; then scattered CRs in extinction.

S 15——First CR after 16 pairings. After 2-week rest, 6 CRs after 31 pairings.

S 12——First 2 CRs after 21 pairings in the 7th sesssion. After extinction following 3 CRs, S showed spontaneous recovery. The next day, 6 CRs in 11 tests with CS alone. After 18 days' rest, S gave 7 CRs to the 1st 9 test CSs.

Conclusion: Some 15-20 paired stimulations were required to establish conditioning to the level of 3 or 4 successive CRs. Experimental extinction, spontaneous recovery, and retention of the CR for about 3 weeks were demonstrated.

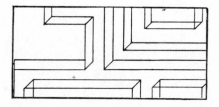

Learning How to Learn

Harry F. Harlow
University of Wisconsin

"The Formation of Learning Sets," *Psychological Review,*
1949, **56**, 51-65.

Learning psychologists have concentrated on the acquisition of specific
habits, ignoring the learning history of their subjects. If learners are
given many experiences with the same kind of problem (with differing
components) they might behave quite differently in the later problem
situations.

Method

Subjects: Twelve normal monkeys, 8 brain-impaired monkeys, 17
children.

*Procedure: S*s were required to uncover 1 of 2 small wells in a tray to

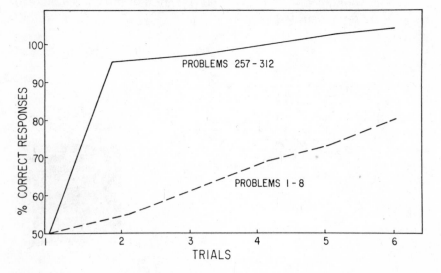

LEARNING IN THE FIRST 6 TRIALS ON EARLY AND LATE PROBLEMS.
(Note that the late problems need only 1 trial for virtually perfect solutions.)

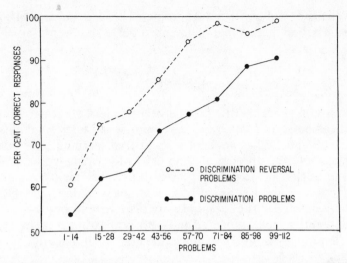

PERCENT CORRECT RESPONSES ON TRIAL 2 FOR A SERIES OF PROBLEMS.
THE 1ST TRIAL BECOMES AN "INFORMATION TRIAL" AND IS A 50-50
PROPOSITION
(Note that the monkeys learn the discrimination reversal faster than the previously experienced discrimination problems.)

find a food reward. The wells were covered with lids varying in size, shape, color, texture, etc. The first trial was always a chance or guess affair. After that, learning could be expected to begin. As each problem was solved, 2 new covers would be introduced to form the next problem. These were "discrimination" problems. A "discrimination reversal" problem could be created by having the object under which the food was found on the last trial be incorrect on the next trial, and so on. Another kind of problem could have a "position habit" solution —e.g., "It's always on the right."

Monkeys were given up to 344 discrimination problems with varying numbers of trials. Both monkeys and children were studied in both simple discrimination and reversal problems.

Results

The first 8 problems were learned slowly by the monkeys. By the 6th trial, they were only about 75% correct in their choices. In the last 56 of 344 problems, the monkeys were 97% correct on the 2nd trial and, in effect, needed only 1 trial to learn. Brain-damaged monkeys learned only a little more slowly than normals. Children 2-5 years old were faster learners in the discrimination reversal situation. After original training on discrimination problems, monkeys were able to solve reversal problems even faster, solving their late problems (99-112) in 1 trial. They also acquired position discrimination in an "orderly and progressive" manner.

Discussion

Problems that appear difficult to solve on the part of the naive monkey or child can be solved in 1 trial with a sufficient background in solving similar problems. What appears to be 1-trial learning, or "insight," actually calls for an appropriate and gradual learning history. What is learned through many experiences with different elements in similar circumstances is what might be called a "learning set." Presumably, social and emotional patterns of response are also learned in the same way; e.g., our ability to get acquainted and work with strangers. The explanation for learning sets probably lies in the gradual elimination of "error-producing factors."

Acquired Distinctiveness of Cues

Douglas H. Lawrence
Yale University

"Acquired Distinctiveness of Cues: I. Transfer between Discriminations on the Basis of Familiarity with the Stimulus," *Journal of Experimental Psychology,* 1949, **39**, 770-884.

Whenever some aspect of a complex stimulus or situation becomes associated with some response, that aspect or feature of the stimulus becomes distinctive; i.e., it will be noticed or responded to more effectively in some new situation than it was originally, especially if some other stimulus features were dominant in the first situation. Whenever any response is associated with some stimulus, there will be two learnings: There will be an association of S and R, but there also will be a modification in the initial order of distinctiveness of the cues in the situation.

To demonstrate such a change in stimulus feature values, suppose that a rat learns to enter a compartment that is white and avoid a black one. There will be other features to the compartments; e.g., the floors could be rough or smooth, the compartments wide or narrow. If the floors and room size varied randomly but the black-white feature was a stable guide to food, the organism would presumably come to ignore the irrelevant cues and the color feature would be come *"distinctive."* Testing the animal in a new situation where the same 3 kinds of cues are available would demonstrate the animal's tendency to rely on the color instead of the other cues. If one of the other cues was correct in the new situation, relying on color would impair learning; it would produce negative transfer. If color happened to be the correct cue, positive transfer would be shown.

Method

Subjects: Fifty-four albino rats, originally trained as 3 groups of 18, then tested in a new situation with 6 groups of 3 in each of 6 testing arrangements.

Apparatus: Two basic pieces of equipment were used, the first for a "simultaneous" discrimination learning, the second for a "successive" learning situation.

The "simultaneous" training device was a box with 2 compartments which could be entered from a small platform that a rat stepped onto from a ledge across a 4½-inch air gap. The 2 compartments could have their walls covered with white, gray, or black cardboard. The walls could be made narrow or wide, and the floor rough or smooth by changing the wire floor material from wide to narrow mesh.

The "successive" apparatus was a T-maze where the same variables could be introduced throughout the maze; i.e., the maze could be all white, all black, all gray, wide, narrow, or in between, and with rough, "normal," or smooth floors.

Procedure: In simultaneous training, rats would have to choose between compartments, i.e., they could enter either. Rewards would accompany one of the features; e.g., white walls. The wall color, however, would vary from trial to trial as far as right or left was concerned. In the "successive" training, animals could go either left or right. Food could be found if, say, a left turn was made and the maze was white, or if a right turn was made and the maze was black.

In general, then, rats were 1st trained in the simultaneous discrimination for 40 trials (10/day) with 1 cue relevant, 1 irrelevant (changing at random), and 1 cue constant, then tested in the T-maze for 90 trials or until 10 correct choices in a row were made. In the training with successive trials, the correct cues would be the same as before, the formerly irrelevant cues, or the formerly neutral cues.

Results

The results appear in the table. It is necessary to consider each group of subjects separately. The A, B, and C in each case refers to whether the Ss were tested with a relevant cue, an irrelevant cue, or a neutral cue in the simultaneous training. Thus, predictions are listed as positive for A groups, negative for B groups, and zero for the control groups.

In general, the results support the positive predictions but fail to support the negative transfer predictions. The latter groups seem to behave more like the control groups. It appears that animals can learn to orient, to look at a specific aspect of a situation, and that such reactions can mediate future problem solving.

Acquired Distinctiveness of Cues

Error Scores on the Successive Discrimination
(N is 3 in each case)

Group	Mean	Predicted Transfer	Group	Mean	Predicted Transfer
IA	9.67	+	4A	19.67	+
1B	22.00	−	4B	29.33	−
1C	26.67	0	4C	22.00	0
2A	25.33	+	5A	27.33	+
2B	30.00	−	5B	41.00	−
2C	37.00	0	5C	39.00	0
3A	13.33	+	6A	24.33	+
3B	24.33	−	6B	25.00	−
3C	14.33	0	6C	28.33	0

The Transfer and Retroaction Surface

Charles E. Osgood
University of Connecticut

"The Similarity Paradox in Human Learning: A Resolution," *Psychological Review*, 1949, **56**, 132-143.

It is commonly held by students of retroactive inhibition that "the greater the similarity, the greater the interference." Yet, the greatest similarity would be represented by *identity*, which is the basic feature of practice. Thus, a paradox exists, which can be stated as follows: "*Ordinary learning, then, is at once the theoretical condition for maximal interference but obviously the practical condition for maximal facilitation.*" This paper is an attempt to resolve the paradox.

Method

Analysis of the retroactive inhibition paradigm indicates that three stages are involved: 1) original learning; 2) interpolated learning; and 3) recall of original. These stages automatically include a transfer condition because we can ask not only what the effect of interpolated learning on recall is, but also what the effect of the original learning on the interpolated learning is? Is it facilitated? Is it subject to interference? The retroactive inhibition paradigm can be considered as three separate paradigms depending on whether we are interested in retroaction *or* transfer; thus:

Transfer

Paradigm A	$S_1 \rightarrow R_1$	$S_2 \rightarrow R_1$	$S_1 \rightarrow R_1$
Paradigm B	$S_1 \rightarrow R_1$	$S_1 \rightarrow R_2$	$S_1 \rightarrow R_1$
Paradigm C	$S_1 \rightarrow R_1$	$S_2 \rightarrow R_2$	$S^1 \rightarrow R_1$

Transfer

In the above paradigms, S_1 and R_1 are presumed to be the same—i.e., identical, in both original learning and recall, although they cannot be precisely the same; no two stimuli or responses ever are. They can only be *functionally* identical. S_2 and R_2 are presumed to be different, but there will be some dimension of similarity, ranging from "identity" to neutrality for stimuli. Responses likewise range from "identity" to neutral, to opposite, even to antagonistic.

By reviewing the literature relating to paradigm A, where S_2 is essentially a *generalization* operation, the following statement appears to be an appropriate summary principle: *Where stimuli are varied and responses are functionally identical, positive transfer and retroactive facilitation are obtained, the magnitude of both increasing as the similarity among the stimulus members increases.*

In paradigm 2, interference appears to be the common finding, and the experimental data in the literature support the following principle: *When stimuli are functionally identical and responses are varied, negative transfer and retroactive interference are obtained, the magnitude of both decreasing as similarity between the responses increases.*

In paradigm 3, both stimuli and responses vary in the interpolated learning. Here the empirical law is: *When both stimulus and response members are simultaneously varied, negative transfer and retroactive interference are obtained, the magnitude of both increasing as the stimulus similarity increases.* These three empirical laws can be represented in a three-function chart, the transfer and retroaction surface.

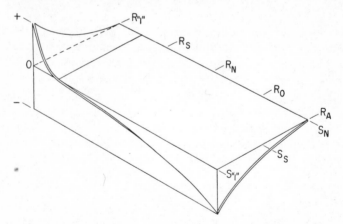

THE TRANSFER AND RETROACTIVE SURFACE.

Note that in this representation, the similarity of stimuli and responses cannot be located with precision because similarity can be defined only operationally for various experimental purposes. The distances, then, represent relative similarity. On the response level, I, S, N, O, and A stand for Identical, Similar, Neutral, Opposite, and Antagonistic. Stimuli are I, S, and N or Identical, Similar, and Neutral.

Observe that the vertical dimension represents positive or negative transfer and facilitation or interference in recall. It can be seen that if stimuli are neutral, there are neither positive nor negative effects, regardless of response variation. Note also that at some point (the line across the surface starting between R_1 *and* Rs) there are no effects of any kind due to stimulus variation.

Kinds of Learning

Edward C. Tolman
University of California, Berkeley

"There Is More Than One Kind of Learning,"*Psychological Review*, 1949, **56**, 144-155.

Conflicting theories of learning may each be correct for some different kind of learning. There appear to be at least 6 kinds of connections or relations which are learned. These are: A. Cathexes; B. Equivalence Beliefs; C. Field Expectancies; D. Field-Cognition Modes; E. Drive Discriminations; and F. Motor Patterns.

A. *Cathexes*. These are connections between drives and objects, dispositions toward or against certain objects (e.g., food, sex, fear-evoking stimuli). Organisms tend to approach positively cathected objects and avoid the negative.

Positive cathexes are probably learned by reinforcement, although the evidence is lacking for both these proposals. It might be obtained by use of an esophogeal dog preparation with a fistula by which swallowed food would fall out and not reduce needs.

Negative cathexes are learned quickly, probably by conditioning, using negative reinforcement. Neither positive nor negative cathexes are forgotten quickly. Extinction of a negative cathexis is probably attained by forcing the organism to remain in the presence of the feared stimulus.

B. *Equivalence Beliefs*. These are connections between positive or negative goal objects and sub-goals or stimuli closely associated with the goals, if such stimuli lead to at least some drive change. Social equivalence beliefs are most important. Positive ones appear to be learned on the basis of primacy, frequency, and intensity of need reduction. Negative ones are apparently conditioned like cathexes, frequently in traumatic episodes.

C. *Field Expectancies*. These are associations made when an organism moves through an environment, or when things happen in succession. "Sets" or cognitive maps are acquired that lead one to expect the next events or environmental features. Field expectancies are what are acquired in latent learning situations. They enable an organism to take short cuts. Field expectancies result from frequency of experience

119

but there must be some motivation for observations. Further, the organism must have some capacity to draw inferences. Expectancies can be extinguished by learning new expectancies; they are also forgotten more readily than cathexes.

D. *Field Cognition Modes*. These are the interacting processes of perception, memory, and inference. New ways of operating in any of these functions can be acquired. An organism can learn to function in probability terms, to tolerate ambiguity, to look for certain kinds of cues, to use rules about time and space, etc. There is little information about how these modes are acquired.

E. *Drive Discrimination*. It is possible, and probably necessary, to discriminate between several drive conditions, but we have practically no data on how these are learned.

F. *Motor Patterns*. These are the only S-R kinds of events comparable to the above described learnings. Motor patterns consist of movements and are probably learned, as Guthrie holds, under conditions where the movements eliminate stimuli present when the movement was started. Thus, motor patterns got conditioned without reinforcement. Such movements are built up into sensory-motor skills.

Conclusion: Reinforcement of the Hullian variety applies only to A and B. Other kinds of relations are learned under different laws, or conditions, most of which are not yet well appreciated.

Proactive Inhibition

Benton J. Underwood
Northwestern University

"Proactive Inhibition as a Function of Time and Degree of Learning," *Journal of Experimental Psychology*, 1949, **39**, 24-34.

Proactive inhibition (PI) was first described by P. L. Whitely in 1927. Since then it has been shown that such factors as similarity and *amount* (number of prior lists) of previous learning increases PI. Does PI vary with the *degree* of learning of prior material? Does it vary with time since learning? Both retroactive inhibition (RI) and PI can be demonstrated after short intervals; does PI increase with time?

Method

Subjects: Four groups of 24 college students in 2 separate experiments. The 2 experiments involved only a difference in time of recall (20 or 75 minutes) after 2nd list learning. (This abstract will report on only the 20 minute *S*s except where noted.)

Materials: Two lists of 10 paired-associate adjectives. The lists can be described as A-B and A-C (the same stimulus words but different response words in the 2nd list). Memory drum with right and left windows. One list was learned with each window.

Procedure: The design calls for 1 group (control) to learn only the 2nd of 2 lists. All other groups learn 2 lists. The learning of the 2nd list can be examined for facilitation or inhibition. The recall of the 2nd list after a time lapse can reveal PI, if any, when compared with the control group.

| | *Groups* | | | |
	I	II	III	IV
Original learning (mean trials)	—	4.33	11.54	20.71
Second list (mean trials)	6.92	6.38	5.46	4.92
(Note "associate facilitation")				
Correct responses on 1st				
test on 2nd list	2.08	1.29	1.67	2.00
(Note "associative inhibition" for Groups II and III)				
Mean recall after 20 minutes	4.75	4.17	3.33	3.33
(Note PI for Groups III and IV, compared with Group I)				
Mean recall after 75 minutes	2.54	2.67		1.67
(Only Group IV shows significant PI)				
Intrusions* in 1st recall after				
20 minutes		3	13	1
Intrusions in 1st recall after				
75 minutes		6	22	21
(Low differentiation; note the greater number in later recall)				

*Intrusions are "B" responses when "C" responses are called for.

121

The control group is labeled I. The 3 experimental groups recalled the 2nd list after learning the 1st list to different criteria: Group II learned the 1st list to a minimum of 3 correct; Group III, 8 correct; Group IV, all 10 pairs correct, plus 5 additional trials. The 2nd list was learned to a criterion of 6 correct. All groups were tested for anticipated recall after 20 minutes. (A similar set of 4 groups was tested after 75 minutes.)

Results

As expected, the higher the criterion for 1st-list learning, the greater the number of trials. Similarly, the greater the degree of mastery of 1st List I, the greater the PI for the 2nd. The table shows the basic findings.

A relearning of the 2nd list showed PI to be transitory. Relearning was relatively the same for control and experimental groups. The data show PI increases with the degree of prior learning. This suggests that when the Ss are unable to *differentiate* the responses, greater associative strength evokes the wrong response (more intrusions, see Group III—20 minutes, where the learning criterion was higher for the 1st list than the 2nd) or where differentiation is high (Group IV), the Ss know the response is wrong and refuse to emit it (note intrusions of Group IV—20 minutes). As time passes, differentiation decreases and more intrusions occur.

Proactive inhibition appears to be a function of degree of learning and passage of time. The essential operation is one of generalization between lists, methods of learning, apparatus, setting, etc., and differentiation. With the passage of time, there is a recovery of generalization and decline of discrimination.

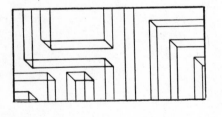

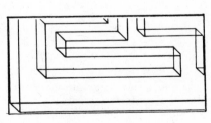

Talking Birds

O. Hobart Mowrer
University of Illinois

"On the Psychology of 'Talking Birds'—A Contribution to Language and Personality Theory," Chapter 24, *Learning Theory and Personality Dynamics*, New York, The Ronald Press, 1950.

In this chapter, Mowrer discusses various aspects of language. This abstract deals only with the section on teaching methods in training certain varieties of birds to "talk."

After experiencing a variety of failures with different procedures, the following procedure seems to work best:

1. Begin with very young birds to make sure they become tame and attached to the trainer.

2. Feed and water the bird by hand, repeating the words or phrase you wish the bird to learn at the same time.

    A. This method appears to work because the words become associated with eating, and will become "good" sounds.

    B. When the bird is alone and makes a sound something like the words previously heard, it "will be rewarded and will be prompted to 'practice' and perfect it."

3. Once the bird has learned to say the word, it is possible to use new procedures.

    A. One can reward the bird for a particular word.

    B. One can reward the bird for saying any word it happens to say.

    C. One can reward the birds for repeating a word spoken by the trainer. (This is a case of imitation learning).

4. Once the bird has learned under food reward conditions it will also respond to the *presence* of a trainer and to the *attention* a trainer may pay to the bird. The bird talks only because talking is rewarding to it.

5. In general, the principle of teaching birds corresponds to the principle involved in human baby speech development. The trainer must behave like a good mother; the bird must become fond of the trainer and like to see and hear him. The trainer is the source of the bird's satisfactions, and words become secondary reinforcers, regardless of their source—bird or trainer.

Transposition in Children

Elizabeth Alberts and David Ehrenfreund
The State College of Washington

"Transposition in Children as a Function of Age," *Journal of Experimental Psychology,* 1951, **41**, 30-38.

One of the best established experimental findings is the inverse relationship between the amount of transposition and the distance between test and training stimuli (see Spence, Abstract 27). In this study, it is assumed that Spence's transposition theory would apply to young, essentially pre-verbal, children but that older children could verbalize a principle like "it's the bigger one" and show no gradient in a test series.

Method

Subjects: Two groups of children, 22 in the age range of 3 years to 3 years and 11 months, and 18 in the range of 4 years and 7 months to 5 years and 5 months.

Apparatus: A panel with 2 cutouts through which boxes could be presented. The 7 boxes could be presented in pairs. Each box had a white door painted on it. The doors varied in size (128, 64, 32, 16, 8, 4, or 2 square inches). The doors could be opened by the *S* or kept closed by *E.*

Procedure: E invited *S* to "find the gumdrop" by opening the correct door. All *S*s were trained to select the 64 square inch door in contrast to the 128 square inch door; i.e., the smaller door was correct. Between trials, the boxes were switched in position randomly. There were 15 trials per day until a criterion of 9 out of 10 trials was reached. *S*s were then tested on the pairs shown in the figure. Ten transposition test trials were given on different combinations of boxes to different numbers of children as shown in the figure. The question to be answered was: Will both the young and older children continue to select the smaller of the 2 test doors? According to the hypothesis, the older children would, but the younger would fail to do so.

Results

The older children required a mean of 30.2 trials to reach criterion. The younger group, 54.8.

Transposition: As is evident from the figure, the older children continued to transpose down to the smallest test items; the younger children began to fail to transpose with the 1st test pairs and continued to fail to transpose in the remaining tests.

The drop in the curves of the older group are due to one child's unusual departure from the group trend. Note that the older children were not tested with the 1st pair of possible test stimuli (the next largest to the training stimuli) because it was assumed they would be almost certain to transpose.

The children were interviewed and some spontaneously mentioned "size" or stated the principle. In the older groups, some expression of size or principle was stated by 88.9%, while only 37.5% of the younger children responded similarly.

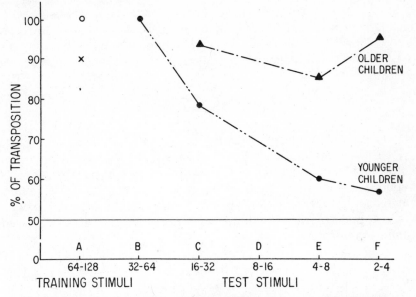

PERCENTAGE OF TRANSPOSITION OBTAINED BY EACH OF THE SUBGROUPS AT THE VARIOUS STEPS TESTED. THE POINT AT X IS THE CRITERION SCORE REACHED BY ALL SS ON THE TRAINING STIMULI. THE SCORE AT 0 IS THE ASSUMED TRANSPOSITION SCORE OF A GROUP HAD IT BEEN TESTED ON THE TRAINING STIMULI.

Conclusion: Older children demonstrated no gradient in transposition. The younger children demonstrated the expected (according to Spence) gradient as test stimuli changed in distance from the training pair. Older children tend to verbalize the cue aspect of size, while the younger do not.

125

Images as Conditioned Stimuli

Clarence Leuba and Ralph Dunlap
Antioch College

"Conditioning Imagery," *Journal of Experimental Psychology*, 1951, **42**, 352-355.

It has been previously shown (Leuba, 1940) that sensations, such as feeling a pin prick, can be conditioned to physical stimuli, like the ring of a bell. The CR is in the form of an image. Can an *image* of the stimulus, used in the conditioning process, evoke a sensory-like or image response?

Method

Subjects: Four college students.

Procedure: As in the earlier experiment, the Ss were deeply hypnotized and given suggestions for post-hypnotic amnesia. While in the hypnotized state, different Ss were given paired stimulations in 2 different sensory modes, e.g., doorbell and pin prick. In all cases Ss were asked to identify the stimuli administered to them. The stimuli were administered from 1 to 3 times.

Results

When Ss were "awakened" they were first asked to imagine various objects and situations unrelated to the experimental experiences. None of these "control" images evoked any reports connected with this experiment. The table indicates the results when E asked the Ss to imagine the events or objects used as conditioned stimuli in the hypnotic period.

Conclusion: "Imagery may occur in response to imagining the stimuli to which it has been conditioned previously."

Post-hypnotic Test

Subject	Stimulus Combinations Used	Asked to Imagine*	Report of S
JL	doorbell and pinprick (3 times)	*doorbell*	"I get a pain; a sharp pain that goes through me . . . in my right hand."
JM (two sessions)	1) finger snap and oil of cloves	*hearing someone snap his fingers*	Nothing.
	2) doorbell and pinprick	*hearing an alarm clock go off*	"I felt a sharp pain in my left hand."
JJ (three sessions)	1) doorbell and pinprick (3 times)	*hearing a buzzer*	"Feels sort of like being stuck by a pin."
	2) arm rub and oil of cloves for less than a minute	*arm being rubbed*	"Some kind of chewing gum— Beechnut or Spearmint—no, not Spearmint. A strong smell, more like cloves.
	3) camphor and card with 2 squares drawn in red crayon (The squares touched at at the corners.)	*smelling Vicks Vaporub*	"This sounds silly, but there is something there, all right; some geometric form, like a triangle. It's red and a square or a triangle." (S then drew an almost exact replica).
JJ		*Retest with arm being rubbed*	Wrinkling of nose; rubbing nose; no additional report.
HW	tin snapper and 3 × 5 inch card with small diamond and letter *s*	*sound of a snapper*	S reported seeing a diamond. To question, "Any color?" he said, "Yes, red; and there's a red *s* in the middle of the diamond."

Subjects were asked to imagine in terms of their own descriptions of the stimuli as these were identified during hypnosis.

Sensory Pre-conditioning

Delos D. Wickens and George E. Briggs
Ohio State University

"Mediated Stimulus Generalization as a Factor in Sensory Preconditioning," *Journal of Experimental Psychology*, 1951, **42**, 197-200.

Sensory pre-conditioning appears to support an S-S interpretation of conditioning. An S-R explanation, however, is readily available. Two stimuli may be conditioned to the same response, which can then mediate some other response which in the S-S situation is conditioned to only 1 of the stimuli. This explanation can be demonstrated by training 2 groups of Ss to make the same response to 2 stimuli. For 1 group, the stimuli would be presented separately, while for the other group the stimuli would be presented together. A transfer test should show no difference. Control Ss would learn a different response to the stimuli presented in isolation. Such Ss should show no transfer in the tests.

Method

Subjects: Forty elementary psychology students.

Apparatus: Semi-soundproof room, chair with arm rest, Watson finger-shock apparatus, ear phones (oscillator tone, 40 decibels above threshold), 6-8 volt light bulb.

Procedure: There were 2 stages: first, pre-conditioning; second, conditioning and testing for pre-conditioning effects.

Ss were divided into 4 groups, each receiving different pre-conditioning treatment. All Ss were told that stage 1 was a reaction time experiment and that they were to respond by saying, "Now" out loud whenever appropriate stimuli were presented. The stimuli for the different groups were as follows:

		Stimulus Used
Group I	Light and tone; say, "Now" when both come on.	15 L + T
Group II	Light or tone; say, "Now" when either occurs.	15 L, 15 T
Group III	Light but not tone; say, "Now" only when light comes on.	15 L, 15 T
Group IV	Tone but not light; say, "Now" only when tone comes on.	15 L, 15 T

Groups II, III, and IV had a total of 30 trials with L and T randomly presented.

All Ss were given 30 conditioning trials in stage 2 with tone as CS and shock as US. They were instructed not to resist any tendency to raise the finger but not to respond voluntarily. Following the CR training, each S was tested for reaction to the light stimulus presented alone.

Results

The mean number of responses to the light alone (transfer test) were 7.6, 7.1, 2.1, and 0.2 for the four groups (I, II, III, IV). Groups I and II were not significantly different, as predicted. Both of these were signnificantly different from the other 2 groups. Note that even though the 2 stimuli had been presented separately to Group II, the Ss showed as much transfer as Group I Ss who presumably were acquiring an S-S association. The Group II Ss demonstrate the operation of mediated generalization; i.e., making the same response to 2 different stimuli, which then permits the transfer of reactions conditioned to 1 of the stimuli to the other.

Abstract **66**

Situational Factors in Retroaction

Ina McDonald Bilodeau and Harold Schlosberg
Brown University

"Similarity in Stimulating Conditions as a Variable in Retroactive Inhibition," *Journal of Experimental Psychology,* 1952, **42**, 199-204.

It is commonly accepted that retroactive inhibition (RI) is a function of the amount of similarity between the materials in original learning (OL) and interpolated learning (IL). But the circumstances under which the materials are learned, i.e., incidental, environmental, and postural stimulation may also be involved. If the interpolated material is learned under different conditions it may not produce as much RI as when it is learned in the same situational setting as is the original material.

Method

Subjects: Seventy-two elementary psychology students, 36 in each of two experiments.

Apparatus: Card-flipping device for presenting learning material (6 lists of 10 paired-associate disyllabic adjectives, 3 lists for OL and 3 for IL; half the stimulus words on the IL lists were synonyms of OL words). The silent card device was used in a well-lighted classroom. Six noisy memory drums were used in the "drum" room, a dingy apparatus store-room. *S*s were *seated* in the card room and *stood* in the drum room. Materials were presented at 4 seconds per pair.

Design: A retroactive inhibition design was followed. In condition A (the control condition for retention), *S*s learned the OL and IL material (long division), and relearning occurred in the same room and conditions. In condition B, the IL (the other 3 lists) was also done under the same conditions as the OL (the RI condition). In condition C, the main experimental condition, OL and relearning took place in one room and IL in the other under different posture and presentation conditions. In effect, there were 2 experiments because 36 *S*s learned their OL in the card room with IL in the drum room for 12 *S*s (condition C) while the other 36 *S*s had OL in the drum room, and 12 of these had their IL in the card room.

Procedure: Each *S* learned an original list for 8 trials. Eight minutes of IL followed, either long division or 8 trials on the IL list. Immediately after IL, *S* relearned the original list to a minimum of 3 trials.

Results

The major finding was a strong retention for condition A (retention control *S*s who had long division for interpolated activity and did all their work in the same room). The other *S*s (condition B and C) showed considerable RI, with condition B (same room and situation) showing more RI than condition C (different room, posture, and presentation). As seen in the figure, after 3 relearning trials, *S*s in condition C were slightly superior to condition A *S*s.

Conclusion: The amount of RI can be reduced by approximately half if the IL is done under different circumstances. No attempt was made in this study to separate the influences of room, presentation apparatus, or posture.

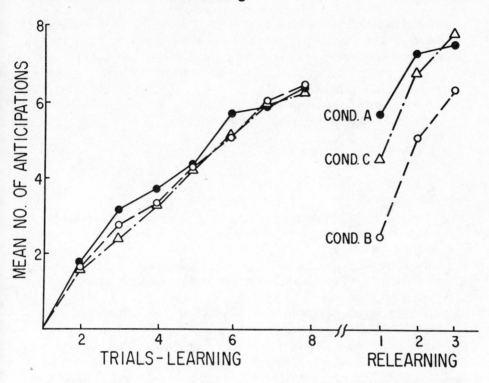

ONLY THE RESULTS OF ONE EXPERIMENT (THE 2ND) ARE SHOWN HERE, AS THEY DO NOT DIFFER GREATLY FROM THE FIRST EXPERIMENT.

Abstract **67**

The Measurement of Meaningfulness

Clyde E. Noble
Louisiana State University

"An Analysis of Meaning," *Psychological Review*, 1952, **59**, 421-430.

Following Hull's systematic program, a connection (relationship) between a stimulus (S) and a response (R) can be considered a habit (H) as indicated: $S \rightarrow R$.

Meanings are also relationships between terms, and for psychological (not necessarily "logical") purposes, meanings and habits can be regarded as the same. Such a view is like Titchener's context theory of meaning which held that a meaning was the conscious context that accrued to a core of sensory content. In the present view, the S would be the core and the R the context. If a given stimulus has many connections with various responses, that stimulus can be considered to be more *meaningful* than some other stimulus with fewer response connections. Such psychological meanings can be coordinated with an operational index, *m*.

Method

Subjects: One hundred nineteen U.S. Air Force recruits.

Materials: After preliminary screening, a list of 78 two-syllable real words and 18 artificial words (paralogs) was prepared. The words were randomly arranged in booklets, 1 word to a page. On each page, the same word was repeated on each line. The paralogs were nonsensical but some looked like words, e.g., ROMPIN, while some words were quite unfamiliar, e.g., BYSSUS. The list contained 20% paralogs, 35% infrequent words (less than 1 in 4 million in the Thorndike-Lorge count), and 45% frequent items (more than 1 in a million).

Procedure: Ss were asked to look at each "word" and write down as many words as occurred to them as responses. Responses had to be related to the original word, and not to a prior response. The time for each writing effort was 1 minute for each stimulus word. The total number of responses to each word or non-word was tabulated and averaged for the 119 Ss.

Results

A table for the 96 items in the word list was prepared, with the finding that, in general, the paralogs generated very few responses, infrequent words a great number, and common words the highest number. Some samples follow (the scores are labeled as *m*):

Word No.	Item	*m*	Word No.	Item	*m*
1	GOJEY	0.99	60	PALLET	3.62
10	QUIPSON	1.26	70	FATIGUE	5.33
20	ICON	1.54	80	UNCLE	6.57
30	TUMBRIL	1.84	90	HEAVEN	7.91
40	CAROM	2.26	96	KITCHEN	9.61
50	ROSTRUM	2.73			

The *m* values ranged from 0.99 to 9.61 with high reliability scores from different *S* samples.

Conclusion: The operational index *m* is a statistical concept, a function of the number of particular S-R connections which are acquired. As an operational measure of meaningfulness, it can be used to develop controlled levels of difficulty of verbal materials in research.

Clustering

W. A. Bousfield
University of Connecticut

"The Occurrence of Clustering in the Recall of Randomly Arranged Associates," *Journal of General Psychology,* 1953, **49**, 229-240.

In prior research on associations, it was observed that items of a similar variety, e.g., chicken, turkey, duck, and goose, tended to be reported in groups or clusters. This clustering may be a consequence of organization in thinking and recall. The present experiment is designed to obtain quantitative measures of the clustering operation.

Method

Subjects: One hundred undergraduate students in psychology. The *S*s worked in a classroom group situation.

Materials: Sixty words, all nouns, made up of 2-syllable items from 4 categories: animals, names, professions, and vegetables. There were 15 items in each category.

Procedure: The words were written on small cards and drawn at random from a box, one at a time. The words were pronounced aloud at 3-second intervals. The *S*s were instructed to attempt to learn the list for subsequent recall, when they would write down as many as they could remember. Three seconds after the last word, the *S*s began a 10-minute recall period during which they marked off each minute as the experimenter called out "Draw a line."

Results

The average recall was 24.97 words (Range: 12-36; S.D. 5.70). The question of concern, however, was the arrangement of the recalled words. Did Ss tend to recall items in category groups or in the random order of their presentation? On the basis of an "artificial" experiment in which 60 colored capsules of blue, green, orange, and white (15 each) were drawn from a box at random, with replacement, for 1000 draws, an estimate of chance clustering was obtained against which the actual clustering could be compared. The comparison is shown in the table.

From the table it can be noted that as many as 18 clusters of 6 items were found where this might occur only once by chance. In general, the chance expectancy favored clusters of 1 or 2, but the differences from chance are strong and reliable once clusters of 3 or more are considered.

The fact of clustering in recall is quite obvious. The finding relative to time is, however, more indicative of what was going on. The Ss showed an initial tendency to cluster well above chance, but this tendency increased only up to the 4th decile of their responses, after which it began to decline. As the Ss exhausted their recall, they would tend to remember items more at random. They also began to report items not in the original list. Categorical intrusions amounted to 7.17%; other irrelevant intrusions made up 3.00% of the recalled items.

Conclusions: The finding of a strong tendency to cluster in recall implies the operation of an organizing tendency. There appear to be two functions operating, one of "habit strength," based on reinforcement before and during list presentation, and a "relatedness increment" or "clustering increment" which is a hypothetical increment added to habit strength—i.e., when an item occurs it tends to arouse items with which it is related whether they actually appeared in the list or not. With these two assumptions of habit strength and clustering increment, the data can be accounted for in their several features.

Number of Clusters of Various Sizes

	1's	2's	3's	4's	5's	6's	7's
Subjects	810	261	164	85	38	18	5
Artificial	1453	343	87	18	4	1	—

Discrimination of Extinction Cues

Donald H. Bullock and William C. Smith
University of Buffalo

"An Effect of Repeated Conditioning—Extinction upon Operant Strength," *Journal of Experimental Psychology,* 1953, **46**, 349-352.

What is the effect on behavior of repeated training and extinction sessions?

Method

Subjects: Six albino rats on a 24-hour feeding schedule.
Apparatus: Skinner box; food pellets.
Procedure: After preliminary habituation in the box, the rats were subjected to the following schedule: For 10 successive days, the rats were placed in the box and allowed 40 reinforcements, each bar press being followed by a pellet. Starting with press 41, no pellets were provided, and a 1-hour period of "extinction" followed. The daily schedule was then one of alternating training and extinction.

Day	No. of presses in first 5 minutes	No. of presses in extinction hour
1	1.0	52.5
2	4.6	21.0
3	6.2	30.5
4	6.5	18.0
5	7.3	27.5
6	7.8	24.5
7	7.2	13.0
8	7.5	14.5
9	7.1	13.5
10	7.8	14.5

Results

By the 5th day, the rats stabilized their pressing performance (see table), and by the 6th day they stabilized their extinction behavior. Thus, the rats demonstrated a discrimination based on the response contingencies. In the extinction sessions, the failure of the appearance of the pellet is considered a response-correlated stimulation which acquires discriminative properties.

Transfer of Training

Albert E. Goss
University of Massachusetts

"Transfer as a Function of Type and Amount of Preliminary Experience with Task Stimuli," *Journal of Experimental Psychology,* 1953, **46**, 419-427.

Miller and Dollard have proposed that when a separate and distinct response is made to each of a number of stimuli, such responses (producing stimuli themselves) will make the original stimuli more distinctive because the response-produced stimuli are added to the original sensory stimulation. In this study, an attempt is made to determine if verbal responses (e.g., naming the stimuli) will similarly contribute to distinctiveness as tested in a transfer of training situation where separate motor responses to a number of visual stimuli are learned. Two other variables, "warm-up" and possible pre-experimentally acquired distinctiveness of the cues, called for controlled investigation in the context of this study.

Method

Subjects: One hundred four introductory psychology students.

Apparatus: Stimulus box with 4 toggle switches and 2 round plastic windows (about 1 inch in diameter). A light of 1 of 4 intensities could be projected through the lower of the windows and a nonsense syllable could be shown in the upper window. The lights used were of 1.5, 1.9, 2.5, and 3.4 foot candle brightness. The 4 nonsense syllables (each paired with a different light) were CUF, JER, NIG, and VOL.

Procedure: All *S*s eventually went through a learning session in which they turned off the different lights by moving one of the toggle switches. Prior to this "motor" task, the *S*s received different amounts and kinds of pretraining. Besides a control group that had no pretraining, the *S*s were divided into 9 other groups, 3 of which were given a verbal-learning task; i.e., they learned to say a particular nonsense syllable to each of the 4 lights. There were 3 such "verbal-learning" groups, trained to different criteria (9 out of 12 correct, 11 out of 12 correct, and an "overlearning" group which had twice as many trials as the 11/12 group plus the 12 criterion trials). Another 3 groups ("seeing and discriminating") with the same number of trials as the above 3 were asked to look at the lights, to pay close attention, to note how many different kinds there were, and to be able to state how the stimuli differed. The last 3 groups (with equal numbers of exposures) were merely asked to pay attention to the lights. This was the "seeing" group.

	Mean Correct Responses	
Verbal Learning	*in 48 Trials*	*Mean Errors**
(1) 9/12 criterion	31.0	21.2
(2) 11/12 criterion	32.0	19.8
(3) overlearning	36.3	14.4
Seeing and Discriminating		
4. Same number of trials as (1).	29.8	24.3
5. Same number of trials as (2).	29.9	24.4
6. Same number of trials as (3).	31.1	22.5
Seeing		
7. Same number of trials as (1).	28.2	27.9
8. Same number of trials as (2).	27.9	28.5
9. Same number of trials as (3).	23.0	36.7
10. No pretraining (control).	18.9	44.3

*More than 1 error could be made per trial.

In the motor-learning task which followed, the Ss pushed 1 of the toggle switches to turn off a given light. There were 48 trials for eacn S.

Results

The results for the 10 groups are shown in the table. All groups with pretraining were superior to the control. The "seeing and discriminating" groups were not significantly better than the "seeing' groups. The "overlearning" verbal group was significantly better than any other. All groups showed a tendency to generalize (in relation to light intensity), with the generalization gradient the steepest for the verbal learning groups.

Conclusion: Warm-up (seeing the stimuli) and acquired distinctiveness from attempted discrimination helped the motor learning up to some limit, perhaps 50 trials (compared with controls), but not as much as verbal learning in the overlearning groups. The latter groups strongly confirmed the initial assumption about the importance of cue distinctiveness as related to correlated responses.

The Backward Learning Curve

Keith J. Hayes
Yerkes Laboratories

"The Backward Curve: A Method for the Study of Learning," *Psychological Review*, 1953, **60**, 269-275.

When a large number of Ss are used in a study, it is awkward to publish individual learning curves, yet "group data are commonly so heterogeneous that the customary type of average curve is bound to give an impression of gradual learning, regardless of the facts." If different Ss arrive at the criterion at different times or in different numbers of trials, pooling all of the Ss for averaging points will automatically result in a negatively accelerated learning curve, even if every *S* arrived at criterion in some single (but different) trial without showing any previous learning at all.

Method

No actual experiment was performed for this paper. Instead, data gathered by other researchers were analyzed. The data are from discrimination studies using rats in one case and monkeys in the other.

Procedure: The original learning data were plotted in the traditional style, beginning with trial 1 and continuing until the criterion was met by all the *S*s. In both rat and monkey studies, "typical" (negatively accelerated) learning curves were obtained.

The data were then plotted "backward"—that is, starting with the criterion trial.

Results

When the data for the rats were plotted backward, a considerable change in the form of the curve was observed. The new, or "backward" curve corresponded to the curves of the individual rats which appeared to follow a pattern of no or little learning until just before the criterion was met, when a sharp rise in learning seemed to occur. The 2 kinds of curves are shown in the figure. The data for the monkeys, when plotted backward, correspond with the pattern shown when plotted in the traditional fashion, and are not shown in this abstract.

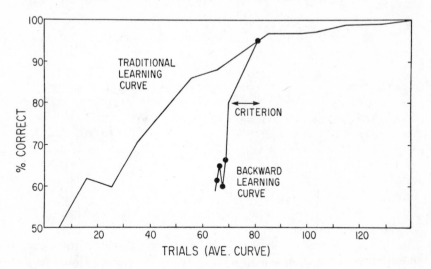

The Rat Data. The points on the curves indicate the percentage of correct choices of a group of 40 rats in a brightness discrimination. Note that when plotted backward the curve shows practically no learning by the group, even after 60 trials. In forward plotting, some animals, having learned quickly, show the curve to be rising for the group.

Conclusion: Learning may occur gradually (the monkey study) or suddenly (the rat study), but plotting the data in the traditional manner will show gradual learning in both cases. Plotting the curves backward will provde a more correct representation of individual performances.

Orienting Tasks and Incidental Learning

Irving J. Saltzman
Indiana University

"The Orienting Task in Incidental and Intentional Learning," *American Journal of Psychology,* 1953, **56**, 593-597.

In previous studies of incidental learning, the incidental learners were given an orienting task not given to the intentional learners. Instruction to learn was therefore not the only variable. In this study, both groups are given the same orienting task in order to assess its role in such experiments.

Method

Subjects: Two groups of undergraduate students, 20 incidental learners and 20 intentional.

Materials: A deck of 32 cards with numerals. The numerals could be classified as above or below 50, and odd or even. An additional 40 cards were used in a recognition test, making a total of 72 cards.

Procedure: All Ss were instructed to sort the 32 cards into 4 groups (above 50, odd; above 50, even; below 50, odd; and below 50, even) by placing them on a table where the positions were indicated on a chart. Three training trials were given. The incidental group then had a 75-second rest followed by 3 more trials. The intentional group had a recognition test (all 72 cards arranged in sequence) after trial 3, and the Ss were then instructed to continue sorting for 3 more trials; but to try to learn the numbers in addition. After trial 6, both groups took the recognition test, and the intentional group had 1 more sorting trial, their 7th.

Results

The groups did not differ on the first 3 training trials. During the following 3 trials, the incidental group continued to improve; so did the intentional group, but not so much. In short, while trying to learn, they lost time on sorting speed. After the 6th trial, the results of the recognition test showed no significant difference between the 2 groups. The relevant data are shown below.

	Sorting Speed			*Recognition Test*
	1st 3 trials	2nd 3 trials	Trial 7	
Intentional	57.9	51.3	35.2	4.60
Incidental	59.4	39.3	(Trial 6: 36.9)	4.49

The sorting speeds in the second 3 trials were significantly different for both groups, but it is clear that the intentional group was taking time for learning in some fashion. Their 7th trial did not differ from the last trial of the incidental group.

An easy conclusion from these data is that instruction or intention to learn does not contribute to the learning, for both groups learned equally well. A sounder conclusion may be that the time factor is repsonsible for differences found in previous experiments; in general, the rates of presentation of learning materials in these experiments were slow enough for intentional learners to learn, but the incidental learners, performing another (orienting) task, did not have the time to learn. In this study, each S set his own speed, and the intentional learners took more time, but not enough additional time (because of instructions to rush), to actually learn more than the incidental Ss.

Intensity of the Unconditioned Stimulus

Kenneth W. Spence
University of Iowa

"Learning and Performance in Eyelid Conditioning as a Function of Intensity of the UCS," *Journal of Experimental Psychology*, 1953, **45**, 57-63.

Studies of the influence of motivation or drive (D) on behavior have varied widely in design. In some experiments, a constant drive is used in acquisition, and Ss are tested later under different drives (differing in degree or kind); in other experiments, different drive levels are used during training periods, and tests are conducted under a constant drive. In some studies, no differentiation is attempted between habit (H) and drive (D), but behavior is observed during training as a function of differences in deprivation time. Inferences are drawn from all such studies with respect to Hull's principle that R = frequency (H × D) where R is a measure of performance or response.

In this study an attempt will be made to determine whether changes in drive (assumed to be related to intensity of the UCS) affect habit strength (H) directly or only affect performance. According to Hull, increments of habit strength are related to the amount of drive or drive stimulus reduction.

Method

Design: The appropriate design to assess the role of D in the R = f (H × D) principle is to train two groups of Ss under different drive levels and to test them subsequently with either the same or different drive levels. Different expectations can be deduced from such a factorial design and these will be stated later.

Subjects: Eighty college students from an introductory course, screened from 97 original Ss. Some Ss were dropped because they showed voluntary CR's, others because they responded to the CS prior to training.

Apparatus: Eyelid movement recording equipment (a microtorque potentiometer) and recording pen amplifiers. The CS was 1.51 apparent foot candles illumination of a 6 inch circular disc. The US was an air puff, either .25 pounds per square inch or 5.0 to the right eye.

Procedure: Each S served for 2 conditioning sessions. On the 1st day, all Ss were given 30 presentations of light and air puff. Half the Ss were given the .25 psi puff, the other the 5 psi puff. On the 2nd day, half of each group was given the same UCS as the day before; the other half was given the other intensity of UCS. This arrangement resulted in 4 sub-groups of 20 Ss. The interstimulus interval was 755 milliseconds. The CS light lasted 825 milliseconds. The UCS lasted 50 milliseconds.

Results

The design and results of the study in terms of mean number of CRs on the 2nd day are shown in the table. (Only the first 20 trials were considered because the Ss were beginning to approach the ceiling of 100% responding in the trials following the first 20 on the second day.)

Mean Number of CRs

Day 1	Day 2 .25 lbs	UCS 5.00 lbs	Means reflecting H
.25 lbs	5.65	8.00	7.23
5.00 lbs	7.45	13.00	10.23
Means Reflecting D	6.55	10.90	

Both row and column means were significantly different. The difference between the row means support the conclusion that different strengths of conditioning (amount of habit strength) developed on Day 1. With a stronger UCS, a stronger drive was produced and, with its cessation, there was a greater drive reduction.

The difference between the column means indicates that the response strength varied with the intensity of the UCS at the time of measurement, reflecting the differences in drive strength of the UCSs.

Thus, the difference between rows (reflecting Day 1 training) indicates that the increment of habit strength is a function of amount of drive reduction as Hull stated. Similar differences on Day 2 reflect the influence of drive level on performance as well. Had there been no difference in row means and a difference only in column means it would have been necessary to conclude that habit strength was not a function of

UCS intensity. On the other hand, a significant difference in rows but not in columns would have forced the conclusion that the difference in response strength reflected only habit strength. This experiment demonstrates that UCS intensity affects both response strength and habit strength.

The CS-US Interval in Avoidance Learning

Leon J. Kamin
Harvard University

"Traumatic Avoidance Learning: The Effects of CS-US Interval with a Trace-conditioning Procedure," *Journal of Comparative and Physiological Psychology,* 1954, **47**, 65-72.

This is a parametric study of the effect of varying CS-US interval in an avoidance-learning situation. The CS occurs only briefly and terminates before US is presented. The paradigm is, therefore, one of *trace* conditioning as compared with *delay* conditioning wherein the CS continues until the US occurs or overlaps the US.

Method

Subjects: Fifty mongrel dogs, 1 to 6 years old.

Apparatus: Shuttle-box with two 45-inch compartments separated by an adjustable barrier to correspond with the dog's height. Each side could be electrified. CS was supplied by a buzzer on each side. The US was a just sub-tetany shock.

Procedure: A dog would be introduced into the shuttle-box for a 10-minute test of "operant" level jumping. No dogs used in the study jumped. After the 10 minutes a 2-second buzzer was sounded. Then, depending on the group (N = 10 dogs), a shock followed either 5, 10, 20, or 40 seconds later. Trials averaged 3 minutes apart on a random 2-, 3-, or 4-minute schedule. Trials continued until a dog jumped the barrier 5 consecutive times to CS. Three minutes later extinction started with the same schedule for 10 trials per day up to 10 days (100 trials) if the dog did not meet the criterion of 5 successive failures to jump.

Control group dogs followed the same procedure, except that no CS was employed until the extinction trials. Five dogs received 7 shocks and 5 other dogs had 17 shocks.

Results

Acquisition: The 5-, 10-, and 20-second-interval dogs acquired the CSs with a systematic rise in trials requiring a mean of 9.4, 16.0, and 25.8 trials to meet criterion. The 40-second group scored a mean of 28.2 trials, but this mean is not representative as the animals in this group engaged in a phenomenal number of "spontaneous" jumps in the CS-US interval, six of them jumping as often as 18 times per minute. "These jumps, however, *did not appear to be elicited by the CS.*" Two of the 40-second animals did not meet the criterion in 70 trials. The 5-, 10-, and 20-second dogs required, respectively, 6.5, 11.0, and 18.7 shocks before criterion, and gave the first CR in 4.5, 5.1, and 6.9 trials. With increasingly longer CS-US intervals, the animals responded with CRs of increasing latency. The median times for the 4 groups in criterion trials were 1.85, 2.70, 6.40, and 6.65 seconds respectively for the 5-, 10-, 20-, and 40-second groups.

Extinction: The longer the CS-US interval, the more rapid the extinction. Five of the 5-second and 2 of the 10-second groups failed to extinguish in 100 trials. The 40-second groups arrived at 0 responses in 4 days; the 20-second group took 6 days. The 20-second group required about 25 trials to extinguish, the shorter intervals correspondingly more.

Emotional Behavior: The short-interval dogs were tense, quiet, and motionless between trials. They appeared to demonstrate a "focalized" emotional pattern. The animals in the longer CS-US groups were continually agitated and showed a more "diffuse" pattern. Control animals did not jump to the buzzer, indicating that there was no pseudo-conditioning or sensitization factor operating in this situation.

Conclusions: The results of the short-interval subjects support the Mowrer two-process hypothesis that the animals learn to fear the CS and jump when it occurs. The termination of the CS provides for reinforcement by anxiety reduction. In this study the CS terminated before the jump for the longer interval animals and anxiety reduction could not occur from its termination. At least 2 different kinds of emotional or "anxiety" reactions must be assumed. The "failure of extinction" appears to depend on short-interval or "delayed-conditioning" situations.

One-trial Learning

Virginia Voeks
Yale University

"Acquisition of S-R Connections: A Test of Hull's and Guthrie's Theories,"*Journal of Experimental Psychology*, 1954, **47**, 137-147.

Hull's theory predicts a gradual rise in amplitude and response probability as a function of N (number of reinforced trials). Guthrie's theory predicts the repetition of a response each time the same stimuli are present. Hull's theory would predict gradual acquisition curves, Guthrie's would predict jump-wise curves—i.e., one trial learning. A test of the theories could be made if exactly the same stimuli could be provided on each test occasion.

Method

Subjects: College students; 25 in preliminary tests; 32 in the main study.

Apparatus: Eyelid reflex camera, devices for stabilizing *S*'s head, spring-loaded telegraph keys. CS: a soft buzzer, .45 seconds before US (puff of air to eyeball). Strength of puff was individually adjusted for a complete eyelid closure.

Procedure: The basic problem is to stabilize the subject so that he will be the same from trial to trial—i.e., all internal and external stimuli must not vary. While this is impossible, one can exercise a number of controls. The following variables were considered and controlled: *S*s sat with back against back of chair, pressing on 2 telegraph keys, head in chin rest, looking straight ahead at ready signal. Ready signal followed breath control routine of inhale, exhale, inhale, and hold. On last "inhale," *S* breathed deeply and pressed the keys on "hold." Pressing the keys started the buzzer-puff sequence.

The trials were run in a sound-proof room. *S*s were relaxed. They were told it was a reaction-time study. Trials were spaced to prevent fatigue, although the response called for little work. Number of trials: Trials varied per *S* from 9-25 (mean = 17.1). Each *S* made at least 5 CRs. Each *S* also averaged 72% CRs.

Results

Of the 32 Ss, 16 showed jump-like acquisition curves. Most of the others had closely similar curves. Once the CR was given, it tended to recur. Ten Ss had 1 failure after the first CR, four had 2, and two had 3 or 4. While the amplitude data tend to follow the direction predicted by Hull, the results are not statistically significant; the blinks do not get progressively larger. The probability data show no support for Hull, either, because there is no gradual increase in rate of CRs.

By checking the response just made, a prediction could be made about the next response; thus, if there were no CR on trial X, one would predict no CR on trial X + 1 and, similarly, the appearance of a CR on trial X would justify the prediction of another CR on the next trial. When such predictions were made, 84% of all the predictions were correct (significant beyond the 1% level). In the 4 quarters of the trials, the predictions were correct 83, 84, 92 and 92% of the time. The predictions for Ss are summarized in the table.

Prediction	Number of S	
90-96%	15	
80-89	9	
70-79	5	
60-69	2	
50-59	1	(This S had a cramp in his leg and shifted posture frequently.)

Conclusion: Most of the Ss showed conditioning in 1 trial. Once the CR was given, they continued to give CRs on the succeeding trials. Learning was "all or none" to the extent that the situation could be controlled.

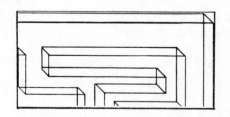

Secondary Reinforcement

Michael R. D'Amato
New York University

"Secondary Reinforcement and Magnitude of Primary Reinforcement," *Journal of Comparative and Physiological Psychology*, 1955, **48**, 378-380.

What variables affect the strength of a secondary reinforcer? Amount of primary reinforcement in the original acquisition period appears obvious, but prior research, using extinction as a measure, has denied that amount of primary reinforcement is effective. This study, using a discrimination procedure, is another attempt to assess the role of amount of primary reinforcement.

Mehtod

Subjects: Twenty male albino rats, 60-90 days old.

Apparatus: A straight alley runway (92 centimeters long) with 2 different goal boxes that could be attached at the end and a T-maze (stem 45 centimeters; cross-way, 70 centimeters), where the 2 different goal boxes were attached. One goal box was painted white, the other black with white stripes. The black box had a black food cup, and a white dish was placed in the white box. Suitable gates at the starting box allowed a determination of starting time in the runway.

Procedure: The animals were given 70 trials in the runway under a 23-hour hunger drive. On half the trials (in one goal box), they found a large reward (5 food pellets), and, on the other half, a small reward (1 pellet) in the other goal box. The animals were allowed 30 seconds in the goal box on each trial. The animals were divided appropriately so that the white goal box contained the high reward for half the *S*s and the black goal box had the high reward for the other half. The starting box was a duplicate of the goal box. There were 8 trials per day for the first 5 days and 10 trials per day for the following 5 days. On the 9th day, the animals were given 15 runs in the T-maze which had the duplicate goal boxes, but these contained no food. On the 1st trial, half the animals were forced to choose the side containing the goal box previously associated with low reward, and half the other.

Results

By the 5th day, 15 of the 20 rats were leaving the starting box which matched the high reward faster than they left the other start box, thus showing that discrimination had developed. In the 15 test runs, an average of 7.5 choices of each box could be expected if only chance factors were operating. The actual average choice was 8.80, a highly significant difference. The animals forced to choose the low reward side on the first trial averaged 8.10 choices of the high reward box, while those forced to the high reward end on the 1st trial averaged 9.50 choices to that end, indicating the influence of the first experience. The procedure of forcing such choices was necessitated to control for positive preferences.

Conclusion: The amound of primary reinforcement affects the relative secondary reinforcing strength of the stimuli associated with the reward.

Abstract **77**

Reinforcement of Verbal Behavior

Joel Greenspoon
Indiana University

"The Reinforcing Effect of Two Spoken Sounds on the Frequency of Two Responses," *American Journal of Psychology*, 1955, **50**, 409-416.

"A reinforcing stimulus is a stimulus introduced following a response that increases the probability of occurrence of that response." Not much systematic work has been done in assessing reinforcing stimuli in human behavior. "The purpose of this research was to investigate the effect of the introduction and omission of two spoken sounds following a predetermined response on the frequency of occurrence of that response."

Method

Subjects: Seventy-five undergraduate students in 5 groups.

Apparatus: Tape recorder, microphone.

Procedure: Ss were seated in front of the E where they could not see him. They were instructed to say as many words as they could think of in 50 minutes. Only individual words (no phrases) were called for. For the first 25 minutes, E would say for Ss in Groups I and III "Mmm-hmm" and for groups II and IV "Huh-uh" depending on the words S emitted. For the control groups, nothing was said at any time following the words. For the last 25 minutes (an extinction period) E said nothing to any S. The four experimental groups were arranged as follows:

Group I:	"Mmm-hmm" for "plural" words.
Group II:	"Huh-uh" for "plural" words.
Group III:	"Mmm-hmm" for non-plural words.
Group IV:	"Huh-uh" for non-plural words.

Results

The data were analyzed by the ten 5-minute periods in each 50-minute session. The Ss spoke in the range of 700-800 words.

The effects of the spoken reinforcers followed expectations; saying "Mmm-hmm" increased the number of plural words emitted by the Ss

Mean Number of Plural Responses for Successive 5-Minute Periods for Control Group and for Experimental Groups in which Contingent Stimulus Was Introduced Following Each Plural Response (Stimulus omitted last 5 periods of experimental groups).

5-minute period	Control Group (No stimulus)	Group I ("Mmm-hmm")	Group II ("Huh-uh")
	Mean	*Mean*	*Mean*
1	15.47	25.50	11.33
2	11.20	22.07	7.17
3	11.00	22.43	2.83
4	10.53	19.07	4.83
5	8.40	20.86	3.83
6	8.13	16.21	7.33
7	8.27	11.64	4.83
8	10.87	10.50	3.00
9	6.67	11.43	7.33
10	8.33	9.50	4.83

and "Huh-uh" decreased this number for Groups I and II. When *E* reinforced non-plural words the results followed the same pattern but not so strikingly (no statistically significant group differences). When the reinforcements were omitted (last 25 minutes) the responses showed a decline (not significant in Groups III and IV). The findings for the control groups and Groups I and II are shown in the table.

It needs to be noted that non-plural words form a proportionally larger class of words than do plurals. When reinforcements were introduced for non-plural words, the class size became a determiner because both kinds of reinforcers increased emission of non-plural words. "Mmm-hmm" thus reinforced both plural and non-plural words, but "huh-uh" decreased only plural words. "The nature of the response is a determinant of the reinforcing character of the stimulus."

Observing Responses in Discrimination Behavior

Kenneth H. Kurtz
Yale University

"Discrimination of Complex Stimuli: The Relationship of Training and Test Stimuli in Transfer of Discrimination," *Journal of Experimental Psychology*, 1955, **50**, 283-291.

With certain sets of stimuli, discrimination develops in two stages: 1) stimuli are recognized as belonging to one or another of several subgroups on the basis of gross distinguishing features, and 2) within subgroups, stimuli are differentiated on the basis of observing responses that make subtle distinguishing features of the stimuli more noticeable. The observing response that "works" for a given sub-group of stimuli depends on the feature that distinguishes them. Development of effective observing responses is by trial and error, and gross features of the stimuli of a given sub-group cue the observing response appropriate to that sub-group. If a person is faced with learning to make a new discrimination, the ease of learning will be a function of which kinds of discriminating responses he has learned to make to similar stimuli in the past. The correct observing response will allow rapid learning, while a conflicting response will hold back learning because the learner is looking for, or at, the wrong properties. Without any prior background, the new discrimination will be based on trial and error. To demonstrate such positive and negative transfer, it is necessary to provide suitable familiarization training prior to a transfer test.

Method

Subjects: Forty Yale undergraduate and graduate students.

Apparatus: Hull memory drum, 16 figures (4 sets of 4) to serve as stimuli for paired associates learning, where color names are responses. Familiarization screen (a card with 2 openings through which the figures could be seen one at a time). The 16 figures are shown in the table.

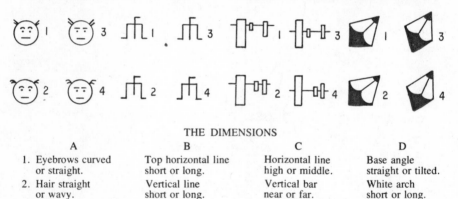

THE DIMENSIONS

	A	B	C	D
1.	Eyebrows curved or straight.	Top horizontal line short or long.	Horizontal line high or middle.	Base angle straight or tilted.
2.	Hair straight or wavy.	Vertical line short or long.	Vertical bar near or far.	White arch short or long.

Procedure: All *S*s first learned to discriminate 6 of the 16 figures (2 from each set) by looking at copies presented in the familiarization screen, where the figures were either the same or different. The different figures could vary in either of the 2 dimensions that characterize each. For example, if 2 faces were shown, they could be the same, or differ in eyebrows or hair. *S*s said "same" or "different" until they could identify all the shown figures correctly.

After familiarization, each *S* learned a list of 8 paired associates where the responses were color names and the stimuli consisted of 8 figures (2 from each set). Two figures were the same as those seen in the familiarization period—e.g., 1 and 2 of Set A. Two others varied in the same

152

dimension as in the familiarization; e.g., if 1 and 3 were used in familiarization (differ in length of top bar), then 2 and 4 would be used in the PA (paired associates) learning. Two more stimuli varied in the dimension not previously noted in familiarization; e.g., if position of the small vertical in Set C were the familiarization variable, then height of the horizontal bar would be the PA variable. The last 2 stimuli were from the set not previously seen in familiarization, and these served as the control stimuli.

	Log Trials to Mastery	Log Correct Responses Minus Within-set Errors*
Identical.	1.026	1.446
Different stimuli distinguished by same property.	1.026	1.426
Distinguished by different property.	1.216	1.196
Control; no familiarization.	1.126	1.306

Subtraction of within-set errors is to correct for guessing. The resulting difference estimates the number of correct responses based on discrimination of relevant stimulus features.

Results

The findings are reported in the table. Note that all of the predictions are confirmed. The negative transfer pairs were most difficult to learn, followed by the control pairs, while the identical stimuli, and those calling for the same discrimination, were easier to learn.

 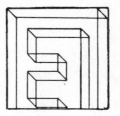

Verbal Chaining via Mediation

Wallace A. Russell and Lowell H. Storms
University of Minnesota

"Implicit Verbal Chaining in Paired-associate Learning,"
Journal of Experimental Psychology, 1955, **49**, 287-293.

Prior research indicated that when *S*s learn an A-B list, a B-C list, and finally an A-C list, the learning of A-C pairs is facilitated by the presumed mediation of the B items or associates which have been previously attached to both A and C. Thus, the *S* hypothetically benefits from a chain of prior learning, and the sequence A—— B—— C runs off with greater ease than if the *S* now had to learn an A-X set of pairs.

The present report deals with an extension of the mediation chain of four units, A—— B—— C—— D, where the *S*s first learn A——B, then A——D. The associations B——C and C——D are assumed to have been previously learned outside the laboratory in ordinary experience. Such associations are readily available from the common responses to Kent-Rosanoff free-association stimulus words. In this study, University of Minnesota norms were used.

Method

Design: The design implied above involved arranging an A-B list where known or presumed common associates to B and C were available. The pairing of A and D items would then provide a test list for mediation. In plan, the design was:

Learn		*Assumed*	*Learn*
Experimental list	A——B	B——C——D	A——D
Control list	A——B	B——C——D	A——X

where the X items were known not to be common associates to C items.

Subjects: Twenty-three sophomore women psychology students completed the basic experiment. Twelve more *S*s served in a control group.

Materials: The materials used are shown in the table; *S*s learned

A——B, where A was a zero-association nonsense syllable and B was a word from the Kent-Rosanoff stimulus list. C and D words were the most common associates to B and C respectively. X words were unrelated to any of the prior words in any row or column.

*Nonsense Syllables, Associative Chains, and Control
Words Used in Forming the Paired-Associate Lists*

A Nonsense Syllable	B First Chained Word	C Second Chained Word	D Final Chained Word	X Control Word
CEF	stem	flower	smell (1)	joy
DAX	memory	mind	matter (1)	afraid
YOV	soldier	army	navy (1)	cheese
VUX	trouble	bad	good (1)	music
WUB	wish	want	need (1)	table
GEX	justice	peace	war	house (1)
JID	thief	steal	take	sleep (1)
ZIL	ocean	water	drink	doctor (1)
LAJ	command	order	disorder	cabbage (1)
MYV	fruit	apple	red	hand (1)

Procedure: Ss learned the A——B list at a 2:2-second rate of exposure in a memory drum. After 4 minutes, they learned the test list which consisted of 5 A——D pairs and 5 A——X pairs. Half the Ss learned List 1 consisting of A——D and A——X pairs; the other half learned List 2 which consisted of A items and unnumbered items in the D and X columns. The control group learned only Lists 1 or 2 without any prior A——B learning; i.e., they learned only 5 A——D and 5 A——X pairs. Learning was to a criterion of 3 perfect trials.

Results

There were no significant differences in the original learning of the A——B pairs among the Ss who were later compared on Lists 1 and 2; nor were there any differences in the latter list learning between Lists 1 and 2. The essential comparisons were between the A——D and A——X items. The table shows the mean number of correct responses for the first 5 items (either D or X) learned in the test list learning for both the main experiment (totalled over the learning trials), as well as the mean difference in the D and X items learned by each S in the first 5 items learned. Note that the control group learned the items equally well, whereas the experimental group showed a significant difference in both the total correct anticipations and the mean differences of kind of association.

	Mean of Successful Anticipation for first 5 Correct Items			Mean Difference of D and X for Individual Ss	
	A——D	A——X	Significance		Significance
Experimental Group	67	48	.04	+3.74 (D——X)	.01
Control Group	30	30		−0.50	

Major Results

It is apparent that previously learned associations served to facilitate (mediate) new learning. There could have been an interference effect for the X items, to be sure, but such interference could only come from the mediational operation. The Ss did not report any awareness of mediational activity, indicating that it may have been "unconscious."

Early Perceptual Experience

Eleanor J. Gibson and Richard D. Walk
Cornell University

"The Effect of Prolonged Exposure to Visually Presented Patterns on Learning to Discriminate Them," *Journal of Comparative and Physiological Psychology*, 1956, **49**, 239-242.

Does perceptual experience in the early environment affect later learning capacity? Such a question has been raised by psychologists concerned with enriched and deprived environments. In this study, a specific perceptual experience was provided for young rats (from birth to 90 days), and the influence of this experience was tested in a discrimination setting.

Method

Subjects: Litters of newborn rats were split to provide 18 experimental groups and 11 control group members.

Apparatus: The rats spent their first 90 days in wire cages identical for all rats in their structure and surroundings. The cages of the experimental rats, however, were decorated with 4 black metal cutouts (2 circles and 2 equilateral triangles). The cutouts were about 3 inches in diameter or side. The cutouts were moved from time to time to different walls.

For discrimination testing, 2 discrimination boxes were placed together so that a correct response allowed the animal to eat in one box and proceed to the other for a 2nd trial. Entry to the boxes was achieved by pushing small doors above which black circles or triangles were painted on white backgrounds.

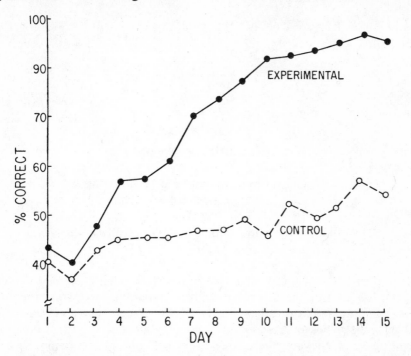

LEARNING CURVES OF CONTROL AND EXPERIMENTAL GROUPS.

Procedure: After preliminary training with the discrimination boxes, the rats were given 10 trials per day for 15 days, using a correction procedure (to assure exposure to each door cue). The learning criterion was 18 correct trials out of 20, with the last 10 correct. The forms were left on the walls during training days. For half the rats, the circle was positive; the triangle was positive for the other half.

Results

Only 1 control animal reached the criterion in 15 days, while 15 of the 18 experimental animals did so. The differences in the number of correct choices is significant at the .001-.002 level. The results clearly show a great difference in ease of learning the discrimination as a function of the rearing environment where no attempt was made to provide any differential reinforcement to the patterns.

Generalization in Pigeons

Norman Guttman and Harry I. Kalish
Duke University

"Discriminability and Stimulus Generalization," *Journal of Experimental Psychology,* 1956, **51**, 79-88.

The form of the generalization curve has been assumed to be some function of the discriminability of stimuli on a CS continuum. The discriminability values for the visible spectrum are available. It remains necessary to obtain generalization test values for different parts of the spectrum and to make appropriate comparisons. Pigeons appear to have about the same relative spectral difference thresholds as humans, and could be suitable subjects.

Method

Subjects: Twenty-four pigeons, 80% of normal body weight.

Apparatus: Skinner box with translucent pecking disc which could be illuminated from the rear, with light passing through a tunable filter to provide a range of hues. The CS wavelengths used were 530, 550, 580, and 600 MU. Test stimuli ranged from -70 to $+60$ Mu around the CSs.

Procedure: Pigeons were first trained to peck at the target key. The 24 Ss were divided into 4 groups of 6 and trained on a given CS for 2 days with 50 continuous reinforcements. This was followed by sessions of aperiodic reinforcement with an average interval of 1 minute. The generalization tests were then conducted under extinction conditions with 11 different hue settings for each original CS. Each value was tested 12 times; the next day, each S was retested in the identical manner.

Results

The basic data are shown in the figure. The several generalization gradients have the same, somewhat steep, form, and show a variation in length and some disparity in left and right aspects, but these variations do not follow the discriminability data. A second generalization showed lower levels of gradients. Individual differences were quite pronounced, although all the Ss demonstrated gradients of generalization. The Ss varied in their individual strengths of conditioning (with the more strongly conditioned birds showing steeper gradients). Later data show that the same function, multiplied by the appropriate constant, will describe gradients from all levels of conditions, from strongly- to weakly-conditioned birds. As the test trials went on and extinction became more obvious, the gradients also flattened out.

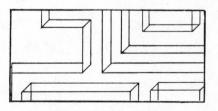

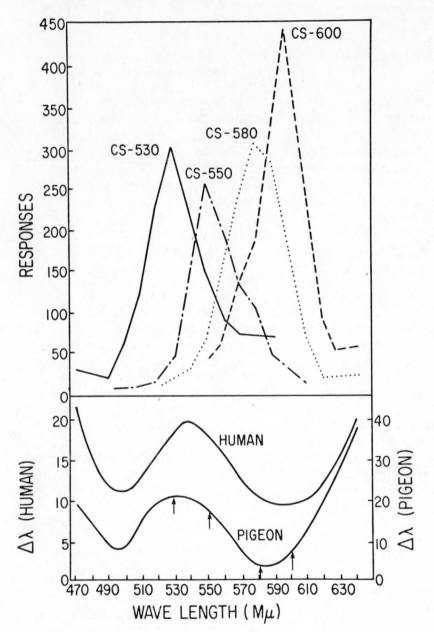

The human data are from E. G. Boring, H. S. Langford, and H. P. Weld, *Foundations of Psychology*, New York, Wiley, 1948. The pigeon data are from W. F. Hamilton and T. B. Coleman, "Trichromatic Vision in the Pigeon as Illustrated by the Spectral Hue Discrimination Curve," *Journal of Comparative Psychology*, 1933, **15**, 183-191.

Learning during Sleep

Charles W. Simon and William H. Emmons
The Rand Corporation

"Responses to Material Presented during Various Levels of Sleep," *Journal of Experimental Psychology,* 1956, **51,** 89-97.

Previous reports of learning during sleep have not monitored the actual states or stages of sleep, which range from fully awake through relaxation, drowsiness, and light sleep, to very deep sleep. At least 8 stages (O, A+, A, A−, B, C, D, E) can be identified by EEG recordings. Being awake is defined as nearly continuous "alpha" waves and being in deep sleep is defined as large "delta" activity. In addition, there is relatively reliable identification of at least 6 transitional states. In this study, Ss were presented learning material through the 8 stages, and the test results were related to sleep stage.

Method

Subjects: Twenty-one male adults (9 scientists, 10 college juniors, 2 policemen), all above average in IQ and all with persistent occipital alpha rhythms when awake (eyes closed). A control group of 40 college juniors and 24 scientists was tested without sleep training.

Materials: Ninety-six questions, on tape, with direct answers and a 5-alternative multiple-choice test on these questions. Three sleeping chambers (3 Ss at a time were monitored); EEG recording equipment; two-way communication system.

Procedure: Ss were first pretested on the 96 questions. They then went to bed with electrodes attached. Suitable sound levels were determined for hearing the questions. Five minutes after retiring, the Ss were asked the 1st question (e.g., "What kind of store did Ulysses S. Grant work in before the war?"), and then given the answer. Questions and answers followed at 5-minute intervals. If Ss heard the question, they were to state so. As the Ss fell asleep, reports of hearing material dropped off to zero. Ss were awakened after the last question, and, after freshening up, they took the direct question-answer test, followed by the multiple choice test. It had been previously determined that 1 hearing of the questions and answers would result in about 86% recall.

Results

The percent of recalled answers is shown in the figure as a function of the 8 stages of sleep. *S*s are not considered asleep until late in the B stage, or in the C stage. Prior to these stages, they report hearing some of the material. Once the *S*s are asleep, the percent of correct answers is virtually zero. Where answers are correctly reported, they correspond with abnormalities in the EEG curves, indicating some degree of arousal. In the multiple choice test, the same pattern appeared.

*S*s scored at chance levels from the B stage on. Chance levels were empirically determined by testing the control groups.

Conclusions: Learning during sleep is impractical and probably impossible. Learning during drowsy states might be feasible. About 30% of the material presented just before sleep onset was remembered, but the efficiency of such learning has not been determined.

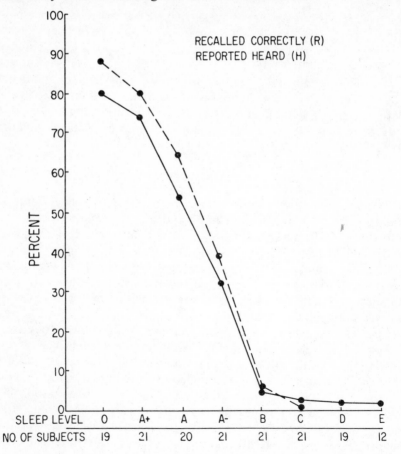

Anxiety and Competitional Learning

Kenneth W. Spence, I. E. Farber, and H. H. McFann
University of Iowa

"The Relation of Anxiety (Drive) Level to Performance in Competitional and Non-competitional Paired-associates Learning," *Journal of Experimental Psychology*, 1956, **52**, 296-305.

In simple conditioning studies, it has been shown that performance is a function of the intensity of the unconditioned stimulus. This has been interpreted as a reflection of emotion (from noxious stimulation), and emotion, in turn, has been interpreted as one of the factors determining level of drive. Granting these interpretations, it could be assumed that emotional subjects would learn more effectively under some conditions than less emotional subjects. One such condition would be the relative ease of the learning task; if the task did not include many competitive responses, then simple or easy associations would be enhanced by the additional drive strength of the emotional *S*s.

On the other hand, if the task contained many competitive response associates and required differentiation, the emotional *S*s would suffer from the intrusion of the competitive associations. The question could be studied if there were a measure of emotionality and a set of tasks involving simple and competitive associations.

The first problem, that of emotionality, might be solved by use of the (Taylor) Manifest Anxiety Scale to discover "high anxious" and "low anxious" *S*s, who would be presumed to have different levels of drive. The second problem might be solved by use of a paired-associate list containing simple or easy combinations and another list with more difficult combinations where the stimuli tended to elicit certain incorrect responses.

Method

Design: Two experiments were performed, each involving high anxious (HA) and low anxious (LA) *S*s. The 1st experiment used a simple learning task, the 2nd, the competitive learning task.

Experiment I

Subjects: Twenty HA and 20 LA introductory psychology students. The HA Ss were in the upper 20% on the Maturity Age Scale, and 20 LA Ss were in the lower 20%.

Materials: Memory drum for paired-associate learning; a practice list to equate Ss in learning ability; paired-associate list of 15 simple associates, such as *wicked-evil, insane-crazy*, etc.

Procedure: Ss learned by the anticipation method with 4-second exposure time for the pairs. Criterion was 2 errorless trials.

Groups	N	Trials	Errors
High anxious	20	8.95	20.95
Low anxious	20	12.60	32.60

Results

The table shows the data of Experiment I. The low anxious Ss were significantly superior to the high anxious Ss throughout the learning session.

Experiment II

Subjects: Ten LA Ss and 9 HA Ss.

Materials: As in Experiment I, except that the stimulus words consisted of 4 key words (*barren, little, roving,* and *tranquil*), each with an easy associate as a response and 2 synonyms of each stimulus word; for *barren*, the additional stimulus words were *arid* and *desert* with unrelated response terms. Thus, the list consisted of 4 high-associate pairs and 8 low-associate pairs whose stimuli would have competitive associations with the easy (but incorrect) responses of the high-associate pairs.

Procedure: Same as in Experiment I.

Results

The results of Experiment II appear in the chart. Note that the high-associate pairs were learned more easily than the low-associate pairs by both groups, although the LA Ss learned at a faster rate.

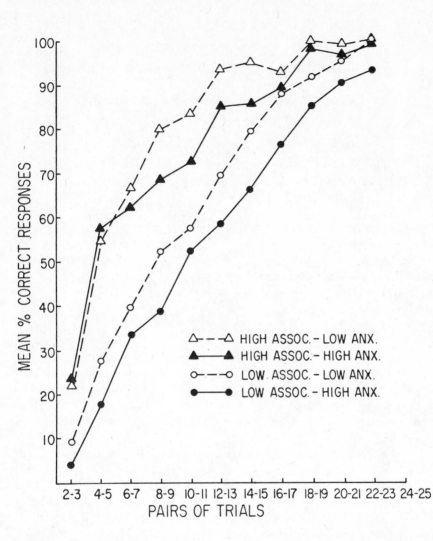

MEAN % CORRECT RESPONSES

PAIRS OF TRIALS

△ — — △ HIGH ASSOC. – LOW ANX.
▲ —— ▲ HIGH ASSOC.– HIGH ANX.
○ — — ○ LOW. ASSOC. – LOW ANX.
● —— ● LOW ASSOC. – HIGH ANX.

The low-associate pairs were learned more readily by the LA *S*s than by the HA *S*s, as predicted, although the difference is not significant. When the total list is considered, the LA *S*s learned significantly faster than the HA *S*s (18.4 trials compared to 23.3). The predictions of the study appear to have been confirmed. High anxious *S*s will learn more slowly in a task with a competitive response feature because the drive (D) factor will multiply all the habit strengths (H) between the stimuli and each competing response, thus adding to the difficulty of differentiation. In simple tasks, such drive factors will assist the learning.

Meaningfulness in Paired-associate Learning

Clyde E. Noble and Deldon A. McNeely
Louisiana State University

"The Role of Meaningfulness (m) in Paired-Associate Verbal Learning," *Journal of Experimental Psychology,* 1957, **53**, 16-22.

Previous work has shown that meaningfulness (m) has pronounced effects on *serial* learning. The *m* scale, however, did not provide enough serial lists for satisfactory tests. The present experiment provides a test of acquisition of single verbal habits as a function of *m*. It is also expected that the value of *m* varies with learning ability.

Method

Subjects: Ninety college student volunteers (28 women).

Materials: Eighteen lists of 10 paired associates were prepared from the 96 items in the Noble *m* scale. Each list ranged in *m* value from .25 to 9.13; i.e., each pair had a different *m* rating so that there were 10 *m* values per list (mean = 4.29). These values are the means of each pair of items.

Procedure: A memory drum with a 3-second exposure time was used. Each *S* first learned a list of paired-associate adjectives. This preliminary practice permitted assignment to a slow, average, and fast learner group. Each *S* then learned 1 of 18 paired-associate lists consisting of paralogs and words. Five *S*s learned each of the 18 lists. Twenty learning trials (anticipation method) were given each *S*, and errors for each pair were counted.

Results

The rate of acquisition was a positive function of *m*. As the *m* value rose, the number of errors dropped off. The table shows the errors for the 10 *m* values used. There were no significant differences among the lists, and so the values in the table are combined across lists. Note that the slow, average, and fast learners vary in their learning as a function of *m*. The slow learners are more sensitive to differences in *m* than

Mean Number of Errors in 10 Meaning Categories for 3 Pre-experimental Ability Levels during Trials 2-20

m value

Levels	n	.29	.79	1.74	2.98	3.92	5.08	5.65	6.51	7.40	8.54
Slow	28	4.64	4.71	4.57	4.79	2.89	2.86	3.00	1.68	1.46	.86
Average	32	4.28	3.38	2.53	3.56	2.66	2.09	1.38	1.31	1.06	1.03
Fast	30	1.73	2.47	1.67	1.67	1.07	1.57	.73	.57	.33	.47
Mean		3.55	3.52	2.92	3.34	2.21	2.17	1.70	1.19	.95	.79
m		.312	.226	.298	.273	.187	.190	.202	.173	.167	.125

are the fast learners. Notice that in the jump between the 9th and 10th values, the slow learners improve greatly, but the fast gain nothing. Most of the differences in learning occur in the first 10 trials; after that the impact of m becomes slight. The rank order correlation between the mean number of errors and m value is $-.915$.

The Role of Repetition

Irvin Rock
New School for Social Research

"The Role of Repetition in Associative Learning," *The American Journal of Psychology*, 1957, **70** 186-193.

While repetition is commonly regarded as essential to learning, it is also commonly observed that some things are learned in a single experience. If a *list* of items (say, pairs of words or nonsense syllables) is to be learned, does repetition gradually strengthen bonds between the items? Or are some pairs learned immediately, and is repetition of the list required because only a limited number of items can be learned in a single trial? One way of answering these questions is to have a group of subjects learn a list in the usual fashion, while an experimental group is asked to work under the following condition: If a list item is known on any trial, it is retained; if it is not known, it will be discarded and a substitute item provided so that on any trial the items will be either already known or new.

Method

Subjects: (Experiment I) Two groups of 25 college students each.
Materials: Fifty cards with letter-number pairs; e.g., B-7, CC-42.
Procedure: The study-test method was used. In any trial, 12 cards were exposed, one after another, for 3 seconds with a 5-second inter-card time. Then the "stimulus" side of each card was presented for 5 seconds (random order). For the control group, the same 12 cards were shown in each trial. For the experimental group, cards that were "failed" were withdrawn and replaced by substitute cards. Inter-trial time was 30 seconds. Groups were matched on the basis of 1st test performance.

Results of Experiment I

The median number of trials to learn the 12 pairs was exactly the same for the two groups, 4.75. Mean errors and standard deviations were as follows: mean errors—4.56 (S.D. 1.9) for the control group, and 4.35 (S.D. 1.2) for the experimental group. The groups were also virtually equal in errors (E = 17.2; C = 17.9).

The same procedure was repeated in Experiment II with nonsense syllable pairs (Glaze association values 47-53%). Experiment II was done to test the relative importance of the familiarity of the materials used in Experiment I and to provide more possible pairs.

Subjects: (Experiment II) Fifteen adults, mostly college students in each group.
Materials: Eighty pairs of nonsense syllables.
Procedure: Same as Experiment I, except for using only 8 pairs instead of 12.

Results

The mean number of trials to learn in each group was identical, 8.1 (S.D. 3.0 for control; 2.4 for experimental). Mean errors for the experimental group: 29.2 (S.D. 12.6), and for the control group: 26.7 (S.D. 11.4). The differences are not significant.

Discussion

The experimental *S*s matched the controls despite seeing the materials once and only once before having them learned (if they forgot later on, the items were dropped and new ones had to be learned). There is no reason to assume that experimental *S*s were getting easier material (random selection from original lists for all subjects). It appears that associations are learned when they are learned—i.e., on one trial, frequently with mnemonic aids. If something occurs to the subject that helps, he learns a pair; otherwise, he has no advantage from just seeing it. Some *S*s attend to only one or a few pairs per trial, while others try to learn them all, without success.

Repetition is important only for learning *additional* associations. It is as if pairs which are not retained by the time of the test leave nothing in the nervous system of any value for future use. Repetition, however, can strengthen associations once they have been formed.

Conditioning Meaning

Carolyn K. Staats and Arthur W. Staats
Arizona State College at Tempe

"Meaning Established by Classical Conditioning," *Journal of Experimental Psychology*, 1957, **54**, 74-80.

According to Osgood, the meaning of a stimulus amounts to a partial, detachable component of the total reaction to the stimulus (sign). Meanings are measured by Osgood by the "Semantic Differential" with three heavily loaded "factors:" evaluative, activity, and potency. If a meaning is a *response*, it should be conditionable. If a nonsense syllable were paired with many words high on one of these factors, it should come to have the same semantic differential value (meaning) as the words themselves.

Method

Subjects: Introductory psychology students divided into 6 groups (see table).

Materials: Six nonsense syllables—YOF, LAJ, XEH, WUH, GIW, and QUG; eighteen positive evaluative words (e.g., beauty, win, gift); eighteen negative evaluative words (thief, sad, enemy); eighteen active words (tense, hot, brush); eighteen passive words (slumber, cool, dull); eighteen strong words (sturdy, robust, brave); eighteen weak words (lame, sick, quiet).

Procedure: Ss were first familiarized with other nonsense syllables and words and then were told they were to learn (test to be by recall) 6 nonsense syllables and 108 words. Ss were told to look at each syllable as it was flashed on a screen for 1 second and to repeat aloud the word spoken by E. The 6 syllables were each paired with 18 different words, but in the case of Group 1, the syllable YOF was paired with positive evaluative words and XEH with negative evaluative words. The other words had no special relationship to the syllables. For Group 2, the relationship was reversed for these 2 syllables. Similarly, for Group 3, XEH was paired with the active words and YOF with passive. For Group 4, the relationship was reversed. For Group 5, YOF had strong words, XEH weak, and Group 6 had weak words for YOF and strong for XEH. Thus, each S heard and spoke 18 different words with the same meaning value for XEH and YOF, although these meanings were presumed to be of opposite value.

After the 108 pairings, Ss were tested for the recall of the syllables and words, although these data were of no interest. The Ss then rated the syllables on the appropriate Semantic Differential scales. The Ss were then asked if they had thought about the purpose of the experiment, and, if they indicated that they were aware of the real purpose, their results were discarded.

Results

Nine of the 86 Ss appeared to be aware of the point of the study. The results for the others are shown in the table.

The syllables XEH and YOF in 18 "conditioning" trials or pairings

Arthur W. Staats made the theoretical analysis, developed the experimental method, planned and conducted Experiment I, and wrote the journal article from which this abstract is derived. Carolyn K. Staats developed the method for statistically evaluating the results, and planned and conducted Experiments II and II. The data form a portion of the results of her doctoral dissertation at the University of California at Los Angeles, 1957.

Group		Variable	N	Mean Ratings				Significance
				XIH		VOF		
				Mean	S.D.	Mean	S.D.	
1 XEH+	YOF−	evaluative	15	4.80	1.80	2.40	1.50	.001
2 XEH−	YOF+	evaluative	15	3.13	1.46	4.73	1.77	
3 XEH+	YOF−	activity	10	4.90	1.70	3.30	2.33	.05
4 XEH−	YOF+	activity	10	3.00	1.79	5.00	2.00	
5 XEH+	YOF−	potency	12	4.42	2.14	6.33	.94	.06
6 XEH−	YOF+	potency	12	4.58	2.25	3.92	2.32	

acquired the characteristics (meaning) of the words with which they were paired, not as "associates" of these words, since there was only 1 pairing with each word, but in Osgood's and Mowrer's sense of the detachable reaction component generated by any stimulus.

Abstract **87**

Durable Secondary Reinforcement

Donald W. Zimmerman
University of Illinois

"Durable Secondary Reinforcement: Method and Theory," *Psychological Review*, 1957, **64**, 373-383.

Secondary reinforcement has been criticized as a relatively weak, transitory, and unstable phenomenon. Actually, the strength and stability may be a function of the procedures followed in developing secondary reinforcement properties. It is already established that partial or intermittent reinforcement can strengthen an operant response. The same intermittency in establishing a secondary reinforcer might have similar effects.

Method

Subjects: Thirsty rats.

Apparatus: Skinner box with a water-reinforcement device; a buzzer.

Procedure: After habituation to the box, a 2-second buzzer is followed by operation of the water dipper at 1-minute intervals. In due course, the animal begins to approach the dipper at the sound of the buzzer. When approach behavior is securely established, buzzer stimulation is no longer reinforced at 100%. A variable ratio schedule is introduced and established at a 1:10 ratio. The bar is then introduced; pressing the bar results in the buzzer sound, but no water. The buzzer is now presented intermittently following bar-presses.

Results

The buzzer begins a signal that "water may be present." When the animal is presented with a bar, it quickly establishes the bar-pressing response (six buzzer reinforcements). After the first 6 responses, a variable interval schedule (1 minute since last response) resulted in continued bar-pressing. Omission of the buzzer resulted in extinction of the pressing. The following day, bar-pressing was reestablished using only the secondary reinforcer (Sr).

Conclusion: By using 2 partial reinforcement procedures (that for the original establishment of the buzzer as an Sr and for the bar-pressing itself), relatively high levels of secondary reinforcement strength can be developed.

Note: The interesting theoretical section of this paper has not been abstracted here, and should be read *in toto*. In a later study Zimmerman demonstrated even more powerful secondary reinforcement effect. (See: David Zimmerman, "Sustained Performance in Rats Based on Secondary Reinforcement," *Journal of Comparative and Physiological Psychology,* 1959.)

The Phantom Plateau

F. S. Keller
Columbia University

"The Phantom Plateau," *Journal of Experimental Analysis of Behavior,* 1958, **1**, 1-14.

In 1897, Bryan and Harter reported that in learning to receive (not send) Morse code, apprentices would experience long periods (weeks) of no apparent progress. They hypothesized that the student first learned letters, but that, after mastery of the individual units, he would have to learn to receive whole words as new units, and later (after another no progress period), phrases and sentences. The periods of no progress in the learning curves were described as "plateaus," and for 50 years they were accepted and expected in a variety of learning tasks, such as typing and foreign-language learning.

During World War I, Rees Edgar Tulloss at Harvard began systematic studies of Morse code with naval recruits and found no signs of plateaus in their training records, and, moreover, the men showed much faster progress than the trainees described by Bryan and Harter.

The present study deals with one subject who was trained in Morse code reception over a period of 10 weeks.

Method

Subject: An 18-year-old high school graduate.

Procedure: For the first 12 days, 1 hour of daily practice. After this, there were 2-hour practice speed sessions daily (7 days per week) for a total of 10 weeks, with the rate of sending rising as the criterion was met. The teaching technique was the code-voice method in which the instructor names each signal a few seconds after sending it, and the student tries to respond during the pause. The trainee practices on letters and digits with 4 kinds of material: E0, random basic signals; E, first order approximation of English (frequency of letters corresponding to English text); Et, nonfiction English; and Ed, disconnected discourse.

Results

The progress of the learner A.S. is compared with that of Bryan and Harter's subject J.S. in the figure. The line at 72 words per minute is the "lowest main line rate." Note that there are no plateaus in the A.S. record. A.S. seems to have no limit, and the sender could work no faster.

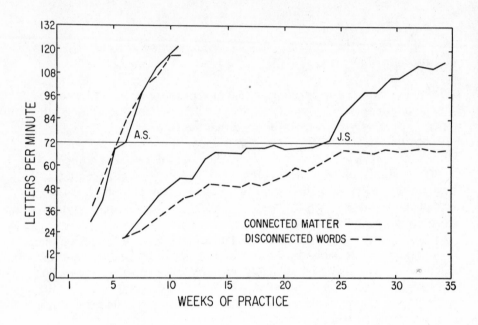

Analysis of the performance of A.S. and of the subjects of Tulloss suggests that the original Bryan and Harter interpretation that *S*s learn different *kinds* of units (e.g., letters, then words, then phrases) is not correct. Because of their very nature, *code* stimuli are never *word* stimuli (except for guesses or when sent at uncommonly high speeds). What happens in receiving code is that the receiver copies "close behind" the speaker, responding letter by letter. The basic steps are these: 1) The subject hears the auditory signal, e.g., di-dah. 2) In early learning, he imitates this by articulating it. 3) He then articulates the translation silently. 4) He writes it out. With practice, he stops articulating the signal and correctly articulates the letter. He then begins to overlap response chains and "copy behind." As some letters appear to become words, the receiver articulates them and records them, but the words are never heard as such from the transmission. The Bryan and Harter curves were the result of faulty training. Their plateaus were phantoms.

The Semantic Differential

**Charles E. Osgood, George J. Souci, and
Percy H. Tannenbaum**
University of Illinois

The Measurement of Meaning, Urbana, The University of
Illinois Press, 1958.

This abstract deals only with parts of Chapter 1 and Chapter 2 wherein
the development of the *Semantic Differential* is described.

When someone is asked the "meaning" of anything, he usually ex-
presses himself in descriptive terms, in adjectives, apparently describing how he is affected by the item. Frequently, reporters run out of
words; in short, they are not very good at the task. That "meaning" is
some kind of internal response seems acceptable. Here it is described as
an r_m, which is described as an internal, or covert, "representational
mediation response" when amplified to read ($r_m \rightarrow s_m$). How such responses can be described and measured is the problem of this investigation. Because words are the usual way of describing meanings, recourse
is had to words.

Method

Subjects: One hundred college students.

Materials: Workbooks with 50 pairs of adjectives in a bi-polar arrangement; e.g., good——bad arranged on each page of the workbook. The
adjectives were selected and amplified from a prior study in which Ss
reported the first 3 adjectives they thought of as responses to 40 words
from the Kent-Rosanoff list.

On each of 20 pages of the workbook there would be 1 word to be
checked off on each of the 50 adjective scales, which had 7 unnumbered
divisions; thus: Lady——rough _ _ _ _ _ _ _ smooth. The 20
words used were lady, boulder, sin, father, lake, symphony, Russian,
feather, me, fire, baby, fraud, God, patriot, tornado, sword, mother,
statue, cop, and America. The bi-polar adjectives will be illustrated
later.

When the 100 Ss had checked each of 50 adjective scales for each of the 20 words, there were 2000 scale values for each of the 50 scales. Numbers were inserted at the check points (1-7) to provide numerical scale values, and each scale value obtained was entered into a correlation table for all 20 concepts for all *S*s to determine the degree to which the scale values correlated. By a process of Factor Analysis, it could be discovered, if there were any common patterns within the scale values for the different adjective sets.

Results

The Factor Analysis indicated that 4 factors would account for .9975% of the common variance, with the 4th factor accounting for only 1.52% of the total variance. The first 3 factors accounted respectively for 68.55, 15.46, and 12.66% of the common variance. Inspection of these factors suggested that names like evaluative, potency, and activity might be assigned appropriately. Examples of adjective pairs with heavy loadings on these 3 factors are:

*Evaluative:*good-bad, beautiful-ugly, sweet-sour, clean-dirty, kind-cruel, pleasant-unpleasant, happy-sad, nice-awful, sacred-profane.

Potency: large-small, strong-weak, heavy-light, thick-thin, hard-soft, rough-smooth, rugged-delicate.

Activity: fast-slow, active-passive, hot-cold, sharp-dull.

A number of these pairs have high correlations with several factors. In general, the findings suggest that most of the "meaning" of a word referring to some person, thing, or concept is measured by the evaluative factor.

When the factor values for any item are marked off on a hypothetical three-dimensional scale (imagine 3 rods intersecting at right angles at the centers), the "location" of that item in "semantic space" can be indicated, with a high probability that no 2 objects will ever occupy the same space.

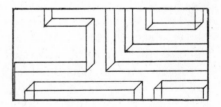

Imprinting

Eckhard H. Hess
University of Chicago

"Imprinting," *Science*, 1959, **130**, 133-141.

Lorenz (1935) first used the term "imprinting" to describe the effects of early social contacts which determine some adult social behavior. He also noted "critical periods" when imprinting was most effectively established. While imprinting has been observed mostly with fowl, some mammals (buffalo, sheep, and guinea pigs) also have been described as demonstrating the effects of early infant experience.

Method

Subjects: Ducklings and chicks. Only duckling data will be presented here.

Apparatus: A circular runway 5 feet in diameter with plexiglass sides. The runway was 12 inches wide. A wooden decoy male mallard duck suspended 2 inches above the runway could be moved about in a circle while a loudspeaker in the decoy kept repeating, "Gock." Colored spheres were also used in place of decoys.

Procedure: As soon as ducklings were hatched, they were placed in boxes and kept there for varying periods of time (up to 32 hours). At varying ages, different ducklings were placed in the runway, the decoy started, and ducklings observed for an hour. Ordinarily, the ducklings would follow the decoy around the runway, but tests of imprinting were made later by releasing the duckling in the runway between 2 decoys (the original male and a female) which could give the normal call of a mother duck. Ducklings were observed to see which decoy was responded to when both were silent or either or both were calling. Positive responses were counted.

Results

Although imprinting can be observed immediately after hatching, the highest test scores were made by ducklings "imprinted" between 13 and 16 hours old. Twenty-four hours after the ducklings hatched, practically no imprinting was observed. A number of additional observations developed around the major study:

1. Colored spheres were just as effective as decoys, but they varied in effectiveness depending on color. Blue, red, and green were better than black, yellow, or white.
2. Ducklings tested outside the laboratory would prefer decoy "mothers" to genuine mothers as objects to stay with and follow.
3. Presenting mother calls (on tape) to unhatched ducklings just before hatching had no effect.
4. When ducklings worked harder (walked farther, crossed hurdles, went up ramps) in the initial exposure, the imprinting was more effective (Law of Effect).
5. Ducklings born from eggs laid by ducks that were good "imprinters" were more easily imprinted than those of poor-imprinter stock.

Conclusion: Ducklings show no fear before about 13 hours and are progressively more fearful after about 17 hours. The critical age for imprinting appears to be related to fearfulness; i.e., the duckling must approach if it is to be imprinted. Drugs that abate fear do not facilitate imprinting. Imprinting may be a form of learning, but it shows strong primacy and poor recency effects. It is more effective under massed than it is under spaced trials. Fowl that can learn visual discriminations under drugs cannot be imprinted in the same state. The proper way to approach the subject of imprinting is to explore it and study it without making assumptions.

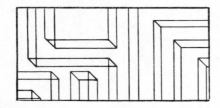

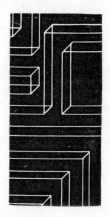

Short-term Memory

Lloyd R. Peterson and Margaret Jean Peterson
Indiana University

"Short-term Retention of Individual Verbal Items," *Journal of Experimental Psychology*, 1959, **58**, 193-198.

During an acquisition process, there may be forgetting because of the decay of some stimulus trace. The amount of decrement of the effects of stimulation as a function of time needs investigation.

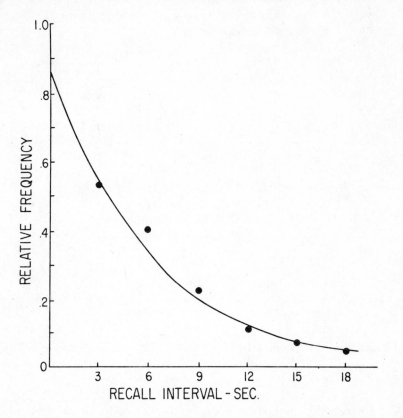

CORRECT RECALL AS A FUNCTION OF RECALL INTERVAL.

Method

Subjects: Twenty-four college students.

Materials: Forty-eight three-consonant combinations (CCC).

Procedure: E spelled out a CCC and started timer on saying the last C and stating a 3-digit number. *S* began to subtract by 3's or 4's from this number. *E* waited for varying intervals (3-18 seconds) and then signalled *S* for a recall. Each *S* was tested 8 times at recall intervals of 3, 6, 9, 12, 15, and 18 seconds. In a replication, *S*s were allowed to repeat the CCC 1, 2, or 3 times.

Results

An increasing percent of *S*s forgot the CCC as the time of recall increased. When *S*s repeated the CCC, retention improved. The improvement was found both for sequences and 1st letter recall. There was no finding of proactive inhibition.

Conclusion: Short-term retention is an important, though neglected, aspect of the acquisition process.

Extinction of Tantrum Behavior

Carl D. Williams
University of Miami

"The Elimination of Tantrum Behavior by Extinction Procedures," *Journal of Abnormal and Social Psychology,* 1959, **59**, 269.

Can extinction procedures be applied to undesirable human behavior?

Method

Subject: A 21-month-old male child who was pronounced medically fit, but who had a history of ill health up to the age of 18 months, and who had required special care and attention. The child would now demand special attention at bedtime, and the parents could not leave the bedroom till the child was asleep.

Procedure: Child was put to bed in a relaxed manner, and the parent (or aunt) closed the door on leaving the room and did not reenter when the child began to scream with rage. The extinction procedure was repeated in a second series after an original 10-day series.

Results

In 10 days, the child accepted the putting-to-bed routine without fussing and appeared to welcome the operation. After about a week, the child again had a tantrum episode after his aunt put him to bed, perhaps a spontaneous recovery. A second extinction, requiring only 7 days, brought about the quiet acceptance again. At almost 4 years of age, the child showed no side effects and appeared to be a normal, friendly person.

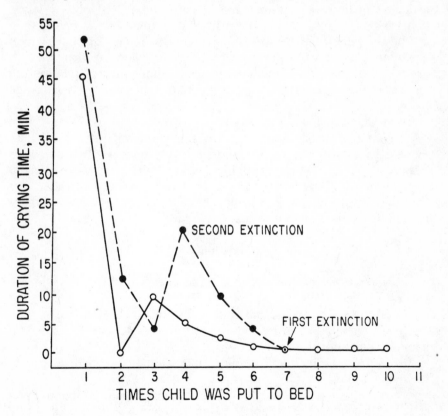

Variables in Paired-associate Learning

William Epstein, Irvin Rock, and Carl B. Zuckerman
University of Kansas   Yeshiva University   Brooklyn College

"Meaning and Familiarity in Associative Learning,"
Psychological Monographs, 1960, **74**, 1-22.

It is generally accepted that meaningful material is learned more easily than non-meaningful. Meaning is, however, frequently confused with familiarity. There are five principal explanations: 1) the *associative* or positive transfer from prior learning (*the number or frequency* of prior associations); 2) the *organizational*—two meaningful items can be re-arranged to make a new meaning or new "whole" (Kohler); 3) the *familiarity*—unfamiliar items must first come to be known before they can be learned; 4) the *transitional probability*—some items have a high expectancy value of following each other or going together; and, 5) *grammatical habits*—items arranged in grammatical structure are learned better, even if nonsense, than items that violate our language habits.

In the above listed explorations, only Kohler (2) is concerned with *referential* aspects of stimuli; the others invoke familiarity, rather than meaning in the sense of implicit perceptual responses which occur when "familiar" objects, events, activities, or abstract concepts are referred to. It is hypothesized that "familiarity" will enhance learning, but "meaning" will enhance it even more because "it makes possible organization or conceptual unit formation."

Method

Subjects: College students in 8 experiments—different Ns in the several studies.

Materials: Familiar and unfamiliar nonsense syllables, meaningful and less meaningful words, pairs of pictures or pictures of 2 items in some organizational form.

Procedure: The procedures and results will be described separately for the 8 studies.

Experiment 1. Forty-eight *S*s learned both 6 pairs of familiar and unfamiliar nonsense syllables. Familiarization was accomplished by pairing syllables with numbers. Later they were learned as pairs for 2 trials (5 seconds/pair). Ss recalled 3.4 familiar and 2.4 unfamiliar, a significant difference.

Experiment 2. Thirty-six Ss learned pairs of nonsense syllables, conjunctions, prepositions, and nouns. There were 6 pairs of each type, 1 trial per pair at 5-second exposures. After a minute, Ss were asked to give the response member when the stimulus was shown. The mean recalls were: nouns, 2.9; conjunctions and prepositions, 1.8; and nonsense syllables, .8. Nouns were significantly better than the other word types which were also significantly better than nonsense syllables.

Experiment 3. The results of Experiment 2 might be due to failure to recall and not failure to learn the poorly recalled material. A matching test might show this. Experiment 3 repeated Experiment 2 with 36 Ss except for use of a matching test with all responses available. Results were the same as for Experiment 2; apparently it is the associative process and not the recall that is affected by meaningfulness and familiarity.

Experiment 4. Learning of conjunctions and prepositions was compared with that of prefamiliarized nonsense syllables for 36 Ss. No differences were found. This suggests that *noun* meaning was the important feature in Experiment 2, as the frequency correct was equal for the 2 types of words.

Experiment 5. It could be argued that common nouns might have some sequential probability and that non-noun words normally do not. The learning of a list of non-noun words with high sequential probability ("here is," "before any," "will have") was compared with pairs of prepositions and conjunctions and noun pairs. The procedure of Experiment 2 was followed. The sequentially arranged words (with less meaningfulness than nouns) were learned significantly better than conjunctions and prepositions, but significantly more poorly than nouns. Transitional probability cannot, then, account for the superiority of the meaningful words.

Experiment 6. The procedure of Experiment 2 was followed for 48 Ss each learning 4 lists of picture-pairs, concrete noun pairs, abstract noun pairs, and verb pairs (6 pairs of each). There were 2 sets of materials to avoid bias—24 Ss learned each set. The mean recalls were: pictures, 3.9; concrete nouns, 3.0; abstract nouns, 2.0; and verbs, 2.3. All differences were significant except between abstract nouns and verbs.

Experiment 7. Four groups of Ss (20 per group) learned the same 6 pairs of nouns with or without (group 3) a connecting word between them. The connecting words for group 1 were "organizational," i.e., logical possibilities (near, on, in). For Group 2 they were irrelevant (how, but, late), and for Group 4 they were suitable transitional words (and, or, without). Procedure of Experiment 2 was followed. Results: Group 1, 3.8; Group 2, 2.7; Group 3, 2.4; Group 4, 2.3. Transitional words were of no help at all, while organizational words helped most.

Experiment 8. Two groups of 20 Ss were exposed by the procedure of Experiment 2 to separate sets of 6 picture pairs. In one set, the pictures were drawn as of 2 separate objects, e.g., pipe and clock. In the other, the 2 objects had some relationship indicated, e.g., pipe on the clock. Results: The organized pictures were recalled with a mean score of 4.9, while the unorganized mean was 3.3, a significant difference.

Conclusion: While familiarity and grammatical sequence do help, the chief factor in verbal learning is meaning in the sense of relationships and references which permit imaginary components in relation to one another.

Presentation Time

Bennet B. Murdock, Jr.
University of Vermont

"The Immediate Retention of Unrelated Words," *Journal of Experimental Psychology*, 1960, **60**, 222-234.

The purpose of this study was to develop a task where the learning curves of individual Ss could be determined mathematically and where the effect of different variables—e.g., length of list, presentation time, practice, auditory or visual presentation, warm-up, group or individual testing, etc.—could be studied. The task chosen was that of *free recall* of common English words. Twelve different experiments were performed. This abstract will deal only with the variable of presentation time.

Method

Conclusions on presentation time were drawn from a number of the experiments, and, therefore, only the general method will be described.

Subjects: College students, in groups and individually—different numbers in different experiments.

Materials: Words chosen from the Thorndike-Lorge list of the 1000 most common words. Lists of words varied in number.

Procedure: Both auditory and visual presentations were employed. Where visual lists were used, Ss were shown words on 4 x 6 index cards, or mimeographed lists were studied for some specific period. Auditory presentation was by tape recording. Different presentation rates (½, ¾, 1, 1½, 2, and 3 seconds per word) were used. Following a list presentation, S would attempt a recall in any order.

Results

From the 12 different experiments, a number of conclusions emerged. Auditory and visual presentations did not differ. Concerning presentation time, the basic finding appeared to be that the amount of recall was a function of total learning time where this total time (t) = L × PT—list length (L) × presentation time (PT).

With a long list of words and a short presentation time, one will recall the same number of words as he would with a shorter list and a longer presentation time, if the total times are the same. Data in support of this conclusion were drawn from several experiments, but only one will be cited.

In Experiment 11, Ss learned lists of different lengths at different presentation times, as shown in the table. By using the t = L × PT formula, a number of predictions from the other 11 experiments were confirmed, and supported the conclusion. Similar evidence from other researches were cited, where total time, list length, and presentation time were available; e.g., it would be predicted from the present data that with a 60-word list at a 3-second rate, Ss would recall about 16.9 words after a 2-minute learning time. The actual finding by Bousfield, Sedgewick, and Cohen was 16.1 words. Again, predicting results from a

List Length	PT	Total time	Number Recalled
20	3 sec.	60	9.3
30	2 sec.	60	9.3
40	1-½ sec.	60	9.6
60	1 sec.	60	8.4

study by Deese and Kaufman with a 32-word list at 1 second per word and a 10-word list at 1 second per word, the recalls should be 8.0 and 6.7 respectively. The actual results were 8.5 and 5.8.

The formula has not been tested to its limits and is not firm at very fast rates of presentation, but, in general, it holds for the kinds of times used in this study. With lists of moderate length, e.g., 20 or 40 words, one would expect the same amount of recall if the 20-word list was presented at 2 seconds per word and the 40-word list at 1 second per word. Usually one finds greater recall with longer lists, but, in such cases, the total learning time must be considered because the longer list takes longer to go through.

Retroactive Inhibition in Connected Discourse

Norman J. Slamecka
University of Vermont

"Retroactive Inhibition of Connected Discourse as a Function of Similarity of Topic," *Journal of Experimental Psychology,* 1960, **60**, 245-249.

In a few earlier studies of Retroactive Inhibition (RI) of prose passages, little RI was found where the RI was measured by retention of facts, not by verbatim recall of the memorized material. In this study the actual verbatim retention of the words previously learned (original learning, or OL) was recorded in an effort to determine the influence of the degree of thematic similarity of interpolated learning (IL). Prior studies have measured the effects of physical similarity or the similarity of meanings of individual words in word lists. Here, the concern is with the semantic or thematic similarity of the contents of two passages.

Method

Subjects: Twenty-eight undergraduates in introductory psychology.

Material: Four 20-word sentences of approximately equal difficulty were selected from a book on *Language*. After preliminary testing by actual learning sessions with other *S*s, 3 more equally difficult sentences were obtained. The 3 new sentences dealt with semantics, mathematics, and government. These were reliably judged to be of high, intermediate, and low similarity to the original sentences. A sample of the original sentences follows: "We must postulate that from strictly semantic points of vantage, most confusions in communication revolve about in-adequate stipulation of meaning."

Procedure: Each *S* participated in 4 experimental sessions (2 a day on each of 2 days). In each session he learned one of the 4 original sentences, and then either a high-, intermediate-, or low-similarity sentence (or none, in the control condition). After the interpolated learning, he was given 4 relearning trials on the original sentence. The sentences were presented by a memory drum with a 3-second rate per word. Learning (OL and IL) was by the anticipation method to a criterion of 1 perfect trial.

Results

Learning the 4 original sentences took 9.8, 10.0, 10.7, and 11.1 trials (the last for the control sentence). These scores should be compared with those for the 3 interpolated learnings (high-, intermediate-, and low-similarity sentences), which were 7.6, 6.3, and 7.0. There were no significant differences within the 2 groups, although the practice effect is obvious.

Retroactive inhibition. When the *S*s relearned the original sentences, their mean recall scores in the 1st relearning trial were as follows: with high-similarity IL, 11.0 words; with intermediate-similarity, IL, 13.5 words; with low-similarity, IL, 15.0 words; and in the control situation, 17.2 words. All the conditions significantly differed from each other, and showed a clear retroactive effect, depending upon similarity of interpolated learning.

It appears, then, that a non-localized variable like a theme can interfere with recall of previously learned material. When two quite different themes are involved, there is little interference, but a similar theme will tend to elicit words from the same circumscribed class and become a source of interference. Because omission errors were strongly related to similarity, it is presumed that (with the 3-second limit) correct responses

187

could not be generated in the short period available—i.e., that latency of correct responses was too prolonged because of competition rather than because of unlearning. Unlearning might have been reflected in intrusion errors but was not clearly reflected in the errors recorded.

Abstract **96**

Imitation of Aggression

Albert Bandura, Dorothea Ross, and Sheila A. Ross
Stanford University

"Transmission of Aggression through Imitation of Aggressive Models," *Journal of Abnormal and Social Psychology,* 1961, **63**, 575-582.

Note: This paper includes much interesting material on aggression. The abstract will deal only with the specific imitation aspects of the report.

A test of imitative learning can be considered more crucial if carried out in the absence of the model and in a setting different from the original situation. In this study, Ss were first exposed to a model in one setting and tested elsewhere without the model present. The study, therefore, involves the generalization of imitative patterns.

Method

Design: Experimental Ss were divided into 2 groups. One group observed an aggressive model; the other group observed a passive or subdued model. A control group did not observe either.

Subjects: Thirty-six boys and 36 girls in a nursery school; ages 37 to

69 months, with a mean age of 52 months. The children were rated and matched on normal aggressiveness. Male and female adults served as models. Data on sex differences, sex of model, and aggressiveness of *S*s were collected.

Materials: Assorted nursery-level toys serving as background items for the toy of major concern, an inflated 5-foot "Bobo" doll.

Procedure: An individual child would be invited to play at an attractive task. Seated at a table, the *S* would begin to work with colored pictures. The model would then go to another part of the room where, for 10 minutes, he engaged in either: a) aggressive behavior (lay Bobo on its side, sit on it, punch it on the nose, strike it on the head with a mallet, toss it in the air, and kick it about the room). These were all considered specific behaviors that are unlikely to occur to a child who is likely to punch the clown doll but not much else. b) The nonaggressive condition. The model assembled a tinker toy and ignored the doll.

After the model left, the experimenter took the child to another building, where the *S* was subjected to a frustrating experience to insure that no inhibiting process would be obscuring aggressive tendencies. The question under study is not aggression itself, but what form it would take. In this room the *S* was shown some attractive toys and allowed by *E* to start playing with them; *E* then told him the toys were for the other children and took the child to still another room where he could play with any of the toys there. These included the Bobo doll and mallet, a dart gun, and other aggressive and non-aggressive toys (dolls, trucks, etc.). The *S* spent 20 minutes in this room with the experimenter, who was busy with paperwork. Two observers watched the *S* through a 1-way mirror.

Results

All *S*s were scored for aggressive responses. In the non-aggressive and control groups, 70% of the *S*s had zero scores. The scores for the various subject breakdowns are shown in the table.

While some general aggression could be expected due to the frustration imposed on all *S*s, the precise form of the aggression is the issue. Where the table refers to imitative aggression, the data represent the number of times the *S*s distinctly repeated the model's behavior, including the repetition of precise remarks made by the model. The differences between the experimental groups were highly significant in such specific imitativeness. In general, boys showed more aggression than girls following exposure to the male model.

Conclusion: The observation of cues produced by the behavior of others is one effective means of eliciting certain forms of responses, which are of a low probability in themselves, without the necessity of reinforcement.

Mean Aggression Scores for Experimental and Control Subjects

Experimental Groups

Response category	Aggressive		Nonaggressive		Control groups
	F Model	M Model	F Model	M Model	
Imitative physical aggression					
Female subjects	5.5	7.2	2.5	0.0	1.2
Male subjects	12.4	25.8	0.2	1.2	2.0
Imitative verbal aggression					
Female subjects	13.7	2.0	0.3	0.0	0.7
Male subjects	4.3	12.7	1.1	0.0	1.7
Mallet aggression					
Female subjects	17.2	18.7	0.5	0.5	13.1
Male subjects	15.5	25.8	18.7	6.7	13.5
Punches Bobo doll					
Female subjects	6.3	16.5	5.8	4.3	11.7
Male subjects	13.9	11.9	15.6	14.8	15.7
Nonimitative aggression					
Female subjects	21.3	8.4	7.2	1.4	6.1
Male subjects	16.2	36.7	26.1	22.3	24.6
Aggressive gun play					
Female subjects	1.8	4.5	2.6	2.5	3.7
Male subjects	7.3	15.9	8.9	16.7	14.3

Anticipation vs. Recall Methods

William F. Battig and H. Ray Brackett
University of Virginia

"Comparison of Anticipation and Recall Methods in Paired-associate Learning," *Psychological Reports*, 1961, **9**, 59-65.

In the "anticipation" method of learning paired-associates, the stimulus item is presented first; then, after a pause, the response item appears. This method has the advantage of immediate knowledge of results and corresponds to the techniques in teaching machine programs where a question is asked, the learner attempts an answer, and is immediately shown the correct answer as a reinforcement. In the "recall" method, both stimulus and response items are shown together in the "study" period; the stimuli are then shown separately to test the learner. No information is provided about the correctness of the results. This method should be poorer than the anticipation method, if immediate knowledge of results is of importance. Prior to this study, however, no direct comparisons have been attempted.

Method

Subjects: Forty summer session students, paid for their efforts.

Materials: Six lists of 12 paired-associates. The stimulus side in each pair was a nonsense figure or shape; the response side was a 2-digit number from 12 to 98 (no double numbers or zero endings). The nonsense shapes were maximally discriminable. The pairs were on photographic slides and could be projected to show only the stimulus side or both sides at once.

Procedure: The S-R pairs were presented for 5 seconds, with the S term appearing for 5 seconds first in the anticipation trials. In the recall trials, the *S* terms were each presented for 5 seconds alone in a random order after *S* had seen all 12 S-R pairs for a 5-second period each. *S*s recited aloud each R term whenever it appeared on the screen in both methods. Order of S-R pairs was unsystematically varied between trials. The intertrial interval was 30 seconds for the anticipation learning, and each test in the recall learning occurred 30 seconds after the list presentation.

Each *S* learned 2 lists, 1 by each method. *S*s were counterbalanced for order of learning. Criterion was 1 perfect performance.

Results

All 6 lists were used and were essentially alike in the learning results. The findings are shown graphically in the figure. In both trials and number of errors, the recall method was distinctly (and significantly) superior. The recall learning averaged 6.85 trials, the anticipation 9.75 trials.

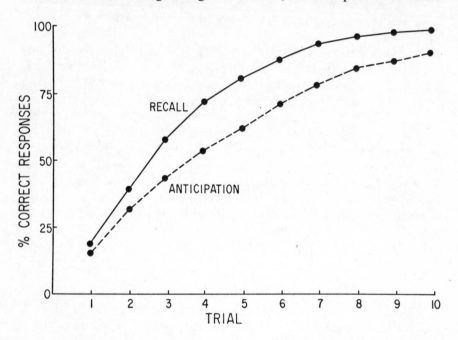

The superiority of the recall method shows no "detrimental effects of delayed knowledge of results." The "legitimacy of treating knowledge of results or 'feedback' in complex human performance as a simple extenstion of reinforcement principles" is questioned. Teaching machine operations might properly be considered somewhat less than optimum. The recall method may benefit from these considerations: 1) There are *two* presentations of each S item, which might aid differentiation of the materials; 2) There was, in effect, a 30-second rest interval in the recall procedure, which might suggest a distribution of practice factors; 3) There may be two behavioral processes involved (learning and testing), and the recall method enhances a separation of these processes.

Cortical Conditioning

R. W. Doty and C. Giurgea
University of Michigan

"Conditioned Reflexes Established by Coupling Electrical Excitation of Two Cortical Areas," J. A. Delafresnaye, A. Fessard, R. W. Gerard, and J. Konorski (Eds.), *Brain Mechanisms and Learning,* Oxford, Blackwell Scientific, 1961.

This chapter (pp. 133-151) of the volume cited, reviews research on cortical conditioning—i.e., studies where two cortical stimulations, one in a sensory area (the CS) and one in a motor area (the US), can be presented via implanted electrodes. A normal CS (external to the subject) can also be presented prior to cortical stimulation in this type of research. It is also possible to arrange for some subsequent instrumental tasks followed by reward. Earlier work by Loucks had suggested that direct cortical conditioning was impossible.

Method

Subjects: Four dogs, 2 cats, 2 monkeys.

Apparatus: Restraining equipment for animals. Implanted platinum electrodes through which suitable currents can be applied to cortical tissue. The electrodes rest on the plial surface. Several pairs are inserted in the motor area to improve the prospects of a definitive movement. Preconditioning tests are conducted to establish the ineffectivenss of the CS prior to training.

Procedure: The CS is presented for 3-4 seconds (1-millisecond rectangular current pulses at a 50/second frequency); then the US is presented in the last 1-1.5 seconds of the CS duration. Six to 10 pairings daily.

Results

Dog Alpha: CS—stimulation of left posterior suprasylvian gyrus. US—stimulation of left postcrucial sulcus. Response: a complex of movements, including head to midline and down. After 108 pairings, first distinct CR (head turn). Subsequently, this CR would be evoked after 8 trials with an auditory click.

Dog Beta: CS—right marginal gyrus. US in right postcruciate gyrus. Response: flexion of left hind leg. On 66th pairing, 1st CR, a 10-centimeter flexion of the leg, was observed. Subsequently, 74 CRs were evoked in 171 CS presentations (including extinction). Some generalization was observed from stimulation in right posterior ectosylvian gyrus. The CR did not extinguish in 84 CS presentations.

Dogs Gamma and Epsilon: Showed similar results in 16 and 85 trials with different locations and responses.

Monkey 1: CS to left occipital pole. US to left precentral cortex. Response: flexion of right arm. Findings: no conditioning with 200 trials at 2-minute intervals. With a 4-minute interval, conditioning was noted at the 67th pairing. Following this, there were 31 CRs in 47 trials. The flexion CR was then placed in conflict with an avoidance response (push a lever to avoid a trial shock). The flexion CR persisted for 25 trials.

Monkey 2: Similar results, but with a stronger US necessary.

Cat 425: No success with a seizure-prone cat.

Cat 489: CS to right middle ectosylvian gyrus. US to right ansate area. Response: left turn of head and flexion of left foreleg. First CR after 39 pairings. At first, the CR was a vigorous left leg flexion, but after 79 pairings the cat flexed the right foreleg more often than the left.

Conclusion: "There can be no question that conditioned reflexes can be established with cortical stimulation as US." And "in the usual sense of the word, there is no motivation involved in the formation of CRs by coupling cortical stimulations." Earlier failures to obtain CRs (Loucks) may be due to too brief an intertrial interval.

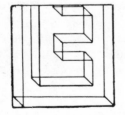

The Role of Syntax

William Epstein
University of Kansas

"The Influence of Syntactical Structure on Learning," *The American Journal of Psychology*, 1961, **74**, 80-85.

Verbal behavior is normally encoded according to a set of grammatical rules (syntax); this makes the learning of natural linguistic units very different from arbitrary arrangements of independent items—e.g., nonsense syllable lists. "The ability to produce and recognize grammatical utterances" does not depend on meaning or familiarity or sequential probabilities of words. This study attempts to show that appreciation of grammatical structure by itself is a factor in verbal efficiency. If nonsense words are arranged in sentence-like form with suitable suffixes (e.g., *s* for plural, *ed* for past tense), they should be learned more effectively than the same syllables in non-syntactical arrangements.

Method

Subjects: One hundred ninety-two students in introductory psychology.

Materials: Six categories (see table) of verbal material. Each category had 2 "sentences." Each "sentence" was typed on a card in the form of a sentence whether it was one or not. In categories I, IV, and V, the 1st word was capitalized and a period closed the sentence. In category I, nonsense syllables were made to look like words by adding suffixes and 2 articles (*a* and *the*). In Category II, the suffixes were omitted. Category III contains the same materials as I, but in random order. In category IV, the suffixes are added to different words, producing sentences which do not follow customary usage. Category V has ordinary English words in grammatical form but is sententially meaningless. Category VI has the same words in random order.

Procedure: The *S*s were divided into 6 groups at random. Each group learned 1 category. *S* was shown each sentence for a 7-second period and given 30 seconds to reproduce it. Trials continued until there was perfect reproduction. Half the *S*s started with the first sentence of each category, half with the other.

Category	Content of the Six Categories	*Mean trials to learn*
I	(1) A vapy koobs desaked the citar molently um glox nerfs.	I 5.77
	(2) The yigs wur vumly rixing hum in jegest miv.	
II	(1) a vap koob desak the citar molent um glox nerf	II 7.56
	(2) the yig wur vum rix hum in jeg miv	
III	(1) koobs vapy the um glox citar nerfs a molently	III 8.15
	(2) yigs rixing wur miv hum vumly the in jegest	
IV	(1) A vapy koobed desaks the citar molents um glox nerfly.	
	(2) The yigly wur vums rixest hum in jeging miv.	
V	(1) Cruel tables sang falling circles to empty bitter pencils.	V 3.50
	(2) Lazy paper stumbled to shallow trees loudly from days.	
VI	(1) sang tables bitter empty cruel to circles pencils falling	VI 5.94
	(2) loudly trees paper from days lazy shallow to stumbled	

Results

The average number of learning trials per category is shown in the table. The following mean differences were statistically significant: I vs II, I vs III, I vs V, and V vs VI. It is obvious that category V is readily learned, even if the sentence has no sense or literal meaning. Category I, however, is also easily learned, although it makes no sense at all. The syntactical structure of Category I sentences apparently facilitates the learning over "sentences" containing the same units, but without the structure.

Conclusion: Syntax facilitates learning apart from the effects of familiarity, meaning, or sequential probability. It may be that syntax provides some opportunities for "chunking" or that Ṣs use different learning strategies when faced with differently arranged materials.

Mediation in Verbal Chaining

David L. Horton and Paul M. Kjeldergaard
University of Kentucky   Harvard University

"An Experimental Analysis of Associative Factors in Mediated Generalization," *Psychological Monographs: General and Applied,* 1961, Whole No. 515.

When two elements (A and B) are associated independently with a third element (C), it is supposed that A and B will acquire some associative connection with each other. Such an assumption underlies thinking about sensory preconditioning, associative chaining, and various mediational theories. The paradigm usually proposed and most commonly investigated is one in which a S learns a pair of items, say A→B, where B is the "response" to A as a stimulus. He then learns B→C, where B is now a stimulus and C the response. Finally he learns A→C, and it is commonly reported that A-C learning is more efficient because of the mediational facilitation provided by B. There are, however, many arrangements of A, B, and C that could be investigated to test several underlying assumptions not always made clear. The possible arrangements and their features are shown in the table.

	Learn	*Learn*	*Test*	*Model*	*Direction of A-C*	*Mediational Item**
1.	A-B	B-C	A-C		A→C forward link	contiguous
2.	B-C	A-B	A-C	chaining	A→C forward link	remote
3.	B-A	C-B	A-C		A←C backward link	remote
4.	C-B	B-A	A-C		A←C backward link	contiguous
5.	A-B	C-B	A-C	acquired stimulus	A←C backward link	remote
6.	C-B	A-B	A-C	equivalence	A→C forward link	remote
7.	B-A	B-C	A-C	acquired response	A→C forward link	contiguous
8.	B-C	B-A	A-C	equivalence	A←C backward link	contiguous

* The relationship of the mediating connection is either close to, or remote from, the response item (C) in the test. Thus, in 1, S goes from A→B→C directly. In 5, e.g., he must go from A→B then to C via B (backward), then to A (again backward), and back to C, or A→B←C←A→C.

197

Note that each paradigm involves directionality of associations and either a contiguous or remote association between the A-C items in the test situation, with the contiguous associations being stronger. The authors assume that directionality is more influential than contiguity and that forward associations are stronger than backward. On the basis of these assumptions, they predict that when Ss are tested in the A-C situation, the several groups would follow this pattern: 1, 2, 6, and 7 will show more facilitation than 3, 4, 5, and 8; 1, 4, 7, and 8 taken together will show more facilitation than 2, 3, 5, and 6 taken together; 1 and 7 will be the most facilitative, while 3 and 5 will be the weakest; and 2 and 6 will show more facilitation than 4 and 8.

Method

Subjects: One-hundred-forty-three female introductory psychology students.

Materials: Twenty-eight relatively infrequently used English words were used to make up 3 lists of 8 words each (A, B, and C words), with 4 additional words left over for control use. Association values of the words ranged from 66 to 93%. The words were randomly paired to make up the A-B, B-C, etc., lists. The control words were randomly substituted for experimental words in the list common to the first 2 stages.

Procedure: The word lists in 5 different orders were exposed in a card master device for 4 seconds (2 seconds for the stimulus and 2 seconds for the response words). Learning was by the anticipation method to a criterion of 3 successful trials for each of the 3 lists of pairs, which were learned in succession. There were 5 trials given for the 3rd stage.

Results

In evaluating the A-C list, the experimental and control words were compared for learning efficiency and the results are reported in the table as the difference in scores between such groups of words. The means (number of correct responses in 5 trials) for the 8 paradigms are reported along with the total number of correct responses on the experimental and control pairs for all Ss.

The data indicate that all of the hypotheses were confirmed for direction of difference, although only the 1st prediction had statistical significance. All of the paradigms showed facilitation, with 1, 6, and 7 the most effective arrangements. Paradigm 3 was the poorest, but might be strengthened with more training trials. Forward associations appear to be stronger than backward ones.

	1	2	3	4	5	6	7	8
Mean difference (E and C)	3.06	2.28	0.44	1.83	2.39	4.00	3.61	3.17
Total correct E	188	149	151	147	146	180	192	178
Total correct C	133	108	143	114	103	108	127	121

198

Non-associative Factors

Solomon E. Asch and Sheldon M. Ebenholtz
Swarthmore College   Connecticut College

"The Process of Free Recall: Evidence for Non-Associative Factors in Acquisition and Retention," *The Journal of Psychology*, 1962, **54**, 3-31.

Since Ebbinghaus, verbal learning and retention has been assumed to be a matter of association. A response (a word, a thought) is associated with some stimulus and later, on repetition of the stimulus, the response is evoked. The phenomena of free recall offer an opportunity to test the association hypothesis (no sequence of recall is required, no stimuli are presented).

Method

Subjects: Twenty-four college students in 3 groups of 8. There were 2 experimental groups and 1 control for a Retroactive Inhibition Study.

Materials: Two lists (A and B) of nonsense syllables; each list had 4 syllables of 47% association value and 4 of 53%. Memory drum with 3-second exposures. Four arrangements were made of the 8-syllable lists; thus, there was not a specific serial order, but 4 separate orders.

Procedure: A Retroactive Inhibition paradigm was followed. Experimental *S*s learned List A and, immediately following this, learned List B. Twenty minutes later, all *S*s (including controls who only learned A) were tested for recall of List A. Experimental *S*s also tried to recall List B. After every learning trial, *S*s tried to recall the items of the list in any order.

One experimental group was directed to recall items from List A first and then items from List B. The other experimental group was asked to recall items from either list in any order after the 2nd list had been learned.

Results

There were no significant differences among the groups in learning List A. The number of trials to learn were 3.9, 5.5, and 4.4. The 2 experimental groups learned the interpolated list in 2.6 and 3.5 trials (difference not significant).

After 20 minutes, the recall scores were 4.8, 5.1, and 7.6 (the last for the control group), showing appreciable R.I. The recall scores for the interpolated list for the 2 experimental groups were 6.5 and 5.8 (difference not significant).

Findings from detailed analysis:

1. Recalled items did not exceed chance frequency as far as number of adjacent items is concerned.
2. The serial position of items was not a factor in recall; items late in the list occurred as readily as items early in the list in the recall order.
3. When pairs of items recalled on early trials were checked for repetition in recall, such pairs were found on only about 25% of the trials. The lack of repetition argues against association formation.
4. Primacy and recency had significant impacts on recall. Taken together, the first 2 and last 2 items were recalled in 73% of the trials.
5. The order of recall in early trials showed no significant effect on later trials.
6. The more frequently an item was recalled, the more likely that it would be recalled subsequently.

Conclusion: The data lend no support to interference or unlearning theories of Retroactive Inhibition. Long-term retention does not appear to be a function of inter-item association. Recall appears to be a matter of availability of items, itself a function of frequency, primacy, and recency.

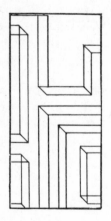
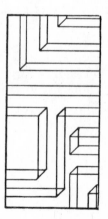
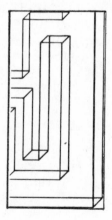

Socratic Programming

Ira S. Cohen
State University of New York at Buffalo

"Programmed Learning and the Socratic Dialogue,"
American Psychologist, 1962, **72**, 772-775.

Proponents of teaching machines or, more properly, programmed instruction, have often referred to the similarity between such modern developments and the Socratic method of teaching. In this study, a sample of the Socratic method is examined from the viewpoint of modern programmers.

Method

Subjects: Two groups of psychology students (N = 32) (N = 33).

Materials: A portion of a Socratic dialogue (Meno) in which Socrates tries to demonstrate that an unschooled slave boy comprehends (by possession of innate ideas) a version of the Pythagorean theorem. The modification can be stated as, "Given a square, another square double its area can be constructed from the diagonal of the first square." The dialogue is here restated in the form of 16 "frames," or questions, that are to be answered in a booklet with answers to each question on the next page. The 16 questions correspond to the 16 questions Socrates asked the boy, although much of the dialogue is omitted.

Procedure: Ss read the questions, write out answers, and, at the end, state the theorem if they can.

Results

Of the 32 Ss, only 17 were able to state the theorem. It is noted that Socrates did not ask this of the slave boy. The "program" as presented by Socrates is obviously inadequate for modern college students. Examination of the locus of errors, inserting some new frames, reversing several in their order, and deleting one, resulted in a new program which was successful for 27 out of 33 Ss.

Conclusion: Socrates had the beginnings of an effective program—

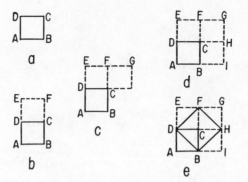

starting from a known point and moving forward by small steps—but, like modern programs, it required revision based on feedback from locating the sources of errors.

Cohen's Adaptation of Socrates' Program

1. Each side of this square, ABCD, is two feet long. Then the size of the square (a) is _____ square feet.
2. Here (b) we have another square, DCEF, equal to it in _____.
3. And here (c) a third square, CHGF, _____ in size to each of the others.
4. Now we can fill up the space in the corner by adding another _____ of _____ size. (d)
5. All four squares, ABCD, CDEF, CHGF, BIHC, are _____.
6. How many times larger is this whole space, AEGI, than the square ABCD?
7. The lines, BD, DF, FH, HB, drawn from corner to corner in each of the squares, cuts each square in _____. (e)
8. The four lines containing the space BDFH are of _____ length.
9. Has each of the inside lines, BD, DF, FH, HB, cut off half of each of the squares? (yes/no) _____.
10. How many spaces of that size (for example, DCF or BCH) are there in BDFH? _____.
11. How many in the square ABCD? _____.
12. Four is how many times two? _____.
13. If our original square ABCD contained four square feet, then how many square feet does the square BDFH contain? _____.
14. From what line do we get this figure? _____.
15. From the line BD drawn cornerwise across our original four-foot figure (ABCD), a square can be drawn which is _____ as large as the original square.
16. Such a line as BD is called the diagonal. To double the size of the square, you may draw a square from the _____.

Transfer of Training

John Jung
Northwestern University

"Transfer of Training as a Function of Degree of First List
Learning," *Journal of Verbal Learning and Verbal Behavior*, 1962, **1**, 197-199.

Previous studies have not resolved the question of what kind, and how
much, transfer occurs in the learning of a 2nd list of verbal material after
different degrees of learning of a 1st list. The composition of the 2 lists
in terms of S-R relationships must, of course, be taken into account. The
2nd learning may profit (or suffer) from non-specific factors like warm-
up, learning-to-learn, and fatigue. Such non-specific factors might mask
possible negative transfer effects; the *S*s might appear to be improving
while actually not doing as well as they might if specific S-R interference factors were not operating.

Method

Design: To evaluate separately the general (non-specific) influence
control, *S*s learn 1 list (A-B) and then another consisting of completely
different items (C-D). The experimental *S*s also learn an A-B list, but
then can be asked to learn an A-C list, a C-B list, or an A-Br list. In the
latter, the response items are the same as in the A-B list, but the pairs
are made up differently—i.e., the B's are assigned to different A's or
re-paired. Suitable comparisons of 2nd list learning are then available.

Subjects: One-hundred-four introductory psychology students in 8
groups. Half the *S*s learned the 1st list to a low criterion (3 out of 6
items correct). The other half learned the 1st list to 1 perfect recitation,
plus 5 more trials of overlearning.

Materials: Two paired-asssociate lists of 6 items for each condition.
All *S*s had the same list for the 2nd learning. The first lists were arranged
so that the 2nd list amounted to an A-C, C-D, C-B, or A-Br grouping.
Stimulus items were 2-syllable adjectives; response items were trigrams.

Procedure: The anticipation method was used for both learnings.
Thirty seconds after either low or high 1st list learning, all *S*s had 10
trials on the 2nd list.

Results

The results on only the first 5 trials will be reported here, although data are presented on all trials in the original paper.

In the 1st learning, the high and low criterion *S*s differed significantly as expected. The 2nd list provides the data of interest.

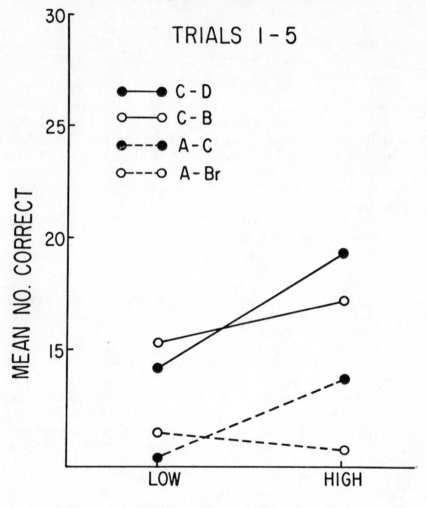

DEGREES OF FIRST-LIST LEARNING.

In the figure above, all groups except A-Br show an absolute improvement, with a higher degree of learning of the 1st list. The differences for the 4 groups, as a whole, are significant. The C-D group shows the greatest impact of greater 1st list learning. If the C-D list (non-specific factors) is used as a base, the *Net* transfer effects for the other groups can be obtained by subtracting the mean number of correct anticipations made by the other 3 groups from the C-D group performance. These results are shown in the figure below. Here it is seen that the

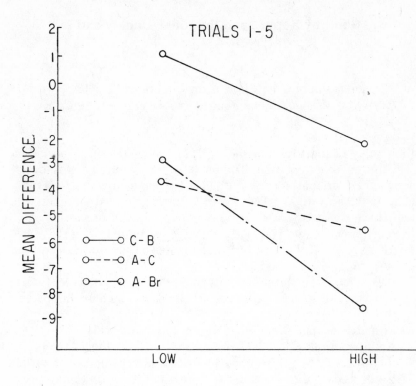

A-Br group suffered the most with greater 1st learning and the C-B group the least.

   Conclusion: There is a tendency for increased 1st list learning to produce negative transfer, varying with the specific stimulus-response features.

Proaction in Short Term Memory

Geoffrey Keppel and Benton J. Underwood
Northwestern University

"Proactive Inhibition in Short-term Retention of Single Items,"
Journal of Verbal Learning and Verbal Behavior, 1962, **1,**
153-161.

In their study of short-term memory (STM), the Petersons reported no
apparent proactive inhibition. The present study is designed to determine whether variables that operate in long-term memory (LTM) function in the same way in STM. Positive findings would eliminate the
potential schism involved in postulating two kinds of memory.

The currently accepted facts about Proactive Inhibition in LTM are:
1. PI is greater if there is a greater number of previously acquired
   associations.
2. PI is reduced if material is relatively well-learned. (In STM studies,
   there may be a learning-how-to-learn effect which might obscure
   PI).
3. PI increases as a function of the retention interval.
4. An interaction of 1 and 3 can be expected—the longer the retention interval, the greater the PI, with a larger number of earlier
   learned associations because of the greater recovery of the latter.

These principles are examined in the context of STM in this study.

Method

Note: Actually 3 experiments are reported. Only the 3rd will be abstracted here, as it represents an improved procedure over the 1st 2
studies.

Subjects: Ninety-six introductory psychology students.

Materials: Six trigrams, association value = 21% (CXP, GQN, HJL,
KBW, SFM, and ZTD) printed on 3 × 5 cards.

Procedure: The *S* was shown a trigram for 2 seconds . At this point,
E pronounced a 3-digit number from which *S* was to subtract backward
by 3s for either 3 or 18 seconds. At a signal, *S* attempted to recall the

trigram shown. Each *S* was shown 5 more trigrams and repeated the process, alternating the 3- and 18-second intervals. Half the *S*s began with 3-seconds, the other half with 18-second intervals.

Results

The finding for the 6 tests of STM are shown in the figure. Note that there is virtually perfect recall of the first trigram, regardless of time of test. After that, the 18-second tests show a consistent decline, demonstrating the expected interaction between number of prior items and length of retention interval. "Severe PI builds up over 18 seconds with successive tests, but this does not happen over 3 seconds. . . ."

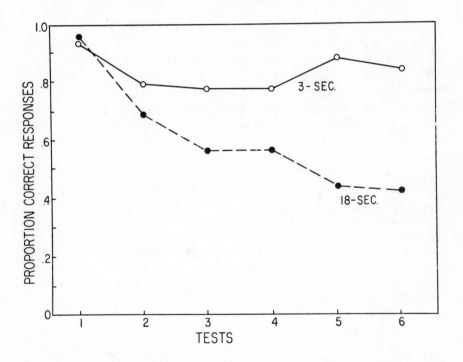

Conclusion: "The results of the present experiment give strong support to the presumption that short-term retention of single items and long-term retention of lists of items are subject to the same laws of proactive inhibition."

Paradigms of Incidental Learning

Arnold Mechanic
University of California, Berkeley

"The Distribution of Recalled Items in Simultaneous Intentional and Incidental Learning," *Journal of Experimental Psychology,* 1962, **63**, 593-600.

There are two kinds of paradigms for the study of incidental learning. In Type I, the Ss in an incidental learning group are not instructed to learn materials on which they are tested later. In Type II, the Ss are asked to learn something but are tested on something else to which they were exposed during the learning session. The present study is of the Type II design. The questions to be investigated are the roles of meaningfulness of materials and practice.

Method

Subjects: One hundred ninety-two college students in 12 groups averaging 13 Ss per group.

Materials: Four lists of 12 trigrams of low (e.g., *dur, hok, kde*) and high (e.g., *wer, und, ter*) meaningfulness, as defined by language frequency. The approximate mean frequencies of the four lists (in a sample of 1,035,000 English words) were 3, 5, 350, and 375. The lists were used to develop 4 arrangements of 12 pairs (1 incidental and 1 intentional trigram per pair), where the pairs were either of low-low, low-high, high-low, or high-high meaningfulness. The lists presented to the Ss contained 24 trigrams in 12 pairs, with one trigram shown above another in each pair. Different Ss were instructed to learn either the top or bottom trigrams, but, in addition, the Ss were told that the trigrams were from 2 primitive languages and to judge or rate their phonetic similarity on a 5-point scale. The pairs of trigrams were alleged to have the same meaning, and the Ss were supposedly testing the hypothesis that words that mean the same also sound the same. Both items in each pair were to be pronounced by Ss quietly. They were to learn 1 (top or bottom) in each pair. The top words were supposedly from 1 language and the bottom from another. Ss were to learn only 1 language set.

Pairs were presented to different groups 2,4, or 8 times at 10 seconds per pair rates. A 5-minute test of free recall was given after the practice session.

Results

The table shows the mean numbers of recalled items in the several groups. There is an obvious practice effect for both kinds of items. It

Average Number of Incidental Items
Recalled by the Various Groups

Incidental Learning Items

	High Meaningful		*Low Meaningful*	
Presentations	High Inc.	Low Inc.	High Inc.	Low Inc.
2	2.31	2.25	1.06	1.44
4	3.56	4.06	2.31	2.62
8	4.94	4.69	3.88	3.19

Average Number of Intentional Items
Recalled by the Various Groups

Intentional Learning Items

	High Meaningful		*Low Meaningful*	
Presentations	High Int.	Low Int.	High Int.	Low Int.
2	5.69	5.19	4.12	4.50
4	7.94	7.25	7.25	6.81
8	8.81	9.19	9.00	8.62

is apparent that intentional items were learned more effectively than incidental, but note that the learning of the incidental items did not vary with the meaningfulness of the intentional items. The incidental items showed a significant effect of meaningfulness in their own right. If we compare the high meaningful and low meaningful combinations, we find the following relative mean differences: low intentional, high incidental —28.52; high intentional, high incidental—38.13; low intentional, low incidental—51.14; high intentional, low incidental—54.20, indicating that the meaningfulness of the incidental items was a significant factor in the recall.

When incidental items are high in meaningfulness and intentional items are low, there is only a small mean difference in recall scores. When both kinds of items are low in meaningfulness, the difference is almost as great as when the intentional items are high and incidental low. When both are high in meaningfulness, again the difference is relatively small, testifying to the role of meaningfulness in incidental learning.

Hypotheses about Serial Learning

Robert K. Young
University of Texas

"Tests of Three Hypotheses about the Effective Stimuli in Serial Learning," *Journal of Experimental Psychology,* 1962, **63**, 307-313.

In serial list learning, the items are presented in a constant order. It has been commonly assumed that each item is the stimulus for the next item in the series, but it could be that, once the list has been started, two or more preceding items, the position of the item in the list, or some other aspects of serial learning might be the functional stimuli. Three experiments were conducted to examine the possibilities.

Method

Subjects: Introductory psychology students.
Materials: Lists of adjectives in both serial and paired-associate arrangements (details below).
Procedures: Serial lists were presented at 2-second rates; PA lists at 2:2-second rates.

Experiment 1

Procedure: Half of 36 *S*s learned a PA list of 14 pairs after having learned a serial list of 14 adjectives. Seven of the pairs were made up of 2 succeeding items in the original serial list, and the other 7 pairs were from a 2nd 14-item serial list learned by the other half of the 36 *S*s. Thus, there were 7 "experimental" and 7 "control" pairs for each *S*.

Results

The experimental pairs were learned in 10.06 trials; the control in 9.06 trials (criterion: 1 perfect recitation). Where one might have expected some positive transfer for the experimental items, none was found after the first few trials. Actually, there were significantly more errors for the experimental items.

Experiment II

A PA list was made up, with 2 successive items from a previously learned serial list serving as stimuli for the 3rd item. There were two 5-pair sublists. Half of the pairs were drawn from a serial list learned by half of the 46 *S*s, and the control half was made up from a serial list learned by the other half of the *S*s.

Results

The mean number of trials to learn the experimental subpairs was 12.04, while the control sublist was learned in 9.65 trials, a significant difference, indicating a negative transfer rather than what might be expected on the traditional basis. Again, the experimental sublist elicited more errors than did the control items.

Experiment III

In this study, the *S*s first learned a test serial list of 13 items after having previously learned an experimental or a control list. The experimental list consisted of items in which all of the even-numbered items would occupy the same ordinal positions in the test list (Group A, N = 21), or the odd-numbered items occupied the same ordinal positions in the test list (Group B, N = 21). The remaining items appeared randomly in the test list. The control list (C, N = 21) consisted of entirely different items.

Results

The mean number of trials to learn the test list for the 3 groups was: A, 12.43; B, 13.86; C, 9.71. These differences were not significant. When the items occupying the same (S) or different (D) positions were compared for the A and B groups, however, the mean for the same ordinal position items was 10.17, while the mean for the different items was 12.14, a significant difference.

Conclusion: The fact that there was no positive transfer in the 1st study, while there *was* negative transfer in the 2nd, suggests that the items in a serial list are not learned as responses to the prior items. The fact that items in the same position in 2 lists were learned more effectively than items placed in different positions in the 3rd experiment suggests that the position in the list is an effective stimulus in the learning of serial lists.

Superstition in Skinnerians

John Oliver Cook
North Carolina State University

"'Superstition' in the Skinnerian," *American Psychologist*, 1963, **18**, 516-518.

Followers of Skinner applied observations of the behaviors of pigeons to the design of teaching machines. Because pigeons have to demonstrate learning overtly, teaching machine programmers require overt responses. Similarly, pigeons must be reinforced; therefore, humans in programmed instruction must be reinforced. However, Cook and Spitzer (1960) found that 35 students learning paired-associates learned faster when they were not required to make overt responses. Similarly, when a group of students was shown the response items before they pronounced them (prompt group), they did better than those shown the

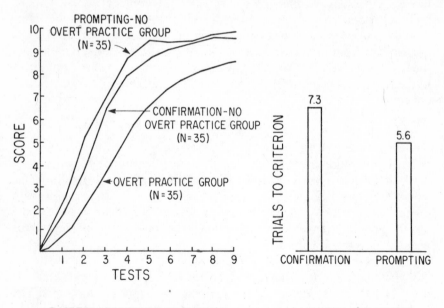

PAIRED ASSOCIATE LEARNING. SERIAL LEARNING.

Cook, J. O. and Spitzer, M. E. Supplementary report: "Prompting versus Confirmation in Paired-associate Learning," *Journal of Experimental Psychology,* 1948, **38**, 168-172.

response items after pronouncing them (confirmation or reinforced group).

In a serial learning task (finding a path through 12 rows of 12 buzzers), 10 subjects did better when shown which button to press next to a light coming on above that button than when *reinforced* by a light coming on above the button when it was correct. Learning was faster when the learner was shown what to do than when he was reinforced for the correct response.

Modeling teaching machines on pigeon behavior represents an unfounded belief that what works in one context will work in another, a form of superstition.

Partial Reinforcement in Classical Conditioning

Robert D. Fitzgerald
Indiana University

"Effects of Partial Reinforcement with Acid on the Classically Conditioned Salivary Response in Dogs," *Journal of Comparative and Physiological Psychology*, 1963, **56**, 1056-1060.

Previous findings with food as the US indicate sooner acquisition and more resistance to extinction with partial reinforcement. The present study extends the research to noxious stimulation (acetic acid).

Method

Subjects: Eighteen mongrel dogs, 2-8 years old. The dogs were surgically prepared with two fistulas, one on each cheek, to supply the acid stimulus and to collect saliva from the parotid duct.

Procedure: The animals were restrained in a Pavlov-type frame. The

CS was a 15-second, 400 cycles-per-second tone, at 75 decibels, delivered through a speaker above the *S*'s head. The US (5 cubic centimeters of acid solution) was delivered through a solenoid operated syringe discharging into a tube connected to the fistula in the cheek. After *S*s were habituated to the shock, *S*s received 24 trials on each of 10 days in 2 daily periods, 3 hours apart. In each period there were 3 conditioning sessions of 4 CS presentations. The animals were treated as 3 groups. One was given 100% reinforcement, one 50%, and one 25%. The partial reinforcements were randomly administered.

Results

Because the recording system allowed continuous monitoring of the secretion, a base line reading (number of drops in 15 seconds prior to CS) was taken for each trial for comparison with CRs.

Acquisition. Both pre-CR and CR performance increased for all groups across trials, although only the 100% group showed a significant increase in *pre*-CS secretion. Conditioned responding increased significantly for all groups across trials. Mean increases in CR performance in drops were (all significant): 100%, 15.14; 50%, 5.76; and 25%, 5.02. The 100% group was significantly superior to both partial groups. At first the dogs tended to salivate more in the first 5 seconds of each 15-second CS period. As training continued, the secretion showed a stronger flow in the last 5 seconds.

Extinction. Only the first day's extinction results are reported because of detachment of the tubes for some animals in later sessions. The loss of CR between the last acquisition session and the end of the 3rd session of extinction was reliable for the 100% group but not for the partial groups. The mean loss (converted into a percentage decrease) was: 100%, 88.5; 50%, 26.8; and 25%, 31.1. The difference in loss between the 100% and the other 2 groups was significant.

Conclusion: Acquisition is poor and resistance to extinction stronger in partially reinforced conditioning with a noxious US. Pavlov's failure with food as US in a 25% schedule may have been due to his scheduling of the US on every 4th trial. Here, US was randomly presented. The shift in the CR amount within the CS interval supports the concept of "inhibition of delay."

Two-stage Theory of Verbal Learning

Richard H. Lindley
Trinity University

"Association Value, Familiarity, and Pronounciability Ratings as Predictors of Serial Verbal Learning," *Journal of Experimental Psychology,* 1963,4, 347-351.

Nonsense syllables vary in rated pronounciability (PR), familiarity, and association value (AV). These measures are also related to meaningfulness.

The question underlying this study is, "Which of the three measures facilitates learning more, and can, therefore, be considered to underlie the meaning dimension?"

Method

Subjects: Eighty men and women college students.

Design: Four groups of *S*s with different kinds of 12-item nonsense syllables to learn.

Group 1. Learn a list of low AV, high PR (hard to pronounce) unfamiliar trigrams.

Group 2. Low AV, Low PR (easy to pronounce), unfamiliar trigrams.

Group 3. High AV, low PR, familiar trigrams.

Group 4. High AV, low PR, unfamiliar trigrams.

A difference between groups 1 and 2 would be due to PR differences. A difference between groups 3 and 4 would be due to familiarity differences. A difference between groups 2 and 4 would be due to AV differences.

Materials: Sixteen lists of 12-item trigrams. Pronounciability was based on Underwood and Schultz ratings (a 9-point scale). Frequency also was taken from Underwood and Schultz. Association values were taken from Archer and Noble's ratings (5-point scale).

Familiarity was estimated by counting the number of times an item was comprised of the first 3 letters in the Thorndike-Lorge list of words that appear 10 or more times per million.

Procedure: Lists were presented by memory drum at a 2-second rate, with 14 seconds between trials. The criterion was 1 perfect anticipation. A limit of 60 learning trials was set. The data collected are based on the first 25 trials of Each *S*.

Each *S* learned only 1 of the 16 lists, which were counterbalanced for order and similarity difficulties.

Results

The number of trials to learn and number of correct responses for the 4 groups appear in the table.

	Groups	Trials	Number correct (in first 25 trials)
Low AV, High PR, unfamiliar	1	27.65	114.55
Low AV, Low PR, unfamiliar	2	38.20	112.70
High AV, Low PR, familiar	3	26.95	156.25
High AV, Low PR, unfamiliar	4	33.40	141.95

It is clear that Group 3 was superior on both measures. Only AV accurately predicted ease of learning (by correct response measure). The pronounciability ratings were not closely related to learning as claimed by Underwood and Schultz. The familiar lists were learned better than the unfamiliar, but familiarity was not, by itself, a significant source of variance as previously reported; this finding may be due to poorer familiarity measures in earlier studies. From an analysis of when a trigram was first reported (first stage or "response" learning) and when it was first correctly reported in sequence (second stage of "association" learning), it appears that meaningful ness has its effects on the "integrative," or response stage, rather than on the association stage. Such a finding offers support for the two-stage theory of verbal learning.

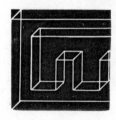

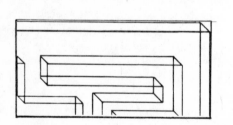

Serial vs. Random Presentation of Paired-Associates

Clessen J. Martin and Eli Saltz
Wayne State University

"Serial versus Random Presentation of Paired Associates,"
Journal of Experimental Psychology, 1963, **65**, 609-615.52

Early studies indicate that if a list of paired-associates was repeated in the same order from trial to trial it would be learned more easily than if the order of the pairs was randomized on successive trials. A prior study by Saltz questioned this conclusion, and the present study was done to make certain that the prior study had been sufficiently sensitive to justify the negative conclusion.

Method

Subjects: One-hundred-twenty introductory psychology students in 6 groups of 20.

Materials: Two lists of S-R pairs, where S was a 47% association value nonsense syllable and R was a high *m* word from Noble's list. List 2 differed from List 1 only in its nonsense syllables.

Procedure: Except for 2 groups of *S*s (groups 5 and 6), all *S*s received 10 learning trials in 2 groups of 5, with a test following each set of training trials. The groups differed in whether the training and test trials followed the same order of presentation or a random order. Thus, a group having the first 5 training trials with the same ordering of the pairs would be labelled S. If the test was also in the same order, it would be labeled S(S). If the next set of 5 learning trials was also in the same order, it would have another S. If the order was randomized for those trials, or for the test, it would be labeled R for training and (R) for randomized test. Four such groups were developed and are labeled as in the table.

The procedure consisted of having *S*s watch pairs presented at 2-second intervals in a memory drum for 5 trials, followed by a test. This operation was then repeated. Groups 1, 3, and 4 were then given 5 learning trials, where only the 10 response words were presented in serial order. They learned by the anticipation method. Half the *S*s learned the

10 words in the same order as they had appeared before in the PA trials; the other half learned a new random list.

Results

The table provides the basic comparisons. It is clear that keeping a constant order does not facilitate paired-associate learning; if anything,

	Paired Associate Learning		Serial Learning	
Mean of First				
	Retention	*Retention Test*	*Anticipation in 5 Trials*	
Groups	Test-1		Same order	Random order
1 S(S)S(S)	4.55	7.50	16.6	10.5
2 R(R)R(R)	5.80	7.90		
3 S(S)S(R)	4.95	7.10	18.2	10.0
4 S(R)R(R)	4.60	7.55	16.4	8.6
5 S(S)	5.7			
6 R(R)	6.1			

it is harmful. On the other hand, there is a significant transfer effect to serial learning of the response items when the order is retained.

In a supplementary study using only 5 trials, with 72 of the original Ss with different lists, and varying the presentation rate (half the Ss saw PA pairs at 1 second/pair, the other half had a 4 second/pair exposure rate), it was found that time for study was a significant factor. But, again, randomizing the order of the pairs between trials had no significant effect.

Conclusion: Contrary to previous belief, it is not necessarily true that serial presentation of PA pairs will facilitate learning.

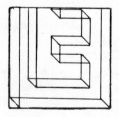

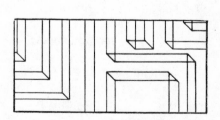

Paradigms of Classical and Operant Conditioning

David A. Grant
University of Wisconsin

"Classical and Operant Conditiong," Melton A. W. (Ed.), *Categories of Human Leaning*, New York, Academic Press, 1964.

The division of learning paradigms into *classical* and *instrumental* is insufficient because each variety contains a number of important sub-classes. The classification here is not ideal nor complete, but it calls attention to experimental factors and manipulations that must be recognized if confusion is to be avoided.

There are at least four sub-classes of classical conditioning:

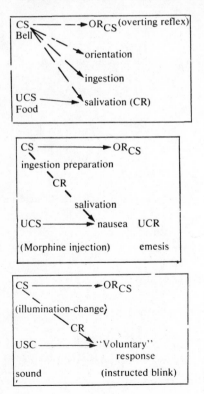

1. *Pavlovian A.* In this sub-class, only a portion of the response to the UCS is evoked by the CS. The CS can be thought of as a *sign* that US is to occur. CR is the orienting response; the US evokes approach and ingestion. CS is not a substitute for US. CR depends on motivation state.

2. *Pavlovian B.* Here, the CS is to a great extent a substitute for UCS. It does not depend on motivation. It is like Watsonian conditioning.

3. *Anticipatory Instructed Conditioning.* This sub-group is like Ivanov-Smolensky's conditioning of a child to squeeze a rubber bulb using the word "Squeeze" and a prior signal. It is like a reaction time study, or like conditioning a voluntary blink (blinking when you hear the sound) to a preceding light.

4. *Sensory Preconditioning*. e.g., the Brogden experiment

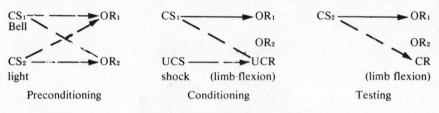

| Preconditioning | Conditioning | Testing |

Instrumental Conditioning

There are at least 8 different experimental designs that are included under the labels of operant or instrumental conditioning. Hilgard and Marquis had 4 categories but did not mention an important class of "omission" training. These are indicated in the table.

A Classification of Types of Instrumental Learning Experiments

Instrumental Types	Cue to Impending Reinforcement	Response	Reinforcement
Reward Training	No	Positive	Reward
Escape Training	No	Positive	Punishment
Avoidance Conditioning	Yes	Positive	Punishment
Discriminated Operant	Yes	Positive	Reward
Omission Training	No	Negative	Reward
Punishment (or Passive Avoidance Conditioning)	No	Negative	Punishment
Discriminated Omission Training	Yes	Negative	Reward
Discriminated Punishment Training	Yes	Negative	Punishment

Illustrations.
1. The Skinner Box or Thorndike situations.
2. Shocking rats on one side of a divided runway; the other side is safe.
3. The Brogden experiment in the conditioning phase.
4. Pressing in the Skinner box is followed by food only if a light S^D is on.
5. Rewarding a child when he refrains from doing something.
6. Shocking cats when they are about to eat.
7. Parent rewards child for not swearing (child doesn't swear when parent is around).
8. "Avoid the appearance of evil." Punishing animals for doing something; e.g., cat scratching furniture is punished by people (it doesn't scratch when people are around).

Proactive Inhibition in Short Term Memory

Bennet B. Murdock, Jr.
University of Vermont

"Proactive Inhibition in Short Term Memory," *Journal of Experimental Psychology*, 1964, **68**, 184-189.

Peterson and Peterson found no evidence for proactive inhibition in their STM study. Keppel and Underwood did. This study is an attempt to resolve the conflict. In this study, PI effects on individual paired-associates were tested with *S*s who were exposed to a series of 6 lists of 6 paired-associates. After each list, a *S* would be tested for 1 of the pairs at any of the 6 serial locations. If PI is involved, one would expect a deterioration between retention interval and practice in the first 5 positions. The 6th item should not show deterioration, since it really measures original learning; it might even improve with practice.

Method

Subjects: Sixty British naval ratings (18-25 years old).

Materials: Six lists of paired-associate common English words. Each list had 6 pairs, but 1 pair—the test pair, was chosen from the following pairs: against-claim; distinguish-Europe; highway-lean; right-speak; delightful-import; reading-anger. Each of these 6 pairs was included in a 6-pair list at a different serial position. For example, right-speak would appear first, second, third, and so on, in different lists. The other 5 test pairs would similarly appear in each serial position. The 5 non-test pairs were randomly selected from a group of 30 other pairs. The pairs were typed on 3 x 5 cards. Lists were all counterbalanced for position of the "probe" item, and, in effect, each *S* had a different list to counterbalance any list difficulties so far as the 5 irrelevant pairs were concerned.

Procedure: For any given *S*, 6 lists were prepared so that he could be "probed" for each serial position in some single list. The *S* was shown 6 cards in one list, one after another, at a 2-second rate, and the stimulus item for one of the cards would then be presented. The *S* would write his response, and the next list would be shown. *S*s were told to expect a probe at random.

221

Results

By testing each of the 60 *S* at each serial position in one list or another, 60 opportunities to be correct occurred in each of the 6 lists, or a total of 360 possible correct answers. The actual correct answers by list were: List (Stage of Practice) 1, 16; 2, 25; 3, 21; 4,21; 5, 17; 6, 17; total number correct, 117. There is little evidence for any striking deterioration in performance as a result of stage of practice, as would be expected by PI theory. If we look at the serial position results (shown later), we see that for serial positions 2-5 performance either stayed the same or improved over the 6 stages of practice, again showing no PI influence. Performance on the 1st position did deteriorate. The last position not only showed no learning-how-to-learn effect, as might be expected, but deteriorated slightly (but not significantly).

Correct Responses at Each Serial Position

Serial Position	Stage of Practice						Total
1	1	2	3	4	5	6	
1	6	5	2	4	0	0	17
2	1	4	2	1	1	1	10
3	1	0	0	1	2	2	6
4	0	3	2	3	3	3	14
5	0	4	8	5	4	5	26
6	8	9	7	7	7	6	44
Total	16	25	21	21	17	17	117

Conclusion: There appears to be no deterioration in performance with practice as PI theory would predict. "Overall, a PI interpretation does not appear to provide a very economical description of the present results."

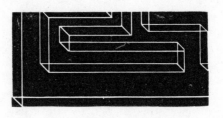

Acquired Distinctiveness of Cues

Erwin M. Segal
University of Minnesota

"Demonstration of Acquired Distinctiveness of Cues Using a Paired-associate Learning Task," *Journal of Experimental Psychology,* 1964, **67**, 587-590.

Previous efforts to demonstrate the acquired distinctiveness of cues (ADC) may have failed because Ss were not reacting to stimulus *features*, but rather to designs or configurations of the stimuli. In this study, Ss first were trained to respond to specific stimulus features or cues and then tested with new displays to determine if the earlier experience would help detect the new items as different from the old.

Comparisons of Correct Responses by Groups

	I	II	III	IV	V	VI	VII
				shape-	shape-	shape-size	
Mean Correct Responses	*shape*	*size*	*position*	*size*	*position*	*position*	*random*
in Original Learning	72.85	62.74	87.45	38.65	55.90	20.55	3.65

Identification Tests

Mean correct per 18 responses*

	I	II	III	IV	V	VI	VII
All-aspects-new	14.10	12.90	17.40	16.20	17.25	16.95	15.20
Position	11.05	10.30	17.40	13.05	16.25	16.30	13.60
Shape	7.00	4.05	2.30	9.75	9.55	9.10	4.80
Size	1.15	2.50	1.39	2.75	.75	2.55	1.45
Filler	1.87	2.37	1.23	2.60	.77	3.23	1.40

*Because there were 9 filler items and only 2 all-aspects-new, the number of correct responses was computed by multiplying the actual number by a factor to make al categories equal to 18.

Method

Subjects: One hundred fifty-two college students from elementary psychology courses.

Materials: A total of 57 triangles differing in size, shape, and location of a cross.

Procedure: Ss first were shown 18 triangles in 5 random orders. They were to learn to "name" each triangle, but different groups of Ss had different numbers of names to use. Thus, a name could be the same for 6 triangles, each with the same shape; another name would serve for 6 triangles, each with the same size; and a third name could serve for 6 triangles, each with the cross in the same location. Other names could serve to identify triangles with 2 common features, or 3. The groups can be designated as shown in the figure.

Group I—3 names for 6 shape differences; the names were D-1, F-6, G-3.

Group II—3 names for 6 size differences; the names were D-1; F-6, G-3.

Group III—3 names for 6 cross positions; the names were D-1, F-6, G-3.

Group IV—9 names for shape and size combinations; the names were combinations of A, B, C, and 1, 2, 3.

Group V—9 names for shape and position combinations; the names were combinations as in IV.

Group VI—18 names for shape, size, and position, or combinations; the names were combinations of A, B, C, VWXYZ, and 1, 2, 3.

Group VII—18 names for shape, size, and position, but the names were assigned at random.

One minute after seeing each triangle plus cross 5 times in the P-A learning sessions, 29 more triangles were added to the 18, and a new test was given in which the S said "same" or "different" as he viewed each of the triangles and judged whether he had seen them before or not. Three tests were run. The new triangles differed in size (6), shape (6), and cross position (6). Two of the new triangles differed in all aspects. Nine of the new were "filler" items because they belonged to the same classes as the original 18.

Results

The basic learning results showed that Groups I, II, and III learned their simple task fairly well; while the other groups learned rather poorly. Group VII could not learn anything to speak of, since

224

there were no clues to guide them. On the tests for identification, however, Groups IV, V, and VI were generally more effective. The position of the cross appeared to be an effective cue. In general, shape was a better cue than size.

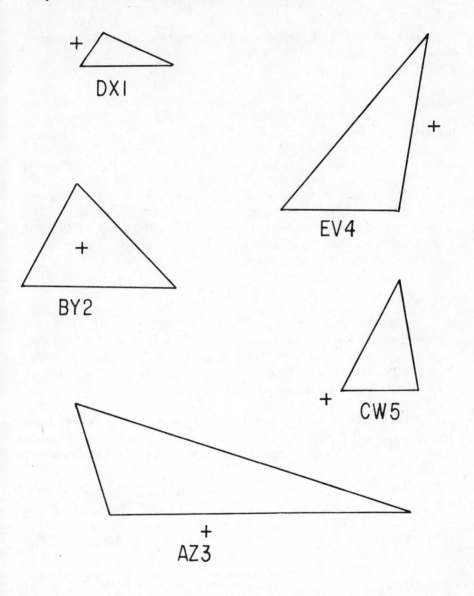

REPRESENTATIVE DESIGNS.

Associative Mediation

James J. Jenkins, Donald J. Foss, and Penelope B. Odom
University of Minnesota

"Associative Mediating in Paired-associate Learning with Multiple Controls," *Journal of Verbal Learning and Verbal Behavior*, 1965, **4**, 141-147.

It has been argued that facilitation effects on verbal learning are not due to mediation, but rather to lessening of interference. In short, it is not so much that the "mediation" groups are helped as that the controls suffer more interference. This experiment is designed to determine the actual degree of positive facilitation and to compare such learning with that of controls, where the degree of interference can be systematically controlled.

Method

Design: The basic design is based on the A-B, B-C, and A-C paradigm, but in this case, as with Russell and Storms, the B-C association is inferred from standard norms. If a *S* learns *Lov-Butter* as A-B, he then learns an A-C list where *Lov* is paired with *Bread*. The Butter-Bread association is assumed.

In the experiment where all *S*s learned the same A-C list, a number of variations in the A-B list were developed to control for several predicted effects. Thus, the *S*s were assigned to various groups as follows (all 1st terms were nonsense syllables; 2nd terms were words):

1. A Facilitation Group—the normal A-B (B-C) A-C paradigm.
2. Warm-up Control—1st list consisted of D-E items (stimuli and responses different).
3. Classical Interference control—1st list A-E (different response words).
4. Associative Interference control—1st list A-Br (the list included the same items as in the 1st group, but these were not arranged in facilitation order; any mediation would arouse some incorrect reponse.

5. Re-paired Control—the 1st list was A-C, where the C terms were not the same as in the final learning.

Note that the design permits evaluating warm-up compared with facilitation. It also allows comparison of the facilitation group with the interference group. Thirdly, classical interference can be com-

Lists Learned by the 5 Groups
First List

		Classical	Associative	Repaired
Facilitation	Warm-up	Interference	Interference	Control
A B	D E	A E	A Br	A Cr
Lov—Butter	Jan—Cheap	Lov—Paper	Lov—Rough	Lov—Smooth
Rus—Dark	Ken—Fast	Rus—Fast	Rus—Tiger	Rus—Lion
Qil—Hard	Sol—Gown	Qil—Little	Qil—Town	Qil—City
Ped—King	Giv—Grass	Ped—Grass	Ped—Table	Ped—Chair
Mon—Rough	Rav—Little	Mon—Cheap	Mon—Butter	Mon—Bread
Fes—Table	Hur—Neck	Res—River	Fes—King	Fes—Queen
Mex—Tiger	Dob—Paper	Mex—Gown	Mex—Dark	Mex—Light
Dic—Town	Wak—River	Dic—Neck	Dic—Hard	Dic—Soft

Second List

	Percent
All Groups	B-C
	Associative
A C	Strength
Lov—Bread	63.2
Rus—Light	82.2
Qil—Soft	66.9
Ped—Queen	74.5
Mon—Smooth	43.6
Fes—Chair	83.3
Mex—Lion	28.0
Dic—City	43.0

REPRESENTATIVE DESIGNS.

pared with mediated interference. Finally, mediated interference (Group 4) can be compared with the re-paired control, where learn- and competing response terms are equated, but with the mediating competitors *presumed* to be in the second response pool while, in the re-paired groups, the competing responses are themselves in the response pool.

Subjects: Eighty undergraduates from an introductory psychology course.

Materials: Six 8-paired associate lists. Stimuli 100% Glaze association value. Responses were words from Minnesota norms with high-strength bidirectional associations. Memory drum with a 2:2-second rate.

Procedure: S learned the 1st list by the anticipation method to a criterion of 3 perfect trials. Following this, he learned the A-C list to 2 perfect trials.

Differences Between Groups in Total Number of Correct Responses on Trial One

	Warm-up	Classical Interference	Associative Interference	Re-paired
Facilitation	31*	36*	53%	55*
Warm-up		5	22*	24*
Classical Interference			17	19
Associative Interference				2

*Significant at .05 level, Newman-Keuls test.

Results

The groups learned the 1st list about equally; no significant dif- ferences. The 2nd list learned, as expected, showed a significant advantage for Group 1 over all of the other groups for the first 3 trials. After the first 3 trials, the Warm-up Control Group (Group 2) and Classical Interference Groups showed no significant differences from the Facilitation Group. The 4th and 5th groups remained consis- tently inferior to the first 3 groups. Because the 1st trial was the crucial one, the data for that trial are reproduced in the table.

Concreteness, Imagery, and Meaningfulness

Allan Paivio
University of Western Ontario

"Abstractness, Imagery, and Meaningfulness in Paired-associate Learning, *Journal of Verbal Learning and Verbal Behavior,* 1965, **4,** 32-38.

In a previous study, it was found that learning a list of words in a noun-adjective order was superior to the normal English language adjective-noun order. The interpretation of this finding was that nouns serve as stimulus pegs, eliciting imagery which can mediate recall of associates. Concrete nouns, being more effective in eliciting imagery, should similarly prove superior to abstract nouns as stimuli in paired-associate learning. The present experiment was designed to test this hypothesis; thus, the comparisons would be among the combinations of concrete-concrete words(CC), concrete-abstract (CA), abstract-concrete (AC), and abstract-abstract (AA) combinations.

Method

Subjects: A total of 100 elementary and secondary school teachers in a summer-session course. They comprised 4 groups of 25.

Materials: Four lists of 16 pairs of words were prepared. Each list contained 4 each of the CC, CA, AC, and AA combinations. Typical concrete words were: tree, dress, pencil, and chair. Abstract words were of the idea, soul, virtue, event variety. All the words were from the A category of the Thorndike-Lorge list (50 or more per million words). The words were rated for imagery by other *S*s not participating in this study on a 5-step rating scale. They were also rated for meaningfulness(m) by Noble's method and for auditory familiarity (F) on a 9-point scale.

Procedure: Word pairs were read aloud to the *S*s, with 2 seconds between pairs. Stimulus words were then read at 8 seconds per word while the *S*s wrote down the response terms. Data from the first 4 trials are reported in the table.

Recall Scores
Response

Stimulus	*Concrete*		*Abstract*	
	Mean	SD	Mean	SD
Concrete	11.41	2.83	10.01	3.21
Abstract	7.38	3.40	6.05	3.59

Results

The table shows the means and SDs for the several combinations of concrete-abstractness. The data were pooled for the 4 groups of Ss, as these showed no differences of any significance.

The predicted order of recall CC, CA, AC, and AA is fulfilled. The effect of stimulus abstractness is clearly greater than that of response abstractness.

Because the ratings of the words were available, it was possible to compare the words in terms of their features. The means of the ratings are shown below.

	Mean Ratings		
	Imagery	*Meaningfulness*	*Familiarity*
Words	I	M	F
Concrete	4.70	14.11	7.70
Abstract	2.90	10.34	6.50

Note that concrete nouns are higher than abstract nouns in all 3 ratings. The several ratings were correlated, with the finding that I and m correlated .90, I and F .76, and m and F .75.

The recall scores of all Ss correlated .74, .75, and .54, with stimulus I, m, and F respectively; and .42, .43, and .31, with corresponding response features. The confounding of I and m creates difficulties for interpretation of the confirmed hypothesis, and their separate roles must be resolved.

Punishment: Duration and Intensity Effects

Erling E. Boe
University of Victoria

"Effect of Punishment Duration and Intensity on the Extinction of an Instrumental Response," *Journal of Experimental Psychology*, 1966, **72**, 125-131.

"Punishment refers to the operation in which the onset of an aversive stimulus is response contingent." Earlier claims about the temporary nature of the depressing effects of punishment have been contradicted by studies using a range of different punishment stimulus intensities or different durations. In this study, both intensity and duration parameters of punishment will be considered.

Method

Two experiments were performed. In the 1st experiment, *S*s were punished for every response during extinction. In the 2nd, only the 1st extinction series response was punished. Otherwise, the procedure was the same.

Experiment I

Subjects: Fifty-five male albino rats, about 90 days old at the start of the experiment.

Apparatus: Thirty-six-inch-long shuttle box divided in the middle by a barrier and a door which could be opened or closed. The grid floors could provide shocks in varying intensities. A timing arrangement could measure the latency of each crossing from the time the door opened.

Procedure: Training. After a water-deprivation schedule of 1 week, animals were given 5 trials a day for 6 days during which they shuttled back and forth (1 minute between trials) for 2 drops of water at the box ends. After 30 trials, extinction began on the same schedule (5 trials per day for 6 days). Failure to cross the barrier in 1 minute on all 5 trials on a given day was the extinction criterion.

Every extinction crossing was punished with different intensities (either .25 milliamp or 2.00 milliamps) and for period of .05, .10, .30, 1.00 or 3.00 seconds. There were 5 animals in each duration and shock group, making 10 groups in all, plus a 5-rat control (no shock) group. The lowest shock would produce evidence of stimulation; the 2 ma and higher shocks would "elicit vigorous motor reaction,, vocalization, and elimination."

Results

The control groups required approximately 25 trials to reach the operant latency as measured in preliminary tests. The shocked rats in the 2.00 ma condition all met the extinction criterion at all duration intervals within 3 days. The .25 ma group reached the criterion in the 1.00- and 3.00-second duration periods. At the shorter intervals in the .25 ma groups, the criterion was not met. In short, brief, weak punishments were not effective, while brief, strong punishments were almost as effective as long, strong punishments.

Experiment II

Because the rats in Experiment I showed some recovery in post-punishment observations in a 3 day test, an additional experiment was conducted, eliminating the short duration punishments, adding a 4.00 ma shock group and using 3 durations (.30, 1.00, and 3.00 seconds). Two new control groups were added—Control II, which received no positive reinforcement at any time in the 6 days of shuttling (this group served to establish the *operant latency*) and Control III, a non-contingent shock group (these animals were shocked 1 minute after being placed in the apparatus instead of after, crossing the barrier and served to determine the contingency relevance). Only 1 shock was given to the 50 animals in this study; i.e., they were shocked only on the 1st extinction trial, and never after that, in the 6-day extinction sessions.

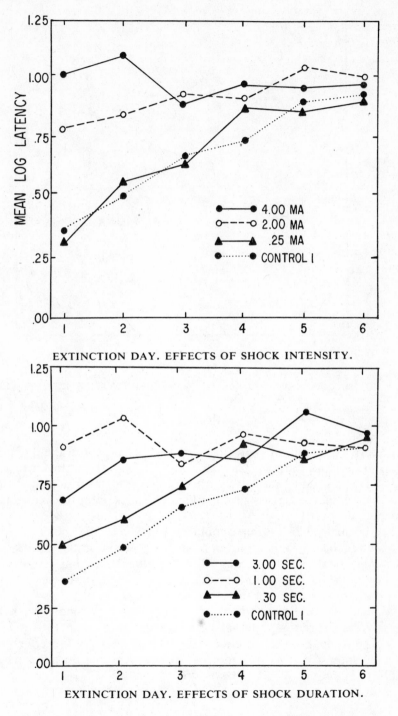

EXTINCTION DAY. EFFECTS OF SHOCK INTENSITY.

EXTINCTION DAY. EFFECTS OF SHOCK DURATION.

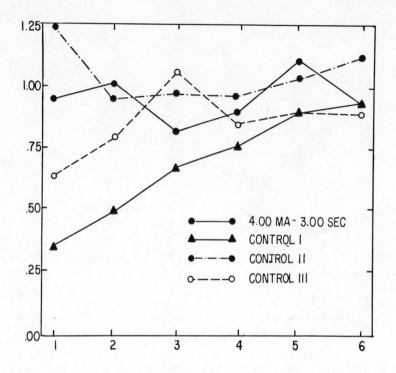

EXTINCTION DAY. CONTROL GROUP COMPARISON WITH STRONG SHOCK.

Results

Under the conditions of this experiment, most of the animals would cross the barrier. The latency of crossing was the measure used. The reaction times were transformed into mean log latencies and appear in the figures as functions of shock intensity and duration.

The normal control group should be considered the standard. The latency reached by this group in 6 days is reached on the 1st day by the long duration and strong shock groups. The non-contingent shock group did not differ significantly from the contingent groups. There was no recovery observed in Experiment II.

Conclusion: One punishment, if strong enough or long enough, is effective in depressing operant performance. From Experiment I, it appears that high levels of either duration or intensity are effective. Varying intensity when duration is long, or varying duration when intensity is strong, seems to have little effect.

234

The Serial Position Curve

Murray Glanzer and Anita R. Cunitz
New York University   Institute for Behavioral Research

"Two Storage Mechanisms in Free Recall," *Journal of Verbal Learning and Verbal Behavior,* 1966, **5** 351-360.

In free recall of a list of words, the Ss usually recall the first and last portions of a list better than the middle. A plot of the results shows a U-shape "serial position curve." This study is based on the hypothesis that two processes, one involving long-term storage, can account for the shape of the curve. The early part of the curve can be attributed to the long-term process, while the latter is a function of the short-term processes. The serial position curve is then really a composite of two curves, one declining from the beginning and the other rising from the beginning. Because long-term storage is known to be affected by at least two variables, repetition and spacing, the first part of the study will be concerned with these variables. The second part of the study will deal with the factor of delay prior to recall, which is presumed to affect the latter part of the curve. Two experiments will be described.

Experiment 1—Method

Subjects: Two-hundred-forty army enlisted men. Ss were used in groups of 20.

Materials: Eight 20-word lists drawn from Thorndike-Lorge AA words. The lists were tape recorded and varied in one of 2 ways. A word would be spoken, and a delay of 3, 6, or 9 seconds would follow before the next word; or a word would be spoken once, twice, or three times at a 3-second rate. The lists, then, varied in "spacing" number of repetitions. Each S heard all 8 lists, and as soon as a list was finished, he would write down all the words he remembered. The results appear in the figure, which shows the effects of spacing. The number of repetitions affected recall in a similar way, in general, but the differences were not as reliable. Note that there are differences in the curves for different presentation rates up to the 16th word. From then on, the differences disappear.

Experiment 2—Method

Subjects: Forty-six army enlisted men.

Materials: Fifteen lists of 15 AA words from Thorndike-Lorge lists.

Procedure: Words were shown on a screen for 1 second, with 2 seconds between words. When a list was finished, *S* wrote down all the words he could recall under each of 3 conditions (5 lists at each condition): 1) No delay; 2) a 10-second delay; or 3) a 30-second delay. During the delay periods, *S* counted out loud from a number shown on the screen.

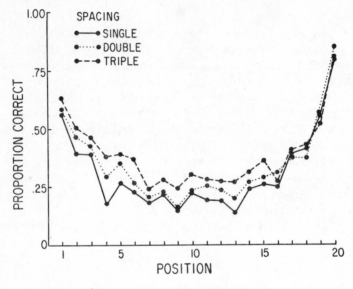

EFFECTS OF SPACING ON RECALL.

Results

The results are shown in the figure, where it is apparent that when there is no delay, the last 3 words are recalled quite effectively. When a delay is introduced, the recall of the 1st items is reduced. The results of the 2 experiments indicate that the 2 predicted changes in the serial learning curve could be effected by experimental manipulations. While repetition (by E) did not affect early item recall, differential spacing did do so. Late item recall was affected by interposing a time-filling task. The hypothesis advanced that there are 2 storage mechanisms operating in free recall is supported by the data.

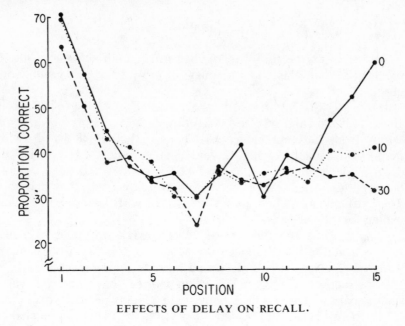

EFFECTS OF DELAY ON RECALL.

Availability and Accessibility

Endel Tulving and Zena Pearlstone
University of Toronto

"Availability versus Accessibility of Information in Memory for Words," *Journal of Verbal Learning and Verbal Behavior,* 1966, **5**, 381-391.

When a person forgets an item known to have been learned previously, it may not necessarily be lost forever because of "decay" or "displacement," but may merely be "unavailable" because it is *inaccessible*. The memory trace may still be intact, but the recaller has no way of retrieving the item because appropriate cues are not present. If aids to recall are provided, the item may be effectively recalled. The present experiment is designed to demonstrate such a change in accessibility as a function of providing appropriate cues.

Method

Subjects: Nine hundred twenty-nine high-school students, grades 10-12, in classroom settings. N = 48 to 56 per group, for 18 groups.

Materials: Eighteen lists of words (6 each of 12, 24, or 48 words). Each 12-, 24-, and 48-word list consisted of groups of 1, 2, or 4 words from different categories. Thus, a list of 48 words with 4 items to a category would have 12 categories. A 24-word list with 2 words per category would have 12 categories. And there would be 6 categories in a 24-word list, with 4 words per category and so on. The extreme case would be a 48-word list with 1 word per category, calling for 48 categories.

Procedure: A practice list of 24 adjectives was read to a class, with instructions to recall as many words as possible. Following this, a list of 12, 24, or 48 words would be read (tape presentation), with the instruction that Ss were to memorize the names of various things, pairs in cases where there were 2 items per category, groups of 4 where there were 4 items per category. They were also told that the words would be preceded by another word or phrase that described the word(s) to be remembered; i.e., a category word would indicate the words to be learned (e.g., the name of a river, a European country, etc.). After a list was read, Ss had 1, 2, or 4 minutes to recall the lists of 12, 24, or 48 words respectively by writing in prepared booklets. Half the Ss learned 1 list of a set of 9, the other half learned 1 of a different set of 9 lists. Half the Ss (non-cued recall) had only blank spaces in their booklets. The other half had the category names listed in the order of presentation (cued recall). A 2nd recall, in which all Ss were provided with category names, followed the 1st recall. Because there were no significant changes from the 1st recall, the results of the 2nd recall will not be described.

Results

The recall data are shown in the figure. The mean number of words recalled increases with the number of words presented for all Ss, but the difference between cued and non-cued Ss is clear-cut and significant at all points except for the 12-word lists with 4 categories. As the number of categories increases, the non-cued Ss do better, while the cued Ss appear to do worse. Note the large difference in the 48-word lists for the single words. Analysis of intrusion errors and comparison with normal associates of the words indicated that the differences between the cued and non-cued groups could not be due to guessing or free associations to the category names. Further analysis revealed that the number of words recalled per category was independent of recall conditions and list length for the 24- and 48-word lists. There was a marked tendency for recall of items in the order in which they were originally presented.

Conclusion: The efficiency of recall depends "on the completeness of reinstatement at the time of recall of the stimulating situation present at the time of input. . . .." The organization of the material (in this cate, categorization by *E*) determines the arrangement of words in storage and their retrieval.

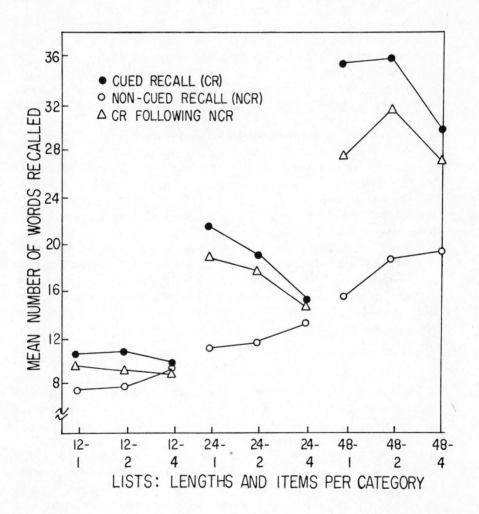

Punishment and Extinction

Erling E. Boe and Russel M. Church
University of Victoria

"Permanent Effects of Punishment during Extinction," *Journal of Comparative and Physiological Psychology*, 1967, **63**, 486-492.

Estes found compensatory recovery of punished responses in only one experiment (A). (In the others, the total time for extinction did not vary from controls.) What are the conditions necessary for compensatory recovery to occur? In this study, 2 variables are explored: shock intensity and contingency.

Experiment 1—Shock Intensity

Subjects: Sixty albino rats, divided into 6 groups which received varying intensities of shock accompanying any bar presses (0, 35, 50, 75, 120, or 220 volts).
Apparatus: Skinner box with grid floor (for shock). Food reinforcement.
Procedure: Rats trained in bar pressing at 100% reinforcement for 2 days; then three 1-hour sessions on a 4-minute FI schedule; then nine 1-hour extinction sessions. Shock was administered during the minutes 5-20 of the 1st extinction session (shock was given only once during a 30-second interval). Animals were then retrained on the FI schedule.

Results

Because of high correlations between the numbers of responses in the last training time and in the extinction sessions, the number of extinction responses is expressed in percentage form in the figure, which shows the cumulative median responses for the 6 groups. It it obvious that the strength of shock is a strong determiner of extinction responses. Compensatory recovery did not occur in the strongly punished groups. It did not occur in the mild punishment groups either, as the rates fall away with additional extinctions instead of rising. It should be noted that the groups with intense shock received fewer such shocks, and the effect of the frequency variable is not indicated in the figure. When the amount of response suppression is computed per punishment, the result is a straight line (log function) indicating that the amount of suppression is a power function of punishment intensity. In retraining, all Ss reconditioned rapidly with no sign of compensatory increases for any groups.

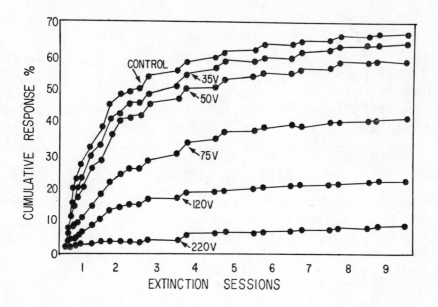

Experiment 2—Non-contingent Shock

Subjects: Sixty rats in three groups of 20: 1) no shock, control; 2) non-contingent shock group; and 3) contingent shock.

Apparatus and preliminary procedure: Same as Experiment 1.

Experimental Procedure: Following the 3rd training day, a 20-minute extinction session was introduced in which 120-volt shocks were given to the 2 shock groups. The non-contingent group was shocked every 30 seconds without regard to responding. The contingent group was shocked only for pressing (no more often than once per 30 seconds). Nine 1-hour extinction sessions followed.

241

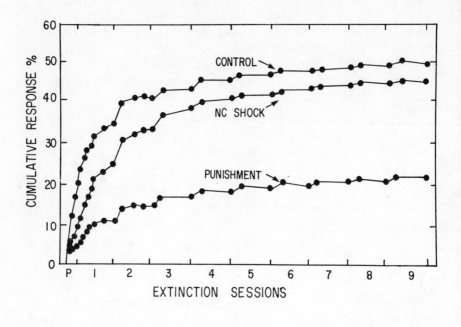

Results

Even though the non-contingent group was shocked more often (30 times, to 8.8 for the contingent group), the contingent group was significantly more suppressed by the end of the brief shock period, and both shock groups were significantly suppressed in comparison with the control group. The shock contingent group quickly inhibited its responses. As soon as the punishment stopped for the non-contingent group, its behavior resembled that of the control.

Conclusion: The intensity of punishment is a major variable in the subsequent suppression of punished behavior. Since compensatory recovery was not observed even after very mild levels of punishment intensity were applied, the results suggest that the range of conditions under which this phenomenon can be reproduced, if at all, is very narrow. The correlation between response and punishment (Experiment 2) is also of major significance.

Studies of Learning to Learn

Geoffrey Keppel, Leo Postman, and Bonnie Zavortink
University of California, Berkeley

"Studies of Learning to Learn: VII. The Influence of Massive Amounts of Training upon the Learning and Retention of Paired-associate Lists," *Journal of Verbal Learning and Verbal Behavior,* 1968, **7**, 790-796.

Previous studies with nonsense syllables have demonstrated that *S*s can improve in their learning skills with serial lists if they learn enough lists. The degree of improvement cannot be estimated correctly because of the inherent interference factors in nonsense syllable letter combinations. Lists cannot be learned in too rapid a sequence because of boredom and fatigue. In this study,.*S*s learned 36 lists 48 hours apart, with recall tests of the previous list prior to learning a new one. This procedure provided data on the question, "Does recall also improve?" Previous work indicated that recall did not improve.

Method

Subjects: Five college-age males in a nutrition experiment, confined to a laboratory through the period of the study.

Materials: A pool of 1000 common English words was used to make up 36 lists of 10 pairs of words. Any words with obvious associations were screened out. The words in each set of 10 appeared on 3 x 5 cards in 4 different orders. Extra cards with only the "stimulus" item was used to test learning in a trial-test or study-recall procedure.

Procedure: In learning trials, the cards were presented at a 1-second rate. In test trials, the rate per card was 3 seconds. Timing was by metronome. Lists were learned to a criterion of 10 out of 10 correct. Prior to learning a new list, 5 recall trials on the previously learned list were given.

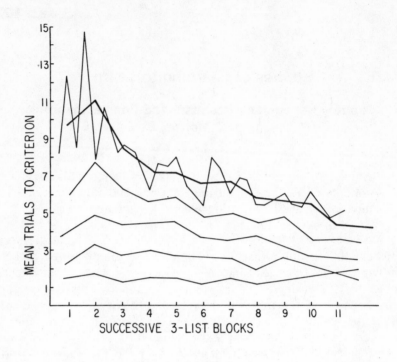

Results

The basic results of the study appear in the figure. The curve for individual lists to the criterion of 10/10 shows marked fluctuation in the early lists but a steady improvement over the training period. In the figure, points are plotted for blocks of 3 lists. Toward the end of the training, plateaus are developing at the lower criteria. Four *S*s actually learned 8 more lists, showing no further improvement in learning. *Errors:* Most of the errors made overtly were based on responses from a current list. Interlist errors amounted to only 1.2%. *Recall:* In recall scores, there was a "precipitous drop over the 1st 3 lists" with a gradual decline as the lists continued, with recall scores approaching zero toward the end of the series. The recall curves bear a striking resemblance to the learning curves, with recall decreasing as learning improves.

Conclusion: The limit of improvement in learning paired-associate words might have been reached in 36 trials. Retention is inversely related to learning skill. The massive decrease in recall is consistent with an explanation in terms of cumulative Proactive Inhibition.

Mediation and Mediator Dropout

George E. Weaver and Rudolph W. Schulz
University of Iowa

"Recall of A-B Following Varying Numbers of Trials of A-C Learning," *Journal of Experimental Psychology,* 1968, **78**, 113-119.

A paired-associate list can be symbolized as A-B, where A refers to the 1st or "stimulus" syllables and B the response syllables. Learning a 2nd list with the same syllables as stimuli, but with different responses, can be called A-C. If the responses of the 1st list are used as stimuli for the 2nd, we have a B-C list. When Ss learn an A-B list, then a B-C list, they commonly do better on an A-C list than they would on an A-D list. Such a learning of A-B, B-C, A-C, is described as chaining (C). A learning of A-B, B-C, A-D would be non-chaining (NC). The improvement in the learning of A-C is usually assumed to be due to the mediation operation of the B items; the final learning is considered to be a matter of the use of B to help evoke the C, so that S is supposed to say "B" to himself (or have B operate in some other way) to evoke C. To support such a thesis, a recall test of A-B after chaining A-C should show good retention of B, at least in early A-C learning trials, as B might "drop out" as unnecessary once the A-C association has been made with its help. A-B might actually be strengthened in A-C learning if it is not at maximum strength in the original A-B learning. This study is an attempt to discover what happens to B items as A-C is learned.

Method

Subjects: One-hundred-sixty college students in 8 groups of 20.

Materials: Paired-associate lists (8 pairs) were prepared in which the A terms were composed of low m paralogs. CVC trigrams served as E or C terms. Common nouns (Thorndike-Lorge AA) served as B terms.

Design: All Ss learned the same A-B list (Stage I). The Ss were then placed into either B-C, A-C (chaining—C), or Be-AC (non-chaining—NC) groups (Stages II and III). Four degrees of A-C learning were arranged for both C and NC groups—0, 3, 7, or 15 trials. Following A-C learning, all groups were tested for A-B retention (Stage III).

Procedure: In all the first 3 stages, a study-test procedure was followed with a 2-second per item interval for study and test in Stage I. In Stages II and III, the test time was 3 seconds per item. Learning in Stages I and II was to a perfect recall criterion. Test trials in Stages II and III were in a 4-item multiple choice arrangement. Immediately after Stage III, *S*s were instructed to recall A-B (Stage IV). The A stimuli were presented at a 1.5-second rate. *S*s were encouraged to guess.

˷ Results

As expected, there were no significant differences in any of the groups in learning either the AB or the BC (or BE) lists to criterion. However, in learning the AC lists, the chaining groups and the non-chaining groups differed significantly at all levels of AC training. The scores by learning level (mean of the total number of correct responses for 20 *S*s in each group) are shown in the table.

Mean Correct

Number of A-C Trials

Groups	3	7	15
Chaining	15.10	40.20	96.00
Non-chaining	10.45	30.35	79.90

In Stage IV (A-B recall), *S*s were equal at the 0 level of A-C learning but diverged immediately in terms of number of A-C learning trials. The chaining group was consistently superior at all levels of A-C learning to the non-chaining group, which dropped off immediately (see figure). Although recall under chaining conditions appears constant, an analysis of the weaker A-B associations (based on AB and AC learning) indicates that the strong A-B associations first rose in strength and then declined (supporting the drop-out thesis), while the weak AB associations gathered strength during A-C learning. In the non-chaining groups, the A-B associations consistently lost strength in the A-C learning.

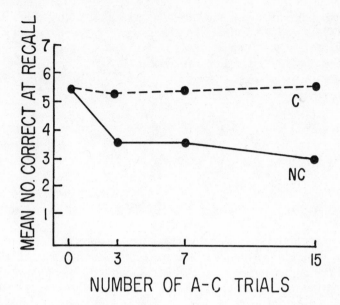

Abstract **122**

Imagery as a Relational Organizer

Gordon H. Bower
Stanford University

"Imagery as a Relational Organizer in Association Learning,"
Journal of Verbal Learning and Verbal Behavior, 1970,
9, 529-533.

"It has been shown repeatedly that mental imagery is a beneficial associative aid." The question of how imagery served this function is unanswered. There are two classes of explanation: 1) Images serve to differentiate stimuli or learning elements making the items "distinctive;" 2) Imagery affects the association process itself.

There are varieties of each view, emphasizing such possibilities as reduction of generalization by more specific encoding, or, in the case of the second type of explanation, that imagery confers "perceptual unity" or generates semantic concepts. This experiment is designed to determine whether imagery functions on the stimulus or cue operation, or on the associative process.

Method

Subjects: Thirty high school graduates (15 male, 15 female, paid for their service).

Materials: Memory drum with 10-second exposure. Pairs of high-imagery words from Paivio's lists. Each S was shown 3 sets of 30 pairs.

Procedure: The Ss were divided into 3 groups of 10. Each group worked under different instructions, but under the general instruction to remember the response words shown with the stimulus words. The instructions were: Group I. Try to form an image of the items shown in some interaction in some vivid way; (Imaginative Imagery) Group II. Imagine each of the items as if they were separated on opposite walls of the room. (Separation Imagery) Group III. Recite each pair of words aloud and repeatedly during the exposure. (Rote Repetition)

Following each of the 3 sets of 30 paired-associates, Ss were tested in 2 ways. The memory drum exposed items on the left (stimulus side, and S was shown 60 words, 30 of which had previously been used as stimulus items, and 30 more "distractor" items. S was to report if he recognized a word as "old" or as "new," and his level of confidence. If he thought the word was an "old" one he was to try to recall the associate.

Results

The table shows the percentages of recognition, recall, and conditional recall (correct responses for only those words that were recognized correctly as old.

Group	Recognition	Recall	Recall Given Recognition
Interactive Imagery	.87	.53	.61
Separation Imagery	.83	.27	.34
Rote Repetition	.84	.30	.36

The differences in recognition scores are not significant, indicating that imagery instructions did not help to differentiate the stimuli over overt recitation. The recall scores, however, are highly significant in both measures, indicating that the function of imagery was to assist in the associative process.

"The benefit due to imagery in associative learning is concerned with the "relational associating part of the process rather than with the 'stimulus encoding' part."

Cue-dependent Forgetting

Endel Tulving
Yale University and The University of Toronto

"Cue-dependent Forgetting," *American Scientist,* 1974, **62,** 74-82.

Memory for an event is a product of information from two sources, a memory trace and the retrieval cue ("information present in the individual's cognitive environment at the time the retrieval occurs"). Something has to remind us of anything we remember. While we cannot be sure that some memory traces do not decay, if an appropriate cue "restores" the memory, the decay theory loses credibility.

Support for the Cue-dependent Theory

1. *Constant traces, variable retrieval.* If *S*s learn PA's, where some of the stimulus words rhyme with the responses (worse-nurse) or are common associates (bark-dog), and are later tested by presentation of the first word, they will forget some of the responses if the list is long enough and if they have only a few trials of learning. Subsequent testing with common associates of the prior rhymed words, e.g., "doctor" or rhymes of the word previously paired with a common associate, e.g., "grog" may bring out the forgotten responses.

In one study, the new rhyme brought out 22% of forgotten responses; new common associates, 30%. When an "obvious" cue fails and another succeeds, it is evident that there may be other cues to the stored information.

In another study, Ss were shown lists of 28 five-letter words. They were tested by being shown the first 2, 3, 4, or 5 letters, and the recall rose progressively with the number of letters in the cue.

In a third study (at another laboratory, by Leah Light), Ss had to recall words presented one at a time or imbedded in sentences. The cues were homonyms, synonyms, or the original words themselves. The results appear in the table. Obviously, different kinds of cues are differentially effective in recall.

Percent of Words Recalled with Different Cues

Original Learning	Identical Word Cues	Homonyms	Synonyms	No Cues
Single word	.92	.81	.51	.32
Sentences	.92	.88	.40	.18

2. *Forgetting in free recall.* Supporters of a dual storage (STM and LTM) model cannot account for a later recall that is superior to an earlier one.

In Retroactive Inhibition studies, it is usually held that the original learning has been either a) unlearned; or b) interfered with. In a study using lists of 24 words (6 categories of 4 words each), different Ss learned different numbers of lists (different categories in each list). After studying each list, Ss had to recall as many of all the words seen as possible, with progressively poorer results as more and more lists were learned. A cued-recall test characterized by mentioning the categories removed all the Retroactive Inhibition. (See the figure.)

3. *Failure of recognition.* Recognition is usually considered easier than recall. In fact, however, the cues for recognition, e.g., the original words themselves, may not be so good as other cues. In one study, Ss were told to learn PA's; then the Ss were asked to write out a few associates of new words which were all related to the original response words. In these association lists, the Ss frequently (70%) included the original response words. When asked to recognize the response, they recognized 24%. When provided with original cue words, they *recalled* 63%. Theories that interpret recognition testing as only requiring decisions are wrong. Appropriate cues are required for recognition as well as recall.

The paper concludes with a discussion of the advantages and possible criticisms or limitations of the theory.

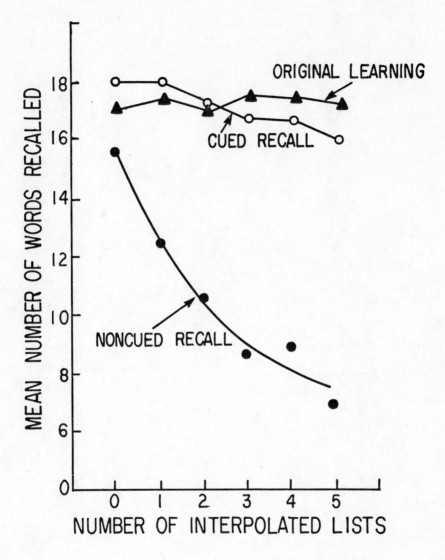

TOPICAL OUTLINE

Note: In 1951 (in S. S. Stevens, Ed., *Handbook of Experimental Psychology,* New York, Wiley) W. J. Brogden divided the subject of learning into three areas: acquisition, retention, and transfer. This classification is the basis of the following outline of the abstracts in this collection. Abstracts are identified by number. Because researchers frequently deal with several topics, some numbers are listed more than once.

Topical Outline

Index of Names

Note: All numbers refer to abstract numbers.

Index of Names

Subject Index

Note: All numbers refer to abstract numbers.

Subject Index

Subject Index

Subject Index

Subject Index